A Better Way of Doing Business?

A Better Way of Doing Business?

Lessons from the John Lewis Partnership

Graeme Salaman and John Storey

OXFORD

UNIVERSITY PRESS

OXFORD
UNIVERSITY PRESS

Great Clarendon Street, Oxford, OX2 6DP,
United Kingdom

Oxford University Press is a department of the University of Oxford.
It furthers the University's objective of excellence in research, scholarship,
and education by publishing worldwide. Oxford is a registered trade mark of
Oxford University Press in the UK and in certain other countries

© Graeme Salaman and John Storey 2016

The moral rights of the authors have been asserted

First Edition published in 2016
Impression: 1

Published in the United States of America by Oxford University Press
198 Madison Avenue, New York, NY 10016, United States of America

British Library Cataloguing in Publication Data
Data available

Library of Congress Control Number: 2016933336

ISBN 978–0–19–878282–7

Printed in Great Britain by
Clays Ltd, St Ives plc

To Olympia and Alexander (GS);
Anne, Rebecca, and David (JS)

Preface

The John Lewis Partnership (JLP) is an extraordinary organization. It is extraordinary in terms of its distinctive features, its longevity, its size, its continuing success, its popularity with staff, customers, and the wider public. Longevity: the first shop was opened 150 years ago and the Partnership was formed nearly 100 years ago; size: the 2015 Annual Report and Accounts show £10.9 billion in sales and over 93,800 partners. The Partnership enjoys increasing appeal to politicians and management-writers for whom it represents a much-lauded, admirable, and moral alternative to the conventional form of business organization. Most of all, it is extraordinary because, when other firms find ways to reduce the number of staff or reduce their rewards and the margins to suppliers, the JLP remains committed not to maximizing shareholder value (and senior management bonuses), but to partners' happiness.

As a revered UK institution and a successful business, the JLP merits our attention. Yet, although admiration for Waitrose and John Lewis is widespread and there is a general assumption that the institution is well 'known', in reality the JLP remains a mystery, a mix of impressions and beliefs—many of them encouraged by current management, some exaggerated, some half-true, many based on reality; for the Partnership is more talked about and admired than it is properly known and understood. The reality is more complex, even more impressive, and more interesting than the image.

The JLP is unusual even within the employee-owned category which, though larger than most people realize, is still a specialist niche. But this does not mean that it cannot teach lessons which apply well beyond this specialist category. The success of the businesses, the popularity of the JLP, and the public's affection for it raises a number of general questions which are of interest beyond the confines of specialists and organizational and business researchers who are interested in the JLP per se.

These questions include: how does JLP work in practice? What is the link between co-ownership, the JLP employment model, and the performance of the businesses? What is the role of leadership and management in its success? Are mutuality, co-ownership, and business performance at odds? What is the significance of democracy within the JLP? And probably most significantly: what are the implications, the lessons to be drawn, for policy makers and for economic agents from this organization? Is it feasible for businesses in the public or private sector to replicate or emulate the JLP model? Even without full replication, we suggest there are indeed many important lessons to be drawn from an in-depth study of this organization which are of relevance to policy makers, practitioners, and academic analysts.

This book is based on detailed knowledge of the JLP and its constituent businesses gathered by the authors over a fifteen-year period. The trigger for the making of this book was unusual. It started unexpectedly with a request at corporate level for advice on management development and organizational development issues in 1999. This led to a succession of assignments by the authors in a series of related projects including board level management development; the introduction of business planning and performance management; John Lewis and Waitrose management board assignments; a values project ('Powered by Our Principles'); a study of branch managers, a study of the role of the registrars; competency profiling; pay systems and human resource management strategy. Each of the projects entailed close involvement as advisers and as participant-observers. This practical work was complemented with in-depth interviews over an extended period of time. The authors' involvement with these projects across the Partnership brought them into contact with many managers and partners at many levels and they visited diverse sites— including head office, branches of John Lewis department stores and Waitrose supermarkets across the UK, and distribution centres.

While this array of activities and projects helped inform the background knowledge and understanding of JLP, the analysis conducted in this book is mainly about the management and leadership of the JLP. The authors, with the approval of top directors, set about an explicit and open attempt to conduct a thorough analysis of the Partnership. Interviews were conducted with virtually all corporate level directors and with directors in the constituent businesses. These were recorded and transcribed. While many other people were also interviewed, including non-management partners, the heart of the analysis in this book is centred on an analysis of managers' accounts. Hence, this book is about managing and about governance. It is not a conventional study of industrial democracy. The views of 'ordinary employees' (non-management partners) are reflected in reports of the annual partners' surveys; we did not seek to add to those results. Our interest and therefore our focus, was upon how managers interpreted the challenge of leading in a high-profile context where expectations extended beyond 'simply' making a profit. At a time when 'stakeholders' rather than only 'shareholders' are deemed to be important, we wanted to use this opportunity to explore how an extant stakeholder organization operated in practice.

The book has a wider relevance and application beyond those who have an interest in the JLP itself whether as a customer, a supplier, competitor, or sector analysts. The book is a detailed organizational ethnography. In the management and academic literature on organizations there are many accounts and histories of business organizations, but there are very few that adopt the kind of research-based approach employed here. We sought to reflect at least some of the characteristics found in, for example, Andrew Pettigrew's study of ICI in his book *The Awakening Giant* (Pettigrew 1985). He carried out research over an eight-year period, and in addition, like us, used retrospective views to extend that period. He too was engaged with his subject through a mixed role as consultant, trainer, and researcher. Few other books offer the kind of rich account we strive for here based on careful analysis of the extended reflections from the participants themselves as they struggle to make sense of their role and the nature of a partnership enterprise.

The book analyses their dilemmas and disappointments, the pleasures of a (mainly) shared commitment to decency and fairness, the burden and possibilities of the Partnership's legacy, the responsibilities invoked by the extraordinary liberality of the founder, Spedan Lewis (son of the original John Lewis), in 'giving away' a large part of his business, and the struggle as they fight to protect and preserve an organization and a way of working. The managers themselves (at all levels and from all functions) tell the story of their sense-making attempts and their struggles. These accounts, presented and analysed by the authors, paint a nuanced, occasionally poignant account of an organization which matters greatly, not only to those who work in the Partnership and who are dedicated to ensuring it survives, but to those who admire its attempt not only to sustain morality in employment and business, but to make it work in the face of increasingly harsh market forces.

The book is an independent analysis by two organizational researchers who have sought to apply their training and experience in academic research methods to develop an understanding of this institution. Punches are not pulled in the ensuing critique. Yet, the research for and the writing of the book was supported by JLP senior management, who typically, did everything to help, and nothing to hinder, the research efforts. Crucially, they sought to apply no editorial influence whatsoever. The authors, though independent in their judgement, are admirers and supporters of the organization but they nonetheless bring to bear a critical perspective. Their admiration for the Partnership has not simply survived their analysis but increased. They appraise and assess the organization as unflinching critical friends.

The book contributes to theory in a number of inter-related domains. From the outset, the analysis is located within the wider context of deep concern about the suitability and fitness-for-purpose of the modern corporation within the US/UK mode of capitalism. We are not alone in raising such concerns. Notable analyses and critiques have been made by Colin Mayer (2014) and Will Hutton (2015a, 2015b). Hutton mounts an impassioned critique of short-termism and transient ownership and proposes a reform of company law and the structure of corporate ownership. In a powerful and influential critique, Mayer, likewise, points to the deficiencies and dysfunctionalities of the modern corporation. This, he argues, has evolved into a rootless, irresponsible, formation which is not acting as a force for good in the way that it could. Mayer's solution to these fundamental ills is a revamped corporate form which is based on a much wider set of values and with commitments to a wider set of stakeholders. A mechanism to help deliver this alternative he suggests is a 'trust firm'. Such firms would align a wider set of interests through a trustee arrangement with an eye on the longer term. The prescription bears a close resemblance to the model practised by the John Lewis Partnership. Our analysis of JLP therefore serves as an examination of the type of firm advocated by Mayer. With our close analysis of one leading exemplar of this 'type', we build on, and add to, Mayer's work by bringing to the surface how actors in these types of firm experience multi-stakeholder pressures and multiple objectives, and how the resulting tensions are managed in practice. We reveal important aspects of the complexities and contradictions inherent in such types.

Another vibrant strand of contemporary theoretical debate in the social sciences concerns institutional theory and the handling of multiple and competing institutional logics (Thornton et al. 2012). In exploring how managers navigate between the dual logics of commercialism and mutualism, the analysis of this book contributes to the wider discussion on 'institutional logics' (Reay and Hinings 2009; Thornton et al. 2012). Having to balance, as they do, commercial objectives and partner objectives, JLP managers face, in a stark way, the tensions associated with 'hybrid organizations' (Battilana and Dorado 2010; Pache and Santos 2013). Hybrid organizations seek to combine competing institutional logics. It has been argued that hybrid organizations are becoming ever more prevalent in late modern societies (Kraatz and Block 2008). Literature in this area notes the different strategies that can be adopted to handle tensions of this kind including 'de-coupling' (for example, handling the partner-interests priority by setting up special departments somewhat apart from commercially driven managers), or for example, more complex attempts to combine competing logics through 'logic blending' (Besharov and Smith 2014). The book explores how JLP managers enact and rationalize such strategies and the degree to which they are successful in handling these potentially competing logics.

The book also makes a contribution to debates on the governance of organizations. This is an aspect explored by others using secondary sources (Paranque and Willmott 2014). JLP has an elaborate array of 'governing authorities' (The Chairman, The Partnership Council, and the Partnership Board). These are presented and treated by most of the players—certainly the senior ones—as a set of checks and balances. But governance in JLP—certainly in terms of accountability—is contentious. Non-executive directors are a relatively new phenomenon on the Board and their role is still uncertain and ambiguous in this 'employee-owned' business. Governance issues are also raised through the dynamics of managers acting nominally as 'agents' of the 'principals' (the employee owners) (Berle and Means 1967). Directors often claim that their role is as 'agents'; yet, in many ways, they act as relatively free agents and assume a principal-like standing and mode of behaviour (Eisenhardt 1989). Similarly, despite the declared commitment to sharing knowledge, there is the problem of asymmetrical information in practice and the danger that agents act in their own self-interest. The emphasis, for example, on growth and expansion and the prioritizing of sales at the expense of returns to partners, is seen by some critics as evidence of just such a tendency. This theme is explored in depth in the book along with similar areas of action such as policy in relation to the pension scheme and decisions about the bonus. The nature and meaning of JLP has, of course, been explored by others. The workings of the democracy were researched in a classic book by Allan Flanders and colleagues (Flanders et al. 1968). The business performance aspects were examined in the early 1990s (Bradley and Taylor 1992). More recently, work by Peter Cox, a former JLP manager has contributed a useful narrative of the growth of the business (Cox 2010). Work by academics, Cathcart, Paranque, and Willmott have raised fundamental issues of the wider significance of the Partnership in relation to capitalism (Cathcart 2009, 2013a, 2013b; Paranque and Willmott 2013).

A further domain of theory illuminated the wider question of the work of managers. As Colin Hales once put the question 'What do managers do?' (Hales 1986). This has been a long-standing debate with important classic contributions from Rosemary Stewart (1976) and Henry Mintzberg (1973). Related work on managers and their work has focused on the theme of managerial identity (Knights and Willmott 1999; Alvesson and Willmott 2002). This book contributes to the debate by shedding light on the detail of managers' daily work and the way they think about their role and the way they conduct it.

A final contribution to theory made in the book that we want to highlight here concerns the handling of contemporary employment relations. The Partnership has gone to unusual lengths in developing elaborate processes of employee consultation and engagement. Considerable investment of time and money is allocated to the maintenance of the supporting institutions. 'Employee voice' is celebrated as invaluable to the realization of the model and to its performance outcomes. The book explores these themes in depth and in so doing contributes to theory on the link between such engagement and performance (Barrick et al. 2015).

In these, and related ways, this book attends to core themes in contemporary business life. It reveals and explores the tensions and dilemmas even in the most well-intentioned of organizations. It anchors common and arguably universal predicaments in tangible decisions relating, for example, to extended opening hours, site closure and redundancy alongside investment in new sites and refurbishment of some existing stock, cost-cutting, new formats, restructuring and delayering, closures of old facilities such as distribution centres and the opening of new ones, choices about employee voice and representation, sub-contracting and off-shoring. Such decisions are the warp and weft of managerial work. Underlying each instance and overlaying the analysis as a whole is the fundamental question: does the JLP way represent a better way of doing business?

Acknowledgements

The nature, and we hope the virtues, of this book stem in large part from the quality and duration of our relationship with an array of articulate and thoughtful people across the Partnership over a number of years. Each, in his or her different way, helped us get the story and the analysis straight about an institution for which they invariably cared deeply. They were generous with their time and with their efforts to help us understand the complex array of interconnecting issues.

It has not been possible to name everyone with whom we talked and we apologize in advance to those whose names are missing. With regard to those who are named below, two points are important to note.

First, some of these were interviewed and consulted for what we describe in the Research Note as the 'business research' phase of the work, that is, the practical project work undertaken from 1999 to 2008 on aspects of management and organizational development. Other names listed are the interviewees for the 'academic research' project phase which took place from 2010 to 2015. Many persons were in both camps and thus were interviewed at least twice.

The second point to note is that the job titles shown alongside names *reflect the roles played by these informants at the time we encountered them.* Given the degree of churn between posts, these designations do not necessarily reflect the current state of play, indeed a number of those listed have since retired and others have moved to entirely different roles, left the Partnership, or died. Others remain in post in the roles as listed. Many, indeed most, moved between a number of positions—for example, Andy Street, currently MD of John Lewis, was formerly Supply Chain Director and Personnel Director at various times during our contact with him. Many of the interviewees had joined as graduate trainees and had worked for as many as a dozen branches and worked in central roles. Most were highly knowledgeable about the Partnership.

Johnny Aisher, Partner Counsellor's Office

Ian Alexander, Finance Director of the Partnership and Deputy Chairman. Died in post

Tom Athron, Waitrose Finance Director then Group Development Director

Kevin Berry, IT Director, Waitrose

Jane Burgess, Partners' Counsellor

Anne Buckley, Registrar, John Lewis; Head of Partner Support

Sally Carruthers, Personnel Director, JL, retired

Margaret Casely-Hayford, Legal Services Director, JLP, until 2014

Marisa Cassoni, Finance Director 2006–2012

Dudley Cloake, Partners' Counsellor and Personnel Director, retired 2003

Paul Coby, IT Director, JL

Rob Collins, Retail Director, Waitrose, Managing Director from 2016

Maurice Dunster, Director of Organisational Development

Steven Esom, Waitrose Managing Director 2002–2007

Judy Faraday, Archivist JLP

David Felwick, Managing Director at Waitrose then Deputy Chairman JLP, retired

Simon Fowler, Managing Director of Oxford Street Branch, then Partnership Registrar on JL Board, Chair of the Employee Ownership Association

Eric Gregory, Systems Director then Personnel Director, JL, retired 2009

Sir Stuart Hampson, Chairman of the Partnership until 2008

Harriet Hounsell, Personnel Director, JL

Ann Humphreys, Properties and Retail Development Director JL, retired 2007

Helen Hyde, Waitrose Personnel Director

David Jones, President of Partnership Council, Waitrose Supply Chain Director, Partnership Registrar, Waitrose Management Board

Nigel Keene, Property Services Director, Waitrose

Tracey Killen, Personnel Director, JLP Board

Alan Lester, Corporate Lawyer (now left the Partnership)

Patrick Lewis, Partners' Counsellor, Group Finance Director

Jill Little, Merchandise Director, retired

Alistair McKay, Deputy Chairman (retired)

Charlie Mayfield, Chairman of JLP

Luke Mayhew, Managing Director of the John Lewis Department Stores until 2004

Richard Mayfield, Head of Partnership Services, left 2012

Angela Megson, Director of Buying, Waitrose, until 2006

Chris Mitchell, Head of Branch, Norwich

Andrew Moys, Director of Communications, Group level

Brian O'Callaghan, Managing Director of JL, retired 2000

Andrea O'Donnell, Commercial Director, JL

Maggie Porteus, Head of Branch, Cheadle, interviewed 2002

Mark Price, Managing Director of Waitrose, Deputy Chairman, retiring April 2016, Minister of State for Trade from April 2016. Baron Price

Dino Rocos, Operations Director, JL

John Sadler, Former Director of Finance, retired

Geoff Salt, Supply Chain Director and then Director of Selling, Waitrose, retired 2009

Andy Street, Managing Director of John Lewis Department Stores

Ken Temple, Chief Registrar and Partners' Counsellor, retired

Gareth Thomas, Retail Operations Director, JL

Peter Ruis, Buying and Brand Director, JL, left 2013

Tony Solomons, Personnel Director then Retail Director, Waitrose 2008–2012

Rupert Thomas, Marketing Director

Laura Whyte, Divisional Registrar, JL, Personnel Director JL, retired

Mark Williamson, Commercial Director, Waitrose

David Young, Deputy Chairman, 1993–2002

Sue Walters, MD of John Lewis Kingston (Branch Manager)

Additionally, the book was strengthened by academic and other colleagues who generously took time to read and comment on drafts of the manuscript as it came together in late 2015. In this regard we are extremely grateful to:

Paul Backhouse, Head of Personnel then Deputy Partners' Counsellor, retired

Imanol Basterretxea, Professor at the University of the Basque Country

David Coats, Founding Director of WorkMatters Consulting and former Associate Director at the Work Foundation

Jean Hartley, Professor of Public Leadership, The Open University Business School

Charles Heckscher, Professor, Rutgers University, New Jersey

Andrew Kakabadse, Professor of Governance and Leadership, Henley Business School and Emeritus Professor, Cranfield University

Acknowledgements

Tom Lawton, Professor of Strategy, The Open University Business School

Colin Mayer, Professor of Management Studies, Said Business School, University of Oxford

Keith Sisson, Emeritus Professor, University of Warwick Business School

Hugh Willmott, Research Professor in Organizational Studies, University of Cardiff

Huainan Zhao, Professor of Corporate Finance, Cranfield University

Finally, other people were of particular importance because they contributed significantly either to the data on which the book is based or to the analysis of these data. Brian Dear worked hard and effectively to gather and make sense of documentary material from the archive and was assisted by Judy Faraday the archivist. He undertook an analysis of many years of the *Gazette*. The financial analyses in the book were enhanced by our friend and colleague Martin Upton, who applied his expertise to the collection and analysis of relevant financial data. Martin is Director of the True Potential Centre for the Public Understanding of Finance, and Senior Lecturer in Finance at The Open University Business School. He was previously Treasurer at the Nationwide Building Society. David Musson, Commissioning Editor of Oxford University Press, was supportive and helpful throughout, gently steering us in directions which have always proved sensible and fruitful and supplying us with valuable advice from a range of informed and insightful referees.

Finally, this book would not have been possible without the support and help of two people within the Partnership. Andy Street, the current MD of the John Lewis Department Stores division, has been a friend and a supporter of our involvement in the Partnership for many years. His encouragement of the analytical work which underpins this book was crucial throughout its gestation. The Chairman, Sir Charlie Mayfield not only allowed us access but actively and positively encouraged his colleagues to give us their time and attention. This support was unwavering and unconditional: he never made any attempt to interfere in our researches or to monitor our conclusions. He gave us something even more valuable than his permission and support—his confidence in our judgement, and trust in our integrity—a living expression of the John Lewis Partnership spirit.

A Note on Research Methods

The research underpinnings for this book are somewhat unusual. They include, among other things, what might be termed 'business research projects' as well as 'academic research projects'. The relationship between these two is of some interest and not only for students of research methods. For this longitudinal work programme, we brought some aspects of academic research methodology into the business research work at the outset. Hence, for example, when working on the initial practical, problem-solving projects, we conducted one to one research interviews with participants using semi-structured interviews which were digitally recorded and then transcribed. The resulting transcripts were used for systematic data analysis. Hence, there was no sharp divide between the methods used for each type of project—research consultancy and academic research.

The business research was constituted by a series of empirically-based projects of an applied nature and were commissioned by a number of senior directors in different parts of the John Lewis Partnership over a period of years. These series of projects started in financial year 1999–2000 and continued through until 2007–2008. Some of these were in the JL department stores, some in Waitrose, and others were at corporate cross-Partnership level.

For example, an early project in the JL department store division addressed the roles and behaviours of branch managers (known in JL as Managing Directors of Branch or Heads of Branch). Another project attended to the workings of the JL Board and reviewed the constituent board members and their roles. This work took place at a vital time when significant changes were being forged under the leadership of Luke Mayhew, who had been brought in with previous experience with British Airways—the classic change management case of the era. He was described in the business press as 'The man who tamed the peculiar beast' (*Daily Telegraph* 23 October 2003).

Other projects were undertaken for Waitrose. These included, for example, a project on the workings of the Waitrose Board and the relations between the work done by Directors and their direct executive reports.

A third set of projects was undertaken for the corporate level (now commonly known as Group). These included a study of the role of the corporate functions in comparison with the constituent businesses, a project on the work of the registrars, and a project on partnership wide values and behaviours. We were also actively involved in projects which were seminal to the transition of JLP around the year 2000 when Business Planning was being introduced and performance management. These professional processes, usually already installed in other leading retailers, were part of the hugely significant shift between the late 1990s to around 2005 that took place in the Partnership. These interconnected innovations brought into sharp relief the tensions between different interpretations of what the Partnership was, and was for. There was a sense, in some quarters, that the Partnership was so different that it could eschew the commercial devices used by competitors. There was pride in the 'instinctive retailer' qualities of some senior managers and a reluctance to import practices such as extended shop hours, advertising, business planning, performance management, and online retailing. The gradual introduction of each of these brought to the surface, and exposed for scrutiny and debate, the nature of the essence and the purpose of the Partnership. We were privileged to see all of this played-out in real-time.

The academic research began in 2010 and continued for five years. The focus of this phase was an apparently simple set of questions: What were the essential features of the JLP model in theory and practice? How did governance, accountability, and management operate in theory and practice? What if any were the linkages with performance outcomes? As part of this academic research phase, we interviewed nearly all members of the senior management teams at corporate level and at business division levels and in the shared services. This group in total amounted to approximately 100 informants. Many of these were interviewed on multiple occasions. To commence this phase, the chairman generously invited a list of directors to cooperate with us in researching the book; this included making themselves available for personal interview and with additional facilitation. Interviews were in the main recorded and transcribed. Much of the analysis in the book is based on this data set—it represents a critical reflection and interpretation of senior managers' own accounts of their understandings and actions. In certain specific areas, we drilled-down into the underlying layers to round-out our understanding of practices in retail trading and the operation of the supply chain.

An additional component of the academic research phase was a project funded by the Economic and Social Research Council (ESRC). This award (code ES/K000748/1) supported work which extended the analysis outside JLP to other 'somewhat like' organizations. The research work designed and undertaken for this ESRC project helped us address the replicability question. We went into 'employee-owned' enterprises in the private sector, former public sector organizations, mutuals, social enterprises, and third sector organizations which had elements of co-ownership and employee participation in decision making. We sought to compare and contrast these cases with JLP. The special focus was on the processes they used to govern and manage themselves. The comparative research also extended to Spain so that we were able to make comparisons with the largest of the Mondragon cooperatives, Eroski, a large supermarket chain. This aspect involved close collaboration with Professor Imanol Basterretxea, from the University of the Basque Country. The range of practices uncovered in these varied organizations helped deepen our understanding of common tensions in managing stakeholder enterprises and helped reveal the considerable variations built around some common ideas and principles. This comparative work was used to inform the analysis of 'replicability' in Chapter 8 of this book.

This admix of applied research, participant observation, and then a separate period of detached independent research is uncommon. It finds some reflection in the work of Andrew Pettigrew who was involved in a similar set of mixed endeavours inside ICI. His work was undertaken over an eight-year period from 1975 to 1983 and was published in 1985 under the title *The Awakening Giant*. He too noted the 'need to balance involvement and distance' as a researcher when engaged in this kind of mixed-mode activity (1985: xiv). Pettigrew's broad objective was to explore 'the role of very senior line managers in creating change' (1985: xv). We had this objective in mind too, though in our case, the focus was upon the special challenges of managing in a stakeholder context where multiple objectives have to be balanced, where there are plural seats of authority and legitimacy, and where there is the weight of a strong and vibrant legacy of ideas and principles underpinned with a written constitution.

We had our first introduction to the John Lewis Partnership in the trading and financial year 1999–2000, when we were invited to help with a management development project at senior levels. This piece of work was followed by a series of consultancy projects which reported to the Managing Directors of both main businesses—John Lewis Department Stores and Waitrose—and subsequently projects at corporate level which reported to the Chairman. These strategic level projects included one on the role of Branch Managers and their development needs; one on the role of the Registrars; appraisal systems for top level Directors; payment systems; a project on core values which became Powered by Our Principles (PboP); and Board level analysis for both John Lewis and for Waitrose.

These various projects, which extended over a decade, involved interviews at corporate head office, in the constituent businesses, in the branches and the distribution centres. The work also involved participation in board meetings and operational meetings as well as participation in management development events.

As noted, this activity was supplemented with academic research work of a more detached conventional kind which was designed explicitly to collect data for the current book. This commenced in 2010. At the outset of this phase we were fully open in raising this objective with the Chairman. In tune with JLP openness and trust, no restrictions were placed upon the researchers. There was no request and no offer to provide a copy of the manuscript prior to publication. It was understood that we approached the task of analysis and critique as critical friends. It can with certainty be assumed that many senior figures in the Partnership will not agree with a number of our conclusions but we are confident that they will treat the diverse interpretations as part and parcel of the ongoing debates in and about the Partnership—the kind of discussions and debates which keep the Partnership alive and vibrant.

Contents

Contents

List of Figures

List of Tables

1

The Big Picture

Something is wrong with the modern corporation and the wider milieu within which it operates. It is prone to periodic crisis and to the persistence, and even fuelling, of extreme inequality. The nature and the sources of the problem have been explored with increasing frequency (Appelbaum and Batt 2014; Gamble 2014; Mayer 2014; Streeck 2014; Wolf 2014). The short-termist outlooks and behaviours of shareholders have been frequently noted (Peston 2013). Corporate leaders feel compelled to dance to the tune of the City financiers. The time horizons of these fund managers and their analysts are notoriously short. The trading of stock has become de-coupled from sensible performance evaluation of firms as electronic trading operates in microseconds based on algorithms constructed by technical wizards—a process graphically described by Michael Lewis in his book *Flash Boys* (Lewis 2014).

In a stark example of distorted 'investment', Lewis reports on the building of a straight-line trench from Chicago to New York to carry a fibre optic cable that would enable trading orders to be sent in milliseconds (less than a blink of an eye). The only purpose was to allow renters of the line to place orders to trade in a manner which gave them advantage over all other market traders (Lewis 2014). To this end, the effort of thousands of people and the expenditure of millions of dollars were allotted. The distorted priorities indicated by such instances suggest some fundamental problems in the workings of the economy.

But the real source of the problem, it has been suggested, is not share-trading per se but the structure of ownership. The holding period of shareholders has declined in almost every country over the past half century—from an average of eight years to about eight months (Mayer 2014). 'Yet outside the UK, short-termism is barely an issue elsewhere in the world, with the possible exception of the US. Indeed, it is often difficult to find a foreign translation of the term' (Mayer 2012). As he argues, the corporation: 'has created more prosperity and misery than could ever have been imagined...the corporation is becoming a creature that threatens to consume us in its own avaricious ambitions'

(Mayer 2012: 1). The corporation, especially the US/UK model, is in trouble. In some other countries the single-minded pursuit of shareholder-value is rather less pronounced. As Hall and Soskice (2001) point out, there are *varieties* of capitalism. These are reflected in their celebrated distinction between liberal market economies (LMEs) as found in the UK, Canada, Australia, and the USA, and the coordinated market economies (CMEs) as found in Germany, Japan, and Sweden. As Hall and Soskice make clear, these varied practices are embedded in wider legal, social, and economic institutional contexts. But for the UK/US contexts most especially, we need to be able to imagine (or re-imagine) an alternative which could possibly work even within the prevailing socio-economic institutions. In this book, through detailed analysis of the John Lewis Partnership (JLP) we seek to suggest that the JLP may be a stronger basis for such an imagining than has been realized. We suggest that while JLP is frequently invoked as a model, it is often characterized as an eccentric, niche residue, and not as a source of major challenges to the 'truths' of the prevailing model. To be clear, our purpose is not to extol, eulogise, or promote the JLP model. Rather, our mission is to subject it to detached assessment. Along the way, we want to assess what would be involved if the type of 'stakeholder' model advocated by Mayer was to be more widely adopted.

At the culmination of the takeover battle of Cadbury by Kraft, the Chairman of Cadbury observed that:

> At the end of the day, there were simply not enough shareholders prepared to take a long-term view of Cadbury and prepared to forego short-term gain for longer term prosperity. Individuals controlling shares which they had owned for only a few days or weeks determined the destiny of a company that had been built over almost 200 years. (Sir Roger Carr, DG of the CBI, address to the RSA, 30 March 2010)

In most other countries, publicly listed companies are better insulated from the effects of movements in stock prices. In the UK, companies are more directly exposed to movements in stock markets because of features of the ownership and control of its companies. In most other countries only a small fraction of shares is held and traded by dispersed shareholders; a much larger proportion is in the hands of families and companies who hold substantial blocks of shares for long periods. Even where shares are traded, control is frequently concentrated through allocating voting control to dominant, long-term shareholders (Mayer 2012). In contrast, the lack of stability and a long-term perspective in the UK firm tends towards a raft of distorted and unhelpful behaviours. Investment for the long-term is discouraged. Lack of investment in modern technology, in infrastructure, and in workforce capability runs alongside cost-cutting and exposure to take-over. In recent years, a plethora of new financial players including hedge funds, sovereign investment funds, and private equity have transformed the commercial landscape. The shift is nicely captured in the title *When Wall Street Manages Main Street* (Appelbaum and Batt 2014), that is, the excessive intrusion into the productive activity of retail, manufacturing, and services by financial manipulations. Financial capital has assumed a more prominent place in Anglo-Saxon economies and all manner of economic assets and activity have been turned into financial instruments which can be packaged and traded. This phenomenon is often labelled 'financialization' (Dore 2008; Batt and Appelbaum 2013). It has been shown to have adverse impacts on employment and employees (Kalleburg 2015).

Likewise, John Kay's review of equity markets for the Secretary of State for Business and Skills, found that these markets were no longer serving Britain's need for investment in long-term growth (Kay 2012). Kay found problems of short-termism, lack of a culture of trust and misaligned incentives. He concluded 'that public equity markets currently encourage exit (the sale of shares) over voice (the exchange of views with the company) as a means of engagement, replacing the concerned investor with the anonymous trader' (Kay 2012: 10). Even some guardians of the establishment are worried. The chief economist of the Bank of England, Andrew Haldane has expressed concern about the unintended negative consequences of the conventional shareholder model.[1] The professional body of chartered management accountants has expressed the same concerns:

> Investment techniques and instruments have proliferated rapidly in recent years. High-frequency trading, short selling, share-lending, hedging and other opaque options have helped decouple investors' title ownership and their true economic interest. Off-market trading, for example, is a recent phenomenon, giving players the chance to buy and sell shares even when exchanges are closed. What looks on paper to be a large owner of a company may only be a renter with a significantly different agenda than that of the true share owner. (CIMA 2014: 2)

The chief executive of the global corporation, Unilever, agrees:

> The recent financial crisis and issues such as climate change, food security and poverty mean that business-as-usual is no longer an option. Leading companies are asking themselves what part they can play in ensuring equitable and sustainable growth for generations to come. A critical requirement for this is to shift the organisational focus to the long term. (CIMA 2014: 1)

The chronic low productivity problem in the UK can be directly traced to such features. There is an inherent underlying bias towards short-term contracts, contingent working, outsourcing, and off-shoring. The approach fuels a

---

[1] Interviewed on BBC2 *Newsnight* 24 July 2015.

tendency towards boom and bust, quick returns, massive inequality and insecurity, and low investment. Could there be a better way? Might organizations like the John Lewis Partnership which claims and pursues contrary values and which has demonstrated sustained commercial success even in the face of fierce competition, offer a demonstration of the alternative pathway as outlined by Colin Mayer and others? A close examination of the case should, at the very least, surface the nature of the challenges faced by such organizations and how they are managed.

The short-termist, 'flash boys', characteristics of the recent period have not always characterized UK capitalism. Things began to change across the economy from the 1970s. Although productivity continued to increase during the period 1973–2011 (by 80 per cent) average wages rose on average by only 4 per cent. During the same period, corporate profits spiked to the highest proportion of national income for sixty years. A new era had dawned and a new philosophy dominated management thinking.

What changed towards the end of the previous century, in the USA and the UK, was the emergence and dominance of a new ideology of the capitalist firm, which carried ideas not only about the firm—what it was for, how it should work, how it should be led, what leaders should be like and how they should behave—but also about the necessary forms of relations between workers and management and the principles which should determine these relations, and about the role of the state in economic life.

This dominant, pervasive conception of the nature and purposes and fundamental logic of the business organization, has played a major role in the current crisis in western economies. And that is why it requires urgent and fundamental critique. But the nature and role of this current pervasive view of the firm in recent events has been insufficiently noted and addressed. This neglect is dangerous: if the problem is not identified and addressed it will recur.

> While the first crisis (the Great Depression of the 1930s) was followed by major reforms, it's not clear that anything comparable will happen after the second. And history tells us what will happen if those reforms don't take place. There will be a resurgence of folly, which always flourishes given a chance. And the consequences of that folly will be more and quite possibly worse crises in the years to come. (Krugman and Wells 2010)

The underpinning rationale of this book is precisely this task: the analysis of the nature and deficiencies of the prevailing US/UK model of the firm. But our approach to this issue is elliptical. We address it not through a direct analysis of the prevailing conception of the firm but through an analysis of an organization which has become, for many managers, commentators, and politicians, an iconic example of an alternative model: one that is increasingly used in policies and debates to exemplify another and successful way of doing business, one that reverses many of the more extreme and—to many—disquieting elements of the conventional model of the firm.

The John Lewis Partnership differs, in fundamental ways, from the prevailing conception of how firms should be organized, structured, and led, and what purposes they serve and how they serve them. It is distinctive with respect to strategies and ambitions, the nature and distribution of power, the ways in which employees and managers relate, the ways in which and the principles by which salaries are determined, the relationship with suppliers, and crucially with shareholders (its employees). Hence, JLP is important not only in its own right but also because it offers a stark and dramatic contrast with, and alternative to, a model that has been proved seriously defective. To take just one indicator, John Lewis was named the best place to work in Britain in 2015 by the Human Resources firm Randstad, ahead of well-known firms such as BMW and British Airways.

We recognize that the current economic crisis in the West is not usually seen as a failure of the dominant model of organization. The diagnosis has normally been the crisis of sovereign and personal debt, of declining competitiveness, increasing social division, and the loss of legitimacy by political institutions. The causes of the crisis also usually include lazy, over-paid workers; an over-active, profligate, and bloated state; excessive regulation and obstacles to enterprise; or reduced demand.

But this list excludes a key underlying factor and misunderstands the nature of the problem and its solution. It not only confuses symptoms (reduced demand, declining competitiveness, rising debt) with causes, it employs as a model of explanation some of the very ideological assumptions which underpin the source of the crisis and the model of the firm: for example, assumptions about the role of the state in economic life. But, most importantly, such explanations avoid the real problem: the pervasive, flawed, and ideological model of the firm in the US/UK. This is a model which, in a number of key respects differs fundamentally from the organization addressed in this volume.

So there is (or there should be) increasing concern about the failure of the US/UK model of the firm. The model is failing, and it is failing because of a series of inter-connected systemic weaknesses and errors. These include: the definition of the purposes of the firm, strategic objectives, the conception of how relations within business organizations and between business organizations and other stakeholders such as employees and suppliers should be designed and managed, the prevailing definition of the nature and role and contribution of leadership, and prevailing views on governance and on compensation.

It must of course be noted that the model of the firm and patterns of shareholding and governance arrangements vary around the world (Dore 2000; Hall and Soskice 2001). They have also varied over time. In the nineteenth century, a number of (usually Quaker owned) businesses existed which differed markedly from the market-oriented, contractual model of employment now dominant. In the mid-twentieth century too, there were major corporations such as Unilever and ICI which worked to a different model (see Storey, 1992). However, the current business model based on short-term, contractualized working, has departed markedly from these examples. As Will Hutton has rightly noted 'It is the great debate about today's capitalism' (Hutton 2015a: 34).

This model may spread across other countries. In his analysis of different modes of capitalism, Ronald Dore argues:

> Firms' increased involvement with the foreign financial community will undoubtedly be one further route by which the shift to Anglo-Saxon notions of economic rationality comes to permeate Japanese management. (Dore 2000: 126)

The dominant US/UK model of the firm is not only responsible for performance failures (chronic and acute) but also for the destruction of value. And it is responsible for a range of internal and wider societal problems including increasing disparity between rich and poor, declining national wealth, declining social-political legitimacy and stability, and ineffective and inappropriate governmental strategies and policies as governments address (inadequately) the symptoms but not the root causes of the problems they face.

Shareholder Value

Politicians and business people like to claim that these problems are not caused by their own policies, decisions, or strategies. They prefer to attribute blame to others: arguing, for example, that declining competitiveness is caused by cheap Asian labour or expensive and inefficient local workers. Measuring the precise impact of cheap imports on employment is complex, but authoritative research by economists from the LSE and UCLA reveals that such imports have impacted mainly on low skilled workers (Kemeny et al. 2013). While certainly a factor, low-cost imports are only part of the story. Another major factor is the persistent pattern of low investment and this can be traced to an excessive focus on 'shareholder value'—that is, a direct consequence of the prevailing model of the firm.

The doctrine of 'shareholder value' seemed to solve the historic tension between owners (investors) and controllers (managers). This tension reflects the possibility that those who control the enterprise may misuse or subvert investors' funds for purposes of their own. 'Shareholder value' apparently resolves this potential conflict by arguing that managers should be rewarded for the degree to which they improve the benefits to shareholders through increase in share price or through distributed profits. Under this logic, managers are rewarded by allocating shares to them in the expectation that their primary objective will be to increase their company's share price.

But, by solving one problem it creates another. In practice, organizations' experience of the consequences of the dominance of the philosophy of shareholder value has been, at best, mixed and in some cases catastrophic. Essentially, what it created was an overwhelming emphasis on value *extraction* at the expense of value *creation*. Profits are maximized through cost cutting; investment is reduced to support the distribution of profits. Shareholder value as an executive priority may apparently resolve the tension between executives and investors but creates a new conflict between investors/executives who emphasize value extraction, and employees and suppliers (and others) who have an interest in the long-term survival, success, and growth of the firm).

According to the Cambridge economist, Ha-Joon Chang, and Massachusetts economist, William Lazonick, firms have tended to under-invest and to distribute instead too high a proportion of their profits to shareholders. Between 2001 and 2010, top UK firms distributed 88 per cent of profits and top US firms distributed 94 per cent in dividends and buy-backs (Chang 2012). Lazonick argues that five years after the financial crisis of 2008, stock markets and profits grew, but the rewards went disproportionately to the top 0.1 per cent and ordinary workers were not benefiting, indeed, good jobs were continuing to disappear. He suggests:

> The allocation of corporate profits to stock buybacks deserves much of the blame. Consider the 449 companies in the S&P 500 index that were publicly listed from 2003 through 2012. During that period those companies used 54 per cent of their earnings, a total of $2.4 trillion, to buy back their own stock, almost all through purchases on the open market. Dividends absorbed an additional 37 per cent of their earnings. That left very little for investments in productive capabilities or higher incomes for employees. (Lazonick 2014: 48)

The consequence was insufficient funds remaining to support investment and growth. When Microsoft recently announced a large investment programme to fund research into innovation, the company's share price fell—because shareholders preferred that they receive these funds as dividends regardless of the implications for the long-term development of the company.

During this post-2000 period, there were a number of catastrophic business failures caused by long decline in investment and competitiveness. Ha-Joon Chang, argued that 'the weakness of [General Motors] management's short-term oriented strategy has been apparent at least from the late 1980s, but the strategy continued until its bankruptcy in 2009, because it made both the managers and shareholders happy even while debilitating the company' (Chang 2011). GM spent $20 billion on share buybacks—money largely spent on boosting share price. This did boost the share price which increased shareholder value but, as a result, GM was essentially bankrupt to the tune of a deficit of $35 billion. The second 'thing' of the *23 Thing's They Don't Tell You About Capitalism* is that 'companies should not be run in the interests of their owners' (Chang 2011).

As Chang notes, 'There are different ways to organise capitalism. Free-market capitalism is only one of them—and not a very good one at that.' Chang's criticism is not of all forms of capitalism but of free market capitalism (2011: 253). In a review of Chang's book, John Gray notes, 'This is clearly right, but the types of capitalism that exist today are not just different. They are also competitors, with conflicting needs and goals. Chinese capitalism, Russian capitalism, Indian capitalism and American capitalism are geopolitical rivals as much as they are different ways of organising the marketplace, and they threaten one another in a number of contexts—not least when they are struggling to secure control of scarce natural resources. Many of the world's conflicts are driven by these geopolitical rivalries' (Gray 2010).

During the period 2001–10, US investment fell absolutely and proportionally; profits, as a percentage of national income, increased and managers' rewards increased but companies languished because of reduced investment and reduced (relatively) average wages. So, ironically, the cult of 'shareholder-value' led to the decline of the firm because in practice many shareholders are fickle and tend to be more focused on short-term measures (share price, dividends) than on the long-term growth of the business. Ironically, shareholders may indeed be the least committed of a business' stakeholders. The average shareholding period is approximately just three months.[2]

The Fetish of the Market

There are different ways of understanding the dynamics of the firm. Fundamental to the prevailing model is the core idea (now broadly held more widely in society and politics—though not without critique) that the market, and market relationships are the best way to achieve efficiency. Market forces, this view argues, represent the only way to ensure that firms improve their products and services in order to compete successfully. Alternative conceptions of purpose (for example, professionals' concern for their

[2] Countries outside the USA/UK have tried to reduce the impact of fickle short-term shareholders. In some countries the government holds shares in key firms directly or through state banks (France, Korea, Germany); in other countries shares have differential voting rights which allows founders to retain control over key decisions; in Japan companies hold shares in each other, ensuring continuity; in Germany employees, who have more long-term interest in the firm have formal rights over decisions.

clients) are downplayed or rejected. But, more than this, the emphasis on the market as a purifying force also applies to relations *within* the enterprise (between managers and employees for example) and between firms and their suppliers. It also has more general applications: for example, for the 'market oriented' competences required by the new manager, for the structures, goals, and philosophy of organizations not previously regarded as involved in commercial relations (public sector healthcare, universities, and schools); for the design of structures and dynamics within organizations where conventional competition is difficult through the installation of proxy competition by the imposition of targets and measurement, with ranked 'scores' of achievement associated with sanctions or rewards—as in universities, schools, hospitals); and for the role and activities of the state where the emphasis on the market results in pressure to reduce the role of the public sector to regulate, to restrict state intervention, and to enlarge the role of the private sector. And even within the rump of the public sector, the prevailing market model has massively intruded in the shape of what has been termed 'New Public Management' (Hood 1991; Pollitt 2014). This model propels private sector principles such as competition, performance measurement, performance related pay, fragmentation, and competitive tendering and contracting-out, to increasingly displace erstwhile public sector principles.

Joseph Stiglitz has described this ideology as 'market fundamentalism' (Stiglitz 2003). He draws attention to the absolute conviction with which an unwavering belief is held by many in the ability of markets to achieve economic growth and other benefits. This is so despite the clear evidence that markets are often inefficient, that public provision is often superior, that deregulation can trigger inefficiencies, that markets can fail, that market relations within the firm or between firms and suppliers can create difficulties and problems. These uncomfortable truths are neglected in the face of a fetishized view of the primacy and inviolability of markets. So deeply is this entrenched, along with the related ideology of the modern corporation, that Colin Crouch argues neo-liberalism will survive the challenge of the financial crisis of 2008 and beyond (Crouch 2011).

One component of this view of the primacy of the market and of the dominant model of the corporation requires special attention: this is the view that state activity threatens enterprise, suppresses business activity and ambition through 'red tape', and regulation and its role must be reduced. Yet, in fact, markets must be regulated, competition must be (and in effect always is) managed, and the state has a major role to play—not only in devising regulations to control markets, but also actively to encourage economic activity. Evidence suggests that national economic growth (for example, in Germany) is not damaged, but positively supported, by state investment in research, development, and training. As one commentator noted: 'German competitiveness is not due only to its lower labour costs (which are not lower when welfare benefits are included) but to its strategic investments in research and development, vocational training, state investment banks that create "patient" finance' (Mazzucato 2012).

And as a leading economist has noted:

> The profit motive is still the most powerful and effective fuel to power our economy and we should exploit it to the full. But we must remember that letting it loose without any restraint is not the best way to make the most of it, as we have learned to our cost. (Chang 2011: 253)

The market, and the profit motive which underpins its use, are thus useful components, but left untrammelled they can be dysfunctional.

Leadership: the God that Failed

In the face of the recent financial crisis, and the collapse or near-collapse of a number of major firms, much opprobrium has been poured on the leaders of these failed businesses. We have seen the catastrophic consequences of these leaders as they destroy businesses through greed, criminality, and recklessness, and many of yesterday's heroes and their achievements are now seen as hollow and illusory, and their once lauded qualities—limitless confidence, single-mindedness, results focused attitude—are reassessed as arrogance, inflexibility, self-centredness, incompetence, greed, and indeed dishonesty. But the failure was less one of individual business leaders, however flawed their decisions or outrageous their behaviour, rather more the fault of the model of leadership which they personified and which legitimated their recklessness and egotism.

Charismatic and transformational leadership was the dominant model of the time. Practitioners of such leadership tend to dominate by their overwhelming, magnificent certainty and self-confidence. Such leaders are prey to serious dangers: their strengths can become weaknesses; confidence becomes arrogance; certainty becomes rigidity; purpose becomes obsession; and conviction becomes intransigence.

A very influential model of leadership in the UK and the USA—readily apparent in the adulatory and ghosted autobiographies and in the large number of training events on leadership—stresses the unique, extraordinary almost magical qualities of the individual leader on whom all depends. Leaders—this view holds—are the main factors behind organizational success, making up for the deficiencies of organization, representing an antidote to organization, by stressing the individual rather than the collective, achieving effects through their 'transformative' behaviour and by personal traits which are the opposite of the qualities traditionally associated with organization—innovative, iconoclastic, anti-regulation, passionate, emotional, individual, personal. The modern business leader overcomes the burden and inertia of organization through enterprise and charisma just as the successful firm must overcome the red tape and burden of excessive state interference.

An implication of this argument is that the dramatic organizational failures we have seen recently are not exceptional events, but are normal in the sense that they are not the result of deviation from prevailing norms of organizational purpose and philosophy and leadership but of compliance with these norms.

How Managers Stole their Businesses

The third component of the prevailing business model, and one that is closely tied both to the focus on delivering/improving shareholder value and the cult of the charismatic transformative leader, is the recent emergence of new structures and principles of executive compensation. Executives are now encouraged by payments systems to behave recklessly and to risk the businesses they lead.

Executive pay levels in both the USA and the UK have increased enormously over the past three decades. In the USA, 'In 1977, an elite chief executive working at one of America's top 100 companies earned about 50 times the wage of its average worker. Three decades later, the nation's best-paid CEO's made about 1,100 times the pay of a worker on the production line' (*New York Times* 2010). A series of individual cases drive home the point: Home Depot chief, Robert Nardelli, received a $210m pay-off when he lost his job in January 2007 even though the shares of his company actually fell during his six years in charge. Carly Fiorina, chief executive of Hewlett Packard from 1999 to 2005, laid-off 30,000 employees during her tenure; she was herself eventually forced out but she was $180m better off despite a very lacklustre performance. Eugene Isenberg, former Chief Executive and Chairman of the oil drilling company Nabors, was awarded $100m in October 2011 merely to surrender the CEO title from his duo Chairman/CEO title. The following year he agreed to waive the payment (*Wall Street Journal* 2012).

In the UK, according to research by the High Pay Centre, an independent think-tank, bosses of the Top FTSE 100 firms in 2014 were earning 130 times the amount of their employees (High Pay Centre 2014). This ratio refers to CEO pay relative to the average employee in the firms in question but, when measured against pay in the UK as a whole, the ratio is even higher at 174 times that of the average employee. The highest ratios were found in the advertising firm WPP where the CEO, Martin Sorrell, earned £29.8m and his average employee earned £38,265—a ratio of 780 to 1, and the retailer

Next, where Lord Wolfson earned £4.6m and the average Next employee earned £10,125—a ratio of 459 to 1. Twenty years ago, a CEO of FTSE 100 company earned 25 times the average wage.

There is rarely a link between directors' incentives and the way a company performs. In the ten-year period 2001–10, the average annual bonus for FTSE 350 directors went up by 187 per cent while the average year-end share price declined by 71 per cent. Even at the deepest point of the latest recession, when pre-tax profit was at its lowest point, the lowest bonus level was still 134 per cent higher than in 2000. Many companies that did not survive the period paid above the odds to their directors. Directors' pay in non-surviving compan-ies went up 1,476 per cent compared with 488 per cent for those in companies which did survive (High Pay Commission 2010). And the trend continues. In its review of the 2015 AGM season, the accountancy firm PwC noted: 'With the median CEO pay out remaining at around 130% of salary for the past three years, and, with almost half of awards showing little change from year to year, can annual bonuses genuinely be described as variable pay?' (PwC 2015).

A report by Incomes Data Services focusing on the link between top pay and the link with performance, found that directors' pay, including bonuses and incentives, far outstripped performance as measured by every conventional performance indicator such as return on capital employed. Comparative ana-lysis of pay data and company performance metrics, found that between 2000 and 2013, the median earnings of a FTSE 350 company director increased more than twice as fast as median pre-tax profits in these companies and four times as fast as the increase in market value of these companies (Incomes Data Services 2014).

By way of contrast, since the late 1970s, the workforce share of GDP has shrunk by over 12 per cent. One consequence is that seven million people, despite being in employment, are identified as living in financial stress (*Guardian* 2012). And while executive benefits soar, for non-management staff, jobs are cut, or outsourced, wages are cut or contained, suppliers squeezed, work intensified; worker insecurity increased, training discouraged, career structures dismantled, psychological contract destroyed, demand reduced, levels of per-sonal debt increased.

These ominous developments—the replacement of stakeholder capitalism with shareholder-value capitalism with its direct implications for widening disparities in reward—matters for a number of reasons both practical and moral. Fair pay within companies matters; it affects productivity, employee engagement, and trust in businesses. Employee engagement is a significant factor in business success, and pay equity influences aspects of lower-level employees' motivation, commitment to management goals, effort, and cooperation. According to research by the Economist Intelligence Unit, some 84 per cent of CEOs said that 'disengaged employees' were one of the three biggest threats facing their business (Economist Intelligence Unit 2010). Yet they actively seek to reduce employees' wages while seeking increased benefits for themselves. The EIU authors note that 'strong opinions might not translate into visible action. A sizeable discrepancy exists between what companies say about the perils of disengagement and how far they will actually go to confront the problem' (EIU 2010: 2).

There are also social consequences (apart from increasing personal debt and reduced demand). As famously argued in *The Spirit Level*, inequality has pernicious consequences for society as a whole, while more equal societies enjoy benefits (Wilkinson and Pickett 2010), more unequal societies have lower levels of social mobility and they foster a whole range of health and social problems. Large gaps between the 'haves and have nots' encourages disengagement and social unrest. Inequality can lead to loss of institutional legitimacy and political instability, with poorer groups pursuing their economic objectives outside the mainstream system. Inequality can also damage the institutions necessary to support the achievement and persistence of national prosperity.

Summarizing the Problems and the Solutions

The extent to which these problems can be resolved by changes to the model of the firm is open to question. Creating shareholders with an interest in the long-term future of businesses and not just in quarterly improvements in share value, would require alterations along the lines already noted. These include regulation, tax incentives and disincentives, and systemic changes to patterns of shareholding. The problem of fickle, short-term-focused shareholders is reduced if stakeholders with a long-term commitment (for example, employees) are allowed formal rights of consultation or even influence over key decisions. And of course, if employees are also shareholders then their interests in the long-term growth of the firm are more likely to be heard.

Decisions on the objectives of the business are central to any model of the firm and are closely affected by controls which limit the fickleness of shareholders, the nature and style (and compensation logics) of leadership, and by the degree to which employees are involved in decision making, or have some degree of ownership themselves in whatever form. New patters of employment relations can be seen as centrally relevant to the underlying problem.

Some issues are clear: the *purposes* of organizations require attention: increasingly, commentators are raising questions about a focus on shareholder value—not, usually, from an ethical point of view but from a practical standpoint. There have been too many corporate leaders whose behaviour, decisions, and team dynamics destroyed their shareholders' funds. They did this while proclaiming their commitment to a strategy of maximizing shareholder value by pursuing this goal in a manner that was in direct opposition to their responsibilities as stewards of shareholders' assets. They created and practised a form of leadership which was at odds with duties of governance and stewardship.

It is necessary to ask some fundamental questions about organizations—questions that have not been properly asked for many years. These questions were once the topic of lively debate (and indeed the JLP emerged during a period of such debate). But the dominance of a particular conception of organizational purpose and of the nature and attitudes and priorities of leaders has been so strong and so pervasive that many important questions about how organizations work and *should/could* work and for whose benefit they should work, were in effect, 'ruled out' by the chorus of support for a model which is now seen as deficient. What are business organizations for? What are their appropriate purposes? Now is the time to bring these kinds of questions back in again: What is the proper function of firms and of their leaders? Why did governance structures, roles, and processes fail? How can boards be held accountable and to whom? What values should underpin the structure, processes, and decisions of organizations? These are big questions. We do not seek in this book to meet them head-on in any macro sense. Rather, we address them by making a detailed critical analysis of one significant organization which has, through radical experimentation, shown a possible alternative way. Indeed, in his influential analysis of the failings of the modern corporation, Colin Mayer (2014) cites JLP as one clear example of the kind of stakeholder capitalism he advocates. In the analysis which follows, we track the advantages, the challenges, and the potential embodied in this alternative form.

The John Lewis Partnership: A Better Way?

The fundamental questions posed in the preceding paragraph are reasons enough to invest time in a close analysis of the John Lewis Partnership because, although no one would claim it offers a universal total solution, it has, over an extended period, sought to grapple with many of the tensions identified. Thus, its foremost concerns have been issues of staff engagement, fair reward, a long-term view, an independence from shareholders, and extended debates about ultimate purpose. The lines of critique we have outlined based around stakeholders, leadership, the limits of the market and the role of managers, are all matters of fundamental concern in the wider economy and they also find resonance and reflection in the internal debates within the John Lewis

Partnership. The Partnership may have some answers to them, even though these tensions and debates are dynamic and rarely fully settled.

The John Lewis Partnership is important to its employees/partners, to its suppliers (with whom, typically JLP establishes and maintains distinctively supportive and mutually beneficial relations), and it is important to its many loyal customers. But its wider importance lies in its potential role as an alternative model of how to do business.

If JLP was simply a bizarre but unique organization, the result of the generosity of an eccentric owner who handed over the business to a trust on behalf of employees and established a number of democratic and consultative mechanisms to limit the decision making of management, then we may admire it and derive some satisfaction. But that would be all. Our interest in JLP stems from another possibility: that the JLP may be seen as a model for other organizations to follow. This idea was implicit in the many calls from senior government figures and numerous others for a shift towards 'a John Lewis economy'. But while many pundits have made such a call, they have invariably done so in a highly abstracted and generalized manner. It is hard to find a resource which attempts a serious close examination of just what such a development might mean. Through a study of this manifestation of a firm which has sought to depart from conventional practices and priorities, we may aspire to a better understanding of the nature and size of the challenge.

In the face of the failure of core elements of the prevailing models of organization and leadership it becomes important and timely to consider alternative ways.

Views on the link between democracy and commitment—that when people work for themselves or their community they invest extra effort and commitment—contribute to the public interest in the JLP model. But the realities of the ways in which JLP partners are able or willing to exercise influence and control over management decisions, or to hold managers to account requires further analysis. There are dangers if the JLP model and its constituent components are regarded uncritically, dangers if rhetoric is confused with reality, dangers too if the possibilities of limits to or paradoxes around the elements of the JLP model are not recognized.

Indeed, some ten years ago, the JLP Partners Survey revealed disenchantment with the Partnership's democratic processes. This was not only because partners thought the democratic institutions did not work well but perhaps also because they didn't know what they would look like if they did work well. They may have been right. Some of the directors of JLP who had been brought in at high level from other businesses told us that in their career with conventional businesses they had rarely felt under so little scrutiny, and with so little accountability, as when at JLP. These questions about the degree of scrutiny and accountability are key and they are accordingly examined in detail in this book.

If the JLP is to act as a model or a source of new ideas on organizational structures, and on governance, leadership, and management processes, it is first important to understand *just what this distinctive model is—how it works, what its core elements are.* For there are hazards with an over-reliance on JLP as an alternative model: unhelpful repercussions for JLP itself if this model is over-used or used in ways which show that the model is not fully known or understood. And there are dangers for those who seek to emulate the structures and principles of the JLP if they do not fully know or understand them or if the model they are emulating does not accurately reflect the realities.

Like all models of organization, the JLP model as set out by its founder is characterized by tensions, some of them deliberately created. These tensions persist despite the remarkable degree of consensus among senior JLP managers about the current JLP model and its impact on the performance of the JLP, and about the necessary and desirable direction of the JLP. One tension arises from the fundamental design of the JLP: for the model deliberately creates a series of countervailing institutions and processes—'checks and balances'—intended to hold managers to account. These include the systemic encouragement and channelling of criticism through various agencies (the democratic bodies, the journalism, and the Partner Survey); the formal capping of executive salaries; and the existence of clearly stated values and principles to guide behaviour. These tensions are actively encouraged; indeed there are mechanisms and even specific roles, responsible for asking questions of managers.

The Partnership is a classic illustration of the playing-out of 'competing institutional logics' (Thornton et al. 2012). JLP managers, past and present, have created, and continue to sustain, a juggling act whereby they emphasize and seek to serve commercial logics while also emphasizing and serving the principles associated with co-ownership. This sustained stance inevitably creates tensions of the kind characteristic of 'hybrid organizations' (Pache and Santos 2013). The literature notes the different strategies that can be adopted to handle tensions of this kind. There are three classic modes of approach:

- de-coupling of the logics by allocating responsibility for each to separate institutional forms (for example, different departments);
- thrashing out the differences until one logic comes to dominate and thus becomes the accepted orthodoxy;
- reconciling in some looser way so that dual logics are accepted as legitimate; combining competing logics through 'logic blending' (Besharov and Smith 2014).

In the case of the Partnership, 'de-coupling' can be seen to be an adopted strategy in so far as special roles and departments are established to defend Partnership principles. This can be clearly seen, for example, with the very considerable investment in the registrars. These, as we will describe in Chapter 2, are unique roles which combine a kind of welfare officer remit with a constitution-defending role which involves a check on managers throughout the Partnership at all levels including the most senior. A danger of this kind of approach is that it might be seen as a licence for managers to focus mainly on the customer and profit agenda, given that 'others' have a prime responsibility to ensure conformance with the defence of partner interests.

Yet, in another sense, it could be said that the Partnership has, in recent years drifted towards a solution of the second kind. Some internal critics argue that the commercial logic has been allowed such an emphasis that it has to all intents and purposes crowded-out the competing Partnership logic so as to render the democratic structures empty shells.

The third solution to the competing logics conundrum, 'logic blending', also has its advocates. This stance suggests that there is a healthy tension between competing logics and it is this ongoing tension which energizes the Partnership and gives it a special competitive advantage.

Other tensions arise from the relationship between the elements of the model and the business aspirations and policies of the businesses. It not only comes into play in the choice of policies to advance the achievement of the businesses' goals, it also introduces—at least potentially—discussions about the *legitimacy* of the goals. These tensions are discussed in later chapters since they go to the heart of the way the JLP works and the extent to which its success is attributed to the JLP model.

We need to know the JLP better if we are to emulate the strengths and benefits of the model.

The first task is to identify the core elements, principles, and relationships of the JLP model. This is not necessarily a simple task since JLP staff and outside commentators do not always agree on the extent to which current arrangements are true to the founder's intentions, or to the core principles underpinning the model. Such differences of view are more likely when JLP has been through a period of considerable change, especially with respect to business and management processes and decisions. The JLP model is not a fixed entity to be copied. It is dynamic: institutions and processes have changed including democratic and consultative and communication pro-cesses. Strategies, business and management processes, governance, and accountability processes have changed. Many new managers have been recruited from competitors (representing a significant change of historic practice). Such changes raise the question: do they represent a development of and a commitment to the historic principles and components of the JLP model, or a diminution or even a rejection of these principles?

What is distinctive about the JLP is that it is 'owned' by its employees (always known as 'partners' inside the firm). Employee ownership is achieved through a mechanism which means shares are held in trust; partners are unable to sell their assets. The owners secure economic benefit as a significant proportion of profits, in the shape of an annual bonus, which is shared among all partners. Between 2007 and 2014, this averaged 16 per cent of salary per annum (11 per cent in 2015). A bonus is paid on top of salary. The bonus rate is the same for all partners—so if the managing directors get 16 per cent so too does a front-line worker. As there are salary differentials, this means that the bonus is worth more in absolute terms to the higher paid. The Partnership has a number of structures and processes which act to ensure that employees have the capacity to hold management to account for their decisions. The partners are represented in the formal governing authorities and processes via two mechanisms: first, five members of the Partnership Board are elected by the partners (indirectly via Partnership Councillors), and second, through the Partnership Council which has an elected membership of seventy councillors. This latter body has the power, indeed the responsibility, to hold top management to account. Top management in JLP is in effect the Chairman. This is an unusual executive chairmanship role carrying significant power and authority. There is no chief executive, but there are managing directors for each division—most notably, Waitrose and the John Lewis department stores. There are also consultative forums at store and divisional levels (for Waitrose the stores are organized on a regional basis).

The founder was alert to the danger that senior managers would be able to use their knowledge and positions to accrue unwarranted power and privilege at the expense of partners in general. To help mitigate this risk he created a set of roles and institutions which he termed the 'critical side'. This included a cluster of roles such as inspectors and registrars' and Partners' Counsellor—who collectively could keep a watchful eye over commercial managers and who could report direct to the Chairman.

And finally, a brief note on pay differentials when compared with the figures shown in the section 'How Managers Stole their Businesses' for executives at large. The highest paid individual in the Partnership is the Chairman. In 2015 his total remuneration, including the Partnership bonus of £104,000, was £1.53m. This represented a 0.6 per cent increase on the previous year. His total pay is 60 times the average basic pay of a non-management partner with three or more years' service. This compares with a maximum ratio of 75:1 allowed for in the Constitution (Rule 63).

It will be evident, from this brief overview, that in a number of ways the JLP model differs fundamentally from the model of the firm prevalent in the USA and the UK. The orthodox model is so dominant that it is seen as natural, inevitable and right, an example of how ideas are deemed true because they are powerful rather than *vice versa*. The JLP differs from this model with respect to strategic objectives, accountability, leadership, and compensation policies.

As noted, conventional firms are increasingly committed to defining all relationships as market relationships—including relations with employees. But within JLP, an organization explicitly committed to the well-being of its staff and other stakeholders, market relations are supposedly less all-prevailing. This raises two issues requiring analysis: by what logic and by what processes is the distinction made between 'internal relations', that is with partners and stakeholders, and 'external relations' with outsourced and agency staff who are not deemed to be partners and to whom partners' benefits are not available and who are treated in ways not wholly dissimilar from conventional businesses? This contentious issue of who is and who should be a 'member' and 'partner' is encountered in many business decisions. And we explore these decisions in detail in later chapters. Asking who should be a partner is tantamount to asking what, ultimately, the Partnership is for, and who is it for?

If the constituent businesses of the Partnership are committed to treating those employees who are *within* the system—the partners—in non-market based ways, that is, more generously than conventional competitors' treat their staff, and if the business is also committed to competing for market share with these competitors, then does this mean that these dual commitments may clash? If they do, when does/should one principle hold more sway over the other, and vice versa?

One argument is that the JLP model has a positive impact on the behaviour of partners and suppliers and through this it generates a superior customer experience which in turn drives sustained sales and revenue. On that reading there is no real clash. This is at the heart of the 'partner–customer–profit cycle' proposition.

But, if the model is expensive—and it is—then these investments while potentially adding to sales certainly also add to costs. A potential tension is thus created, especially during difficult times. As the MD of John Lewis commented candidly when discussing the drop of profits during 2009, 'Our operating model is too costly.' So, how in practice is this tension resolved? It is only through a close examination of specific instances where managers were faced with competing real choices in concrete situations that that question can be answered. In other words, it has to be answered empirically.

The prevailing model of leadership in the US/UK firm has been described. It differs in some important ways from the approach of leadership within the JLP. Within JLP, leaders are held accountable, have to deal with elected directors, must respond to criticism and above all, must comply with explicit values.

This initial overview of some of the core elements of the JLP model indicates the kind of issues at stake. For example, are democracy and accountability still strong? Is the critical side still vigorous? Do these institutions still work as they did or as they were intended to do? Further, if there is a link between the model and performance how does this linkage work? And if it works now, has it always done so, and if not, what intervening factors are required to ensure the model generates and supports successful businesses? Is the model as a totality the key, or are certain elements of the model more important than others? How is leadership exercised in the Partnership?

There are other fundamental issues. How should success and performance be measured? What are the objectives and ultimate purpose of the Partnership? The first paragraph of the Constitution is admirably clear:

> The Partnership's ultimate purpose is the happiness of all its members, through their worthwhile and satisfying employment in a successful business. Because the partnership is owned in trust for its members, they share the responsibilities of ownership as well as its rewards—profit, knowledge and power.

There is also an explicit emphasis on the Partnership making 'sufficient profit to sustain our commercial vitality and distinctive character'.

John Lewis and Waitrose are seen as successful commercially and their success is attributed to customers' appreciation of the qualities they experience when shopping at the Partnership and these qualities are somehow related to the distinctive features of the JLP model. In that narrative, the 'distinctive character' of the Partnership, while valuable and admirable and important in its own right is also seen as *a means* for the achievement of good commercial performance, whereas, in the founder's statements, the distinctive character is seen as an *end* in itself (although one that must be balanced with 'commercial vitality').

Our analysis of the JLP is organized around four core themes which run throughout the book and which can be expressed as key research questions:

1) What are the crucial elements of the JLP model, how is leadership exercised and how, within such a model, are managers held to account? This question domain also addresses issues of governance.

2) What are the implications of the model for business performance?

3) How do managers view the nature and importance of partner engagement and democracy?

4) What are the lessons to be drawn from this case example of stakeholder-oriented organization for policy makers and practitioners and can the positive attributes of the model be replicated elsewhere?

The analysis begins in the next chapter with a profile of the John Lewis Partnership. This provides an introduction to each of its main distinctive features. In later chapters the features are subject to more detailed critical scrutiny and assessment.

2

An Introductory Profile of the John Lewis Partnership

This chapter provides an overall profile of the John Lewis Partnership and describes the key features. Each feature is explored and examined in greater depth in the chapters that follow.

This chapter is organised into four sections. The first provides an outline view; the second offers a brief history; the third describes the customer proposition; and the final section discusses the partner proposition including governance, democracy, and benefits.

An Outline View

The John Lewis Partnership (JLP) is a large UK retailer with two major business operations: John Lewis department stores and Waitrose supermarkets. In addition, it has launched additional businesses such as insurance and travel but the department stores business and the supermarkets business remain, by far, the dominant operations. The retail businesses operate through stores and online. They have expanded their offer across a range of formats including large, full-range stores with a wide assortment of goods and smaller cut-down versions.

JLP is owned by its employees (known always as partners). The shares are held in trust. It is not quoted on the stock exchange; it raises investment capital by borrowing and by its own revenues. This independence is seen by senior managers as crucial: they continually emphasize that they can take the long view as they are not subject to quarterly reviews by the City. The partners have a voice in the running of the Partnership which includes a structure of representational democracy culminating in a Partnership Council and partner representatives elected to the main Board. There are three 'governing authorities' at the pinnacle of the Partnership: the Chairman, the Partnership

Council, and the Partnership Board. The relationship between these is intended to be a system of checks and balances.

John Lewis and Waitrose enjoy an enviable media profile, a high consumer reputation, and a loyal customer base. They are notable for the quality of their customer service, the full-range assortment in its department stores, the quality of their supermarket food, the favourable locations, the modern feel of their fixtures and fittings, and for the employee-owned character of the enterprise. All recruits become partners from the outset and they are entitled to their share of the annual bonus. In recent years, the businesses have outperformed the market, as least as far as sales are concerned and John Lewis and Waitrose are often used by the media as a 'barometer' for the weather on the 'high street'.

As of February 2015, the Partnership operated 322 Waitrose branches in the UK and 41 John Lewis stores. The internet businesses—johnlewis.com and waitrose.com—are both thriving. There is a small overseas presence and Waitrose offers its goods in a number of outlets such as garage forecourt stores and motorway services. Not all such outlets are staffed by partners. The Partnership also owns and operates a production unit and a farm. The production unit, Herbert Parkinson, is based in Lancashire. This unit manufactures own-brand furnishings, fabrics, and curtains. Herbert Parkinson also makes John Lewis's own-brand duvets, pillows, furnishing fabrics and ready-made curtains, and provides a made-to-measure curtain services. There is also a small on-site fabric weaving operation which creates exclusive designs for John Lewis. Founded in 1934, Herbert Parkinson became part of the John Lewis Partnership in 1953. In September 2015, the first new full-range department store in five years was opened, located at the heart of a new shopping centre in Birmingham. The year 2015 also saw further international expansion with the opening of shops in Singapore and the Philippines. JL already had stores in Korea.

In addition to the two main business divisions, there has been recent growth in a shared business services division called Partnership Services which serves the whole of the Partnership. This division delivers processes and systems to support suppliers and internal partners. It provides shared services in finance including payroll and expenses, fixed assets, cash management, accounts payable and receivable, general ledger and pensions administration. The corporate level, called Group, is also important. It is based in a headquarters building adjacent to the JL division head office in central London near Victoria railway station. Group consists of the various governance and strategy functions such as the Chairman's Office, Development, Taxation, Treasury, and Legal. While some of these Group responsibilities are found in other businesses, JLP Group activities include what they describe as 'the Partnership Difference' such as Registry, Partner Strategy (within the Director of Personnel's team), and a team of professional in-house journalists. With divisionalization and the establishment of shared services, the importance of these areas has increased.

The Partnership is by far the largest and most successful co-owned business in the UK. In 2015, there were over 93,000 partners employed. The total revenue was £10.9bn and this was a 5.7 per cent increase over the previous year. But operating profits were down by 7.5 per cent to £442m. The partners' bonus was 15 per cent of pay in 2014 and 11 per cent in 2015. The tendency for overall profitability to be lower than that of some of its competitors continues.

The image of huge success which the Partnership currently enjoys has not always been available to it. When, in December 1995, the BBC broadcast a programme about JLP, the image was of a rather eccentric institution struggling to fit in with wider social change. Yet, when the BBC broadcast another series, *Inside John Lewis* in 2010, the message had changed: it was portrayed as a serious contemporary player willing and able to tackle major competitive challenges in a principled and commercially adept way. The fact that the Partnership is not answerable to shareholders or the City is seen as a key feature which allows its senior managers to make decisions free from short-term constraints. In addition, senior managers believe that the 'collective reward' elements and the co-owner status are among the more central distinctive characteristic features.

The Partnership gained even more attention and approval as it survived and thrived during the recession which followed the financial crisis of 2008. As many rival retailers went to the wall, JLP was seen to prosper. Politicians of all persuasions and many observers began to praise and recommend it as a seeming benign solution. Most famously, the then Deputy Prime minister, Nick Clegg, called for a move towards a 'John Lewis economy', that is, an economy populated with many more organizations characterized by the values and practices associated with JLP.

A Brief History

History matters to John Lewis much more so than to most other businesses.[1] One indicator is the retention of a paid archivist and a significant archive facility. Remarkably, many of the distinctive features of the Partnership today such as the sharing of power, knowledge, and profit were designed and installed by the founder, Spedan Lewis from 1920 onwards. He was influenced by a number of social and political thinkers such as John Ruskin (1819–1900) and Robert Owen (1771–1858) and he adapted their ideas in practical form. He

---

[1] A fuller historical account can be found in Peter Cox (2010) *Spedan's Partnership: The Story of John Lewis and Waitrose*, Labatie Books.

was prescient in recognizing the huge risk of the dilution of the democratic and enlightened ideas enshrined in his vision and he took steps to install checks and balances to preserve the experiment.

He was alert to the risks of future erosion of the principles, observing:

> Once you admit the idea that it may be necessary, or at all events right, to give ground sometimes, once you admit the idea that it may sometimes be necessary, or at all events right, to diminish the degree of democracy that your particular Partnership has in fact attained, you will have no good enough foothold against folly or cunning. Bit by bit you will be pushed and wangled back into unnecessary inequality, privilege, and selfishness. And selfishness is apt to take root quickly and deep. (Spedan Lewis 1948: 214)

History matters too in JLP because the senior managers—and the elected representatives—tend to refer very frequently to the founder, his principles, and the way these are embodied in a written Constitution as yardsticks by which to judge their actions or proposals. There is an unusual awareness about and emphasis on, the legacy. The living culture in JLP as expressed through discourse, behaviour, and by norms and values, reflects, in a highly conscious way, the principles and ideas that stem from that history. One manager noted that Spedan's books used to be issued to newly-appointed Senior Managers: 'When I joined in 2000, I was given them by my Registrar on my first day but this practice lapsed several years later'. When conducting our business research activities, we too were given copies of these books.

The roots of the business (in its original privately-owned form) go back 150 years. John Lewis, the father of the founder, set up his first shop in the 1860s. His main operational base was a department store on Oxford Street, London. He put his son, Spedan Lewis, in charge of an acquired store in West London, Peter Jones, and it was at this store that Spedan began to introduce more enlightened employment practices. Father and son were at odds on many business matters. It was Spedan who transformed the business into a 'Partnership' and became its founder when he took the highly unusual step of giving away a large portion of his ownership of the business to his employees in 1929. He placed these shares in a trust using an 'irrevocable settlement' (Spedan Lewis 1954). Spedan was a deep thinker. He read widely and he gave detailed consideration to how a co-owned business might operate. He authored some notable books including *Partnership for All* (1948) and *Fairer Shares* (1954). An anthology of his extensive writings on trading policies, including pricing, stock control, ticketing, and many other of the minutiae of retailing was gathered together and published by the Partnership under the title *Retail Trading*.

Spedan took the unusual step of producing a written Constitution for the Partnership. This survives and is influential to this day; it is updated periodically in accord with a formal set of procedures. It sets out underlying principles and also the rules of operation. Each element is designed to maintain the desired balance between commercial viability and the model of partner engagement and democracy. As already noted, one important clause states that the Partnership's ultimate purpose is 'the happiness of all its members through their worthwhile and satisfying employment in a successful business'. It goes on to suggest that because the Partnership is owned in trust for its members 'they share the responsibilities of ownership as well as its rewards—profit, knowledge and power' (JLP Constitution, p. 7).

The Constitution establishes a system of 'rights and responsibilities', which places on all partners the obligation to work for the improvement of the business in the knowledge that they share the rewards of success. The Constitution defines various mechanisms designed to provide for the management of the Partnership, with checks and balances to ensure accountability, transparency, and honesty. It established the representation of the co-owners on the Partnership Board through the election of partners as directors (elected directors). The Constitution, as revised in 2009, states that the Partnership 'aims to make sufficient profit from its trading operations to sustain its commercial vitality, to finance its continued development, to distribute a share of those profits each year to its members, and to enable it to undertake other activities consistent with its ultimate purpose'.

The stocks and shares as a whole are held in Trust and they are administered by a group of trustees on behalf of all partners. They cannot be traded on the stock exchange and no one can sell any of the shares. Whether this amounts to 'ownership' or even 'co-ownership' in any strict sense is a moot point. Allocating assets to beneficiaries in this way represents a modified form of Anglo-Saxon Trust law. The arrangement seems to exemplify the kind of 'corporate trusteeship' advocated passionately by Colin Mayer (2014).

There are, however, some managers who believe that the term 'co-owner' is misleading. As one senior informant said to us 'it implies a decision-making authority or even just an involvement in decision making which, to be frank, is not really there'. But others sought to affirm the reality of co-ownership; it is, they said, what they have always believed was the case. Others were content to accept it was essentially a 'perception', a kind of emotional identity and they seek to rebadge it as something like 'membership' instead. So, this crucial and pivotal concept of co-ownership remains inherently ambiguous and fluid.

The founder created a governance system, set out in a Constitution that was, and remains, both commercial in orientation and, in the founder's own terms, 'democratic' (see Figure 2.1). Indeed he referred to JLP as 'An

Figure 2.1. Voting at Partnership Council

experiment in industrial democracy' (Spedan Lewis 1948). The extent to which it can truly be described as a vibrant democracy in practice is another area for debate. In the founder's own words:

> In the John Lewis Partnership, democracy, the sharing of power, has been carried out as far as is practicable. If other people can see how to do it better, let them start another partnership and show how far they are right. (Spedan Lewis 1954: 10)

Spedan's own thinking and writing, although remarkable and singular, were reflective of certain social and political movements of his time. The trade union movement was growing and the Russian Revolution had reverberated throughout Europe. Spedan's own writing positioned his partnership experiment in the context of wider social and economic ideas and initiatives including the work of Robert Owen, the Rochdale Pioneers, and the 'colossal consumer cooperative movement' (Spedan Lewis 1954: 5). He worried about extreme inequality, observing 'apart from fears of a breakdown of society, more and more of the well-to-do are genuinely troubled because so many of their fellow-citizens are so badly off' (Spedan Lewis 1954: 4). He positioned the Partnership as 'an attempt to devise and demonstrate upon a fairly impressive scale a feasible technique for such a change in the private enterprise of the business world . . . an attempt to succeed where after a brilliant promising start, Robert Owen failed' (Spedan Lewis 1954: 5).

Ironically, like his father, Spedan was also often personally autocratic and domineering in his interpersonal relationships. Yet when he was given charge of the Peter Jones store he instigated enlightened personnel policies including a shorter working day, rest breaks, longer holidays, and the introduction of committees for communication with employees. He even introduced the staff journal, the *Gazette*, at Peter Jones in 1918 and this innovation survives to this day. Then as now, the journal allowed and indeed encouraged anonymous letters which challenge management practices. The directors who find themselves challenged and questioned in this way are expected to reply in writing in a reasoned and respectful manner.

Spedan's father, John Lewis, was a traditional employer characteristic of the time. He resisted trade unions and was robust in the face of strike action. When in 1920 his Oxford Street store faced a strike by 400 employees, John adamantly refused them the right to return and he took active steps to keep the store running using strikebreaking labour. Meanwhile, at his store in Chelsea, Speden was experimenting with new ideas including paying bonuses and renaming employees as 'partners'.

Spedan's father died in 1928. In the following year, the First Trust Settlement was made and the Partnership was formed. It was underpinned by a formal Constitution extending to 268 pages. Under the terms of the settlement, profits were to be distributed to all partners as a percentage of their pay. The new policies also introduced a sickness payments scheme and access for staff to the country house and estate at Odney, an idyllic rural retreat on the River Thames.

The pattern was set in these early days to recruit top graduates and talented recruits from the military and the civil service—persons who would not normally have considered a role in retailing or any similar 'trade'. Expansion through acquisition occurred during the 1930s; other established department stores such as Jessops in Nottingham were purchased and so too were ten Waitrose stores in the suburbs of London in 1937. The Partnership also had its own factories—making bedding, furniture, hats, and fabrics for its stores. John Lewis department stores tended to be located in major city centre locations. However, as part of the expansion plan under the Chairmanship of Peter Lewis (1972–93) the first full-range store was opened in a new development shopping centre. This was opened at Brent Cross in North London in 1976 (Figure 2.2).

The Partnership held on to old fashioned trading practices up until around the year 2000 (to give just a few examples, there were restricted opening hours, stores closed early on Saturdays and remained closed until Tuesday each week, there was very limited advertising, a refusal to take credit cards, a lack of business planning, and legacy systems out of step with those of competitors). At that time, JLP was often seen as reliable and trusted but rather dull, old-fashioned, and unadventurous. It was even compared with the

Figure 2.2. John Lewis at the Brent Cross Shopping Centre in the 1970s

National Trust. The top management cadre and recruitment into that group was untypical of the profile for the retail trade at that time. Many members of the top echelon were highly educated graduates from Oxbridge and a number joined from the civil service and even the secret service. For example, the Cambridge mathematician Gordon Welchman who played a pivotal role at the government code-breaking centre at Bletchley Park (later to become GCHQ) was recruited after the war as Director of Research at John Lewis. His predecessor in that role was Hugh Alexander another Bletchley codebreaker, chess champion of his day, and contemporary of Alan Turing. Welchman later emigrated to the USA where he helped develop the first computers for air traffic control and air defence.

A new Chairman, Stuart Hampson, was appointed in 1993 and remained in post for fourteen years until 2007 when Charlie Mayfield became his successor. Hampson had joined the Partnership in 1982 from the civil service. As chairman he helped to instigate growth and modernization; he was knighted in 1998. In 1999, during a time when privatization and de-mutualization were fashionable, there was an attempt to demutualize the Partnership. The media ran stories suggesting very large sums would be available for each worker if the Partnership was sold. Proponents suggested that this would reinvigorate the business and reward each partner with tens of thousands of pounds. Hampson resisted this strongly. There was a tense exchange of letters in the *Gazette* and a full-blown debate on the issue in the Partnership Council. These were testing times indeed for the Partnership and the debate even brought to the surface awkward questions such as whether the owners could sell or not and if not then were they truly proper owners. In the event, the Council debated the issue and rejected the idea.

A signal of a new, wider, outlook came with the appointment of Luke Mayhew as Managing Director of the JL department stores in 2000 following the retirement of Brian O'Callaghan. He was formerly with Thomas Cook and then British Airways. He had joined John Lewis in 1992 as development director and director of research and expansion. Mayhew was seen as a new broom and he instigated a set of changes which seemed to signal a new order. These included investment in Ocado, the internet grocery business which formed a partnership with Waitrose. He was involved in the acquisition of buy.com whose employees did not become partners for a period of time. This enabled key entrepreneurial leaders at buy.com to continue receiving individual bonuses and remain to lead knowledge transfer to JL. All these buy.com leaders left within a few years. However, it enabled JL to make a step change with its online capability. Notably, Mayhew also oversaw seven-day-a-week opening at most of the stores. He additionally set in motion the move to a single brand, with the exception of the historic flagship store, Peter Jones. He also championed a series of significant investments in big store refurbishments.

Luke Mayhew, as a significant change-agent in a milieu unused at that time to such disturbance, was a somewhat controversial figure. He resigned as Managing Director in December 2004 after a relatively short tenure. He received a significant pay-off for 'loss of office'. This denoted a payment made on the basis of a decision to quit, but with the company fixing the time of departure. In effect it was a compromise agreement. It was argued by some that Mayhew, an 'outsider', was ahead of his time. Following his departure, the same direction of travel was pursued by others. He had served his purpose by stirring things up.

We found a lively controversy both inside and outside the Partnership about the interpretations of the relative performance of the business pre- and post-Hampson reforms following the appointment of Luke Mayhew. The argument that the JLP of the pre-Mayhew era saw a period of poor performance which indicated the need for radical change (of the sort initiated by Hampson and Luke Mayhew in John Lewis) is problematical. In fact, profits at certain times in the 1990s were exceptionally good. In the financial year 1997/8, John Lewis achieved a profit of £197m which was 11 per cent of sales. With such a performance there is clear ground for refuting the notion that the 1980s and 1990s were a time of sedate decline. However, the Partnership's profits did decline for four years after 1997/8 which suggests that the results in 1997/8 were a peak and not sustainable. Also important is the fact that the market in which the JLP businesses compete has changed greatly since the late

1990s. The very considerable investment since that time in both businesses has not resulted in higher levels of profitability (although certainly generating very significantly greater overall profits in absolute terms) but this needs to be seen in terms of the transformation of the competitive landscape both in terms of intensity of competition and radical changes introduced by e-commerce.

So, one narrative is that the past two decades have witnessed a heroic and radical revitalisation of the commercial viability of the business. An alternative, more critical view, has two strands. One of these is that the growth has come at the price of profitable return; and a second is that the true nature of the democratic partnership has been sacrificed for commercial success of a more conventional kind. Unpicking these summations is not to be done lightly. The different interpretations are examined throughout the book by attending to relevant evidence both in terms of actions and outcomes.

From 2000 onwards, there was a programme of investment and growth in internet shopping and a website was launched in that year. An early and controversial strategic initiative was an investment in Ocado, an online grocery shopping venture. This new company was a joint venture with two former merchant bankers from Goldman Sachs. It started trading in 2002 and supplied Waitrose goods for home delivery across the Greater London area. The venture lost money for many years and the investment was much criticized by partners in letters to the *Gazette*. In due course, however, it moved into profit. The company was floated on the London Stock Exchange in July 2010. In November 2008, the John Lewis Partnership transferred its shareholding of 29 per cent into its staff pension fund. It also agreed a five-year supply deal with the business and then in May 2010 this was replaced with a 10-year branding and supply agreement. In February 2011, the John Lewis pension fund sold off its entire £152m Ocado shareholding, while Waitrose continued to supply Ocado.

Hampson had signalled his intent to give a sharper commercial edge to the Partnership with his appointment of Luke Mayhew as MD of JL. Together, they instigated a set of reforms and embarked on expansion. Until that time, the Partnership had followed the founder's own predilections. For example, and rather ironically in view of later prowess in this area, the Partnership was opposed to advertising and marketing. This is ironic because, today, John Lewis is noted for stylish and prolific adverts and especially notable for its Christmas commercials. Likewise, the Partnership persisted with quaint and restricted opening hours. Until the early 2000s, the John Lewis stores were closed on Sundays and Mondays and they only worked until lunchtime on a Saturday. The ways in which the partners were persuaded to move first to a five day week, then six and eventually seven, is indicative of its ways of operating.

Luke Mayhew insisted that all stores had the right to discuss and then vote on the proposal for extended opening hours. Some branches resisted, but their managers were asked to re-open the debates and re-run the ballots. In due course, all branches voted in favour.

Hampson and Mayhew also presided over the introduction of business planning. Remarkably, unlike most other businesses of its size it had not utilized modern management techniques such as business planning or performance targets and appraisal. The general approach was incremental improvement on the previous year's work. The authors of this book were present at the divisional board meetings at this time when these business plans were being tentatively introduced and when, in accord with this, the management boards were being professionalized. There was a bold programme of investments including an extraordinary spend of £100m invested in the refurbishment of the flagship Peter Jones store in fashionable Knightsbridge. In addition, £65m was invested in the refurbishment of the Oxford Street store, another flagship of the Partnership. Elsewhere in the country, the erstwhile family-named stores were rebranded with the corporate John Lewis name in 2002. Around this time there was a new concerted effort to modernize supply chain management which until that time was out of step with developments elsewhere. As part of this, new automated distribution centres were built and the current Managing Director of John Lewis, Andy Street, was appointed as supply chain management director. He was followed by Patrick Lewis who then became Director of Partnership Services, a shared business services function, and subsequently Group Finance Director.

Later, the company also moved towards an extended range of own-brand goods in electrical, home, and fashion items. In addition, there was ambitious investment in new-build prestige stores. The significant presence, as 'anchor stores', in the new retail developments at Bluewater, Trafford Centre, and Westfield (see Figure 2.3 for examples of the 'new look' of these out of town stores) were indicative and so to was the new city centre store in Cardiff. In addition, there was experimentation with new formats. This included 'John Lewis at Home' (not full range, these smaller stores focus only on the home, electrical, and home technology assortment). Further, there were new smaller department stores as in Exeter which opened in 2012 and York which opened in 2014. Each of these outlets, and the Waitrose branches, support the online click and collect service.

This narrative of success is challenged by some former high-level insiders. We interviewed a number of retired senior directors who were able to provide an oral history of the continuing unbroken link between Spedan and his immediate team, and the transition to the next generation and the one after that. Through this mechanism they argued, the influence of that team extended well into the 1960s and 1970s. For example, Spedan appointed Bernard Miller, with a first class in history, direct from Oxford University

31

Figure 2.3. The new look out of town shopping centres, circa 2005

and Max Baker, was recruited with a Cambridge degree in Natural Sciences. Sir Bernard Miller took over as Chairman in 1955 and retired in 1972. Under his leadership, the Partnership increased profits six-fold, yet with very little expansion of stores. Paul May and Max Baker were described to us as influential in modernizing the business including the introduction, for example, of centralized buying. The retired directors described with admiration, respect, and affection how these key players handed over the reins to the next generation. This latter cohort included Peter Lewis who became Chairman from 1976 to 1993. As a result of these appointments, the founder and the family continued to have a profound influence long after Spedan's own departure.

In turn, the retirements of that second wave was followed by 'a mix of senior learners and a graduate intake provided finance, trading and principled management expertise at the top of the business that fully respected its founding objectives'. This observation was given to us by one retired senior director and it was a sentiment echoed by others. The 1980s witnessed a fresh intake of fast-track players amongst them Stuart Hampson, David Young, Ian Alexander, Luke Mayhew, and David Felwick. Throughout the 1990s, change began to surface under Hampson's chairmanship. Initially it began with a wish to engage both the press and city in a form not sought by earlier administrations. Other changes soon followed with revision of the rules and regulations and, as the new decade arrived, a wholesale reshaping of the democratic institutions. In many ways, the changed nature of the *Gazette* reflected the scale of what had occurred.

Post-2000, Waitrose sought to move beyond its former niche as the quality food specialist located in affluent areas. Meanwhile, Luke Mayhew's move to the JL department stores resulted in investment on an unprecedented scale both in terms of refurbishment and new space. The management consultants Bain were brought in (allegedly as a result of Mayhew's insistence). Their recommendation began to upturn the previous long legacy. Max Baker's buying and selling template was discarded and replaced by a chain format. The assortment (the range of items) was pruned by a third. Around this time also store opening hours were increased.

As a consequence of this radical modernizing venture, there was an enlarged trading footprint for the JL department stores division and a multi format Waitrose was formed. But this is where the narrative as told by incumbent managers and some of their predecessors varies. While one narrative refers to the need to play catch-up and to modernize a relatively complacent enterprise, another narrative suggests that 'The meagre post-2000 profit performance of the departments stores division tells its own story'. In other words, the decline in profits is seen to denote something other than a neat story of reform and success. Reference was made to Self-ridges which, without similar expansion 'achieved £1 billion turnover and a 13 per cent bottom line that puts the lie to the case for the economies of scale in the DS sector'. The argument here is that it is distinction that matters. Similarly, these retired players note that while Waitrose bottom line has improved, the performance outcomes accompanying the rapid development raise questions: 'The decisions to compete with the majors on all fronts may not prove to be a better option than sticking with the specialist food operator trading in prime locations' (retired senior director).

The critique continues with attention drawn to the scale of the Bain impact on the numbers of posts in central offices and the degree of centralized control. This line of analysis also reflected clear discomfort at the increase ('escalation') in marketing costs and 'the advertising addiction now gripping both divisions'.

The retired senior players acknowledged the 'spectacular nature' of the investments in online trading but they expressed reservations about the impact of the internet business on the Department Stores assortment. It was argued that the supply and delivery chain logic of the online model tends to emphasize simplicity and a packaged product and that can have a 'dumbing down effect' on the furnishing assortments. Likewise, the seven-day delivery commitment in furniture is also seen to carry deleterious consequences resulting from the part reliance on third-party contractors. These conflicting perspectives about business models, reflect sincerely held and passionate stances concerning the way the John Lewis Partnership ought to operate. They reflect the healthy and honest and open debate about retailing strategy in a partnership/stakeholder organization.

There was also a critical stance taken by some former senior players which suggested that a fundamental change had taken place in the Partnership in respect of the principal and agent dynamic. It was suggested that a misfit had occurred between capital expenditure and return—in other words that investment and growth had been prioritized over profit. Critics also contended that the 'constant restructuring' was driven by a need to negate the rising costs that stemmed from the ambitious development programmes. There was criticism too about the changes made by the management consultants from Bain and Company 'outsiders who did not understand the uniqueness of John Lewis'. Complaints were also made about the loss of security of tenure which was revealed as redundancies were made to cope with the economic downturn. The freeze on pay in the JL division over a three-year period around 2009–12 went beyond anything that could have occurred in previous decades and caused considerable concern across the Partnership. According to one of our sources, the 'sanitising of the *Gazette* to a good news only propaganda sheet was a further consequence of the shift in approach'. Doubt was also cast on the modus operandi of the new democratic institutions. The critical view of these former key players was that there had been a 'weakening of accountability'.

The interpretations just outlined differ markedly from the ones held by the current senior team. These diverse analyses are highly significant. They reflect the contested nature of 'proper and responsible management' in a multiple stakeholder organization as well as reflecting, of course, the more normal disagreements about appropriate retailing strategy that could exist in any retail business. In part, the debate reflects changed times. The high level of retained profits achieved in a number of years in 1990s is not disputed. But, what is open to debate, is whether those returns were sustainable without new investment and growth. Likewise, the validity of comparing performance measures in one very different period and context with those of another very different period and context is open to question. The underlying dispute, however, goes deeper than this. It reflects sincerely held divergent views about how to safeguard the soul of the Partnership.

The Customer Proposition

When the shopping public is asked about its impressions of John Lewis and Waitrose, one of the features it mentions is customer service. The stores are noted for their well informed and helpful partners who have unusual product knowledge. Indeed, this has been accepted to the extent that some competitors have sought to turn the tables by advertising which mockingly urges the consumer to go talk to a helpful assistant at John Lewis and then make the purchase cheaper elsewhere without the service wraparound. But JLP gains enormously from its sustained policy of value-for-money, honesty, and fair trading. Its two-year guarantee on electrical goods is a market differentiator, especially as that is backed-up with a no-questions asked fulfilment of that guarantee. However, the number of knowledgeable assistants is lower than was formerly the case. The extended opening hours and seven-day trading has inevitably meant employing more part-time staff. This has raised issues about their level of product knowledge, and some concern about the opportunity to pass-on and assimilate partnership values. Interaction with the appraising line manager may also be reduced due to rota patterns. The sales assistance expert can still, however, be found in specialist areas such as curtains and electrical. Notably, there was awareness and concern among senior managers about the potential dilution of partner identity as a consequence of extended hours and more part-time staff, such that an initiative was launched to try to address this. Labelled the 'Three Commitments' this initiative sought to embed the philosophy: 'take responsibility for business success, build relationships powered by our principles, and create real influence over our working lives'. Partners at all levels were involved in focus groups to construct and deliver this drive.

These features contribute to the value of the brand. As one director said:

> If we were valuing this company on the stock exchange, a key element in the calculation would be our customer franchise and the many things we have done to build that loyalty and trust even if we do not monetise it to maximum effect in the short term. (JLP director)

A key part of the build-up to that loyalty from customers is the discretionary effort expended by partners which in turn is traced back to the Partnership model of co-ownership and shared reward. But the success is not only traced to this, there is also the skill of managers in knowing where to trade and how. Ultimately, it is a subtle mix of co-ownership and commercial acumen. The partner–customer–profit cycle is seen as fundamental.

Senior managers accept that the harmony between these mutually-reinforcing elements work best in the long term and that in the short term there could be gains to be made by sacrificing the 'partner piece' in pursuit of short-term financial gain. But they are also aware that this would amount to what they often termed, 'throwing out the baby with the bathwater', and such a move they said would be a signal failure of leadership. The key to Partnership management, they claim, is about 'playing the long-game'.

There are, however, occasional challenges to this generally positive and enviable reputation and supportive media coverage. A series of complaints to the *Guardian* consumer editor about poor service with regard to goods delivered from the online service fulfilment provider led to an adverse article headline 'Has John Lewis lost the digital age plot?'[2] The complaints about poor delivery and home fitting services were attributed to the outsourced supplier for home delivery and fitting for appliances such as washing machines. One suggestion was that outsourcing of services to firms—such as Capita who provide online aftercare with a contract worth £93.5m—may be responsible. This again raises the significance of the 'who is a member?' question.

The 'Never Knowingly Undersold' strapline which started as far back as 1925 offers a further point of distinction. Its precise meaning is open to question as there are conditions. The claim does not extend to Waitrose supermarkets. Indeed, on certain baskets of goods there is a price premium to be paid at this quality supplier. In general, loyal Waitrose shoppers know this but they are attracted by the concept of 'quality at the price offered'. Waitrose also trade on an ethical sourcing policy and a known provenance for meat and other sensitive products. To counter the threat from discounters such as Aldi during the recessionary years, Mark Price, the MD of Waitrose, introduced the Waitrose Essential range which offers own-brand goods at competitive prices. But, in the main, the Waitrose offer is not so much low price but rather the idea of 'Quality Food, Honestly Priced'. The store environments are clean, brightly lit, and uncluttered. The service standard is high.

Likewise, the JL department stores have 'entry price' variants on products such as kettles and toasters, but in the main the emphasis is once again upon value at medium to higher price points. Many customers are persuaded to part with cash way beyond the baseline price because they trust the brand and they have a concept of value that goes beyond low

---

[2] The Guardian ran a story on 31 January 2015 which suggested that JL was losing its reputation in the 'digital age' as outsourced service companies were letting them down: http://www.theguardian.com/money/2015/jan/31/john-lewis-customer-services-digital-age?CMP=share_btn_link.

price. Another attractive feature of the department store offer is the wide assortment. Despite a management–consultancy-led exercise around a decade ago which 'rationalized' the lines offered, there is still an attempt to retain the notion that a wide array of items such as ribbons and buttons and general haberdashery which is hard to source elsewhere would be found in a John Lewis-bound shopping expedition. The buyers are crucial to the appeal of John Lewis. They are charged with sourcing sensible but stylish products.

There is high trust in both John Lewis and Waitrose. This stems from a number of reasons. The claim of 'satisfaction or money back' is widely believed and delivered more so than with most competitors and there is a liberal attitude to returned goods. There is generally a high standard of relationships between suppliers and buyers which includes an encouragement to build and foster long-term relationships.

Customers also extend goodwill to the Partnership because they believe that the employee-owners will seek to offer a more dedicated service. There is also recognition that John Lewis pays its taxes. The 'Powered by our Principles' slogan is seen to have some real meaning. The customer experience in both Waitrose and the John Lewis department stores is generally one where the staff are perceived as civilized and 'nice'. Indeed, many customers enter the stores and perform their own active roles as participants in a shared performance of civilized shopping. That in itself is part of the value of the offer.

The Partner Proposition: Ownership, Democracy and Benefits

The JLP website states:

> All 90,000 permanent staff are Partners who own 43 John Lewis shops across the UK (31 department stores, 10 John Lewis at home and shops at St Pancras International and Heathrow Terminal 2), 336 Waitrose supermarkets (www.waitrose.com), an online and catalogue business, johnlewis.com (www.johnlewis.com), a production unit and a farm. The business has annual gross sales of over £10bn. Partners share in the benefits and profits.

The Partnership is certainly now of large size. It is by far the largest employee-owned business in the UK. It is also the case that the vast majority of workers are partners—they are truly 'members' and not simply employees. There are, however, a few non-members who work in outlets trading in JLP goods (mainly in retail outlets such as Boots and in petrol forecourts) but the numbers are small. By way of contrast, the famous Mondragon cooperatives in Spain employ many more non-members.

Is the Partnership democratic? It declares, without qualification, that:

> We are a democracy—open, fair and transparent. Our profits are shared, our Partners have a voice and there is a true sense of pride in belonging to something so unique and highly regarded. (JLP website)

The extent to which the democratic claim can be substantiated is the subject of a later chapter in this book. There is certainly a continued and unusual investment in democratic-like machinery. There are elected worker representatives on the main Board, this in itself is a distinctive feature that marks a contrast with most companies. In addition, there is a tiered structure of committees from branch level through to divisional level and then corporate level to enable the partner voice to be heard—and indeed, to use a classic Partnership phrase, 'to hold management to account'.

With 'employee ownership' comes the expectation that the organization will have a distinctive purpose and a set of objectives which differ from a conventional PLC. One key question deriving from this, is the stance adopted towards the pursuit of profit. Will this be central or will it be but one objective alongside more distinctive others? The official position, as publicly stated in its written Constitution under the section on main Principles, is as follows:

> The Partnership should make *sufficient profit* to sustain our commercial vitality and distinctive character, allow continued development and distribute a share of profits each year consistent with Partners' *reasonable expectations*. (JLP 2015 The Constitution of the John Lewis Partnership, June, p. 9, emphases added)

This is a classic JLP statement. It leaves open for further discussion just what level of profit should be deemed as 'sufficient' and what level of expectation is 'reasonable'. There may be caution nowadays in claiming the Partnership to be an industrial democracy but the founder had no such qualms in claiming to seek to establish, as indicated above, a 'far reaching experiment in industrial democracy'.

The elaborate structure of governing parties and of participatory mechanisms with voting, and time away from the trading floor in order to engage in scrutiny and debate, are all part of the system of checks and balances.

There is a conscious attempt to install high standards of corporate governance. The system, it is claimed, 'gives our management the freedom to be entrepreneurial and competitive in the way they run the business for long-term success, while giving the company's owners, the Partners, the rights and responsibilities of ownership through active involvement in the business' (JLP website accessed 29 October 2015). The extent to which, and the ways in which, partners can actually hold managers to account is examined fully in Chapter 7.

Benefits

Another distinctive feature of the partner offer is the package of benefits. All workers at all levels enjoy access to a benefits package which includes the opportunity to stay at company-owned hotels at subsidised rates, and to use leisure facilities and clubs. Each branch used to have a person responsible for organizing the social and the benefits scheme but this role has become regionalized and it covers both Waitrose and JL staff. Partners enjoy benefits in the form of 'amenities' such as the residence and grounds at Odney on the Thames, the Ambleside Park Hotel on Lake Windermere and hiking and canoeing at Lake Bala in Wales. Bala was bought for £3m in 2008 and was the first new such facility in decades. Research shows that these facilities are mainly used by lower-paid staff and the qualifying period to use them has been reduced from one year of service to just three months. Other companies which had facilities of this kind have tended to close them. Partners in branches have access to choirs, to evenings out with entertainment, and to a variety of clubs and societies. At Partnership level there is a music society and a sailing club with its own yachts. In addition, there are other benefits and learning opportunities as well as services for retired partners. Such a package might be open to a charge of paternalism. But the partners whom we interviewed, at all levels, tended to support and value these efforts. And survey data reveals that 94 per cent of partners place a high value on the benefits provided; this puts the Partnership in the top 10 per cent of UK employers according to ORC benchmarking. The Partnership also has a generous sabbatical scheme which enables long-serving partners with twenty-five years' service to take a six-month break. This further sets the Partnership apart from other employers. In 2006 the scheme was extended to the over 50-year-olds. Around 40 per cent of the JLP workforce is over forty-five years of age so this is a significant benefit.

The Leckford Estate covers 4,000 acres and contains a farm which produces crops, milk, meat, fruit, and vegetables sold in Waitrose supermarkets (Figure 2.4). It also has leisure facilities for the partners, including golf courses and fly fishing. It is one of five locations around the UK exclusively for partners with one year's service and their families and friends, who can take holidays there for a subsidized rate.

There was (until) 2015 a generous non-contributory final-salary pension scheme. There are now doubts about whether it is sufficiently funded in order to meet future liabilities. Between 1998 and 2008, annual contributions to the pension fund increased from £48m to £98m—a rise of 55 per cent but doubts remained from some critics as to whether the pensions fund was being properly underwritten. Pensions are, in a sense, in competition with the bonus. We discuss this issue more fully in Chapter 5.

Figure 2.4. The JLP country estate at Leckford, Hampshire

Pay rates were an issue from the outset. Spedan Lewis, in what can be seen as a far-sighted way, talked of a 'living wage' for the lowest paid. His deliberations were as prescient as ever and resonant of the modern living wage debate. Even the current concerns about the ratio between high pay and low pay were rehearsed. The Partnership Constitution used to refer to salary differentials between the highest paid and the average basic pay of partners which equated to a 25 times ratio. More recently as we noted above, this was increased to a 75 times ratio before tax. This equates, at the top end, to around £1m including pension entitlement. As we saw in Chapter 1, competitor companies pay much more to their top earners.

Ownership, Governance, and Democracy

The 'experiment' in democracy and in the distribution of power and knowledge is effected through a complex array of structures, procedures, roles, and rules. Together they claim to add up to the famous 'checks and balances'. These comprise an unusual set of governance arrangements supplemented by a set of democratic arrangements and opportunities for the expression of partner voice. Oiling the wheels across each of these and indeed across employee relations more widely is the performance of a certain kind of management.

As noted, there are three 'governing authorities' at the pinnacle of the Partnership: the Chairman, the Partnership Council, and the Partnership Board. In addition, there is the 'Trust Company'. The shares are held in trust so the trustees act as guarantors of that ownership and they also have a place in the Constitution as guardians of the Constitution.

The concept of 'ownership' in JLP is rather complicated. This appears to be as intended by the founder to safeguard the long-term interests of the Partnership and to prevent 'carpet-bagging'—that is, opportunistic and self-interested exploitation. As the shares are held in trust they cannot be sold by individual shareholders. When partners leave their employment they retain no ownership rights. There is a byzantine ownership structure with shares being held in the Trust Company which sits alongside JLP plc. Under the Constitution, the main purpose of the Trust Company is to protect the Constitution and democracy of the Partnership. The Trust Company has five directors: the Chairman and Deputy Chairman of the Partnership and three directors elected by the Partnership Council. Collectively they are known as the Trustees of the Constitution. John Lewis Partnership Trust Limited ('the Trust Company') holds the Deferred Ordinary Shares in the capital of the Company, in trust, for the benefit of the partners. As part of the checks and balances there are different types of shares. The Chairman is the only one holding shares with full voting rights. There is cross-ownership of shares between the trust and JLP plc.

One of Colin Mayer's key recommendations for a reformed corporate form was the creation of 'corporate trusteeships' which could extend purpose beyond the primacy of shareholders and which could take a long-term rather than a short-term perspective (Mayer 2014). The John Lewis Partnership exemplifies just such a trustee arrangement already in existence.

The Chairman is a very powerful figure and is unlike the role played in many PLCs where he or she is likely to be a part-time non-executive director. In JLP, the Chairman's role is very much full-time and is, in effect, an executive chairman. The role carries huge prestige. A knighthood is normally part of the package. The Chairman is recommended by the outgoing Chairman and he (it has always been a he) is appointed for a ten-year period (it used to be 'for life' until a change was made in 2007 following a controversial and contested succession process). As we have already noted, the Chairman holds a crucial vote with respect to the shares. The only way to remove the Chairman is if the Partnership Board or the Partnership Council was to hold a no-confidence vote. The Chairman appoints each of the managing directors and he even used to appoint all of the directors on the divisional boards. This has now changed so that these divisional directors are appointed by the divisional Managing Directors (MDs)—a move which helps to consolidate the underpinning divisionalization. Each of the directors also used to be directly responsible to the Chairman and he conducted their appraisal. Each of these features reflects the highly unusual, hands-on, influence and power of the JLP Chairman. However, increasingly over recent years, the separate businesses have grown in independence and strength and are responsible for, and manage, the commercial activity of their respective divisions. They develop their own strategies and business plans although subject to scrutiny and oversight by the Partnership Board and with the underpinning of the shared services function. This reflects the ongoing tension between the corporate level and the constituent businesses—a phenomenon common to divisionalized companies in general, but with an added significance in a partnership.

The Partnership Council, along with divisional, regional, and local democratic bodies which culminate in that Council, offer partners a voice and are said to hold management to account. The Partnership Council also elects five of the directors who sit on the Partnership Board. The Chairman is directly accountable to the Partnership Council. He reports to them on both commercial and partner matters and answers their questions and responds to their challenges. Each year they have to decide whether to approve his reports. This is the way in which the Partnership holds the Chairman to account. What all this means in practice is explored in detail in later chapters of this book as we look at specific decision areas.

Business strategy and operational level oversight is undertaken by management boards which oversee each division, such as Waitrose and John Lewis department stores. To help the Chairman in overseeing the corporate level and the Partnership as a whole, there is also a Chairman's Committee with senior figures representing business and Partnership interests.

The Partnership Board is different from PLC boards. It is unusual because it has five places reserved for democratically elected partners. The other places are held by directors appointed by the Chairman and also three non-executive directors—again appointed by the Chairman. At the time of writing, these were Keith Williams, formerly chairman and chief executive of British Airways; Baroness Sarah Hogg, former chair of the Financial Reporting Council and former head of the Prime Minister's Strategy Unit 1990–95; and Denis Hennequin, former President of McDonalds Europe. The Partnership Board is responsible for the overall management and performance of the Partnership. It has a duty to assess risk and it can approve or disapprove of divisional business plans.

The 'Critical Side'

A curious term, almost unheard of in conventional businesses, is the widely-used notion of the 'critical side'. It was instigated by the founder and was elaborately staffed by a number of high-level director posts and an infrastructure of registrars extending outwards across the operational parts of the businesses. Its express purpose was to try to offset what Spedan recognized would likely be a tendency for senior managers, over time, to accrue to themselves more and more power and to pursue commercial objectives which were potentially rather more in their own interests than the interest of partners in general. This critical side used to comprise a Partners' Counsellor, a Chief Registrar, and an Inspector General while other roles, such as Finance Director, had a 'critical' responsibility. The critical side is now much reduced.

This purposeful creation of an institutional counter-weight to the commercial functions and priorities offers a perfect example of the 'de-coupled mode' of handling competing institutional logics (Mullins 2006; Reay and Hinings 2009; Thornton et al. 2012).

Today, these various roles have been reduced to just one main role—that of Partners' Counsellor. The purpose of that role is to seek to ensure that the Partnership remains 'true to its principles and compassionate to individual Partners'. The Partners' Counsellor also monitors and seeks to uphold the integrity of the business, its values, and ethics as enshrined in the Constitution. The Councillor is a member of the Partnership Board and performs the role of senior independent director in their interaction with partners. The Partners' Counsellor is also charged with supporting the elected directors in their contribution to the Board and helping to underpin their independence. At least once each year, the Partners' Counsellor convenes meetings with the elected directors without other executive directors being present.

Within each division there is also a registrar sitting on each board with a remit to safeguard partner interests. There is also a Partnership-wide registrar, whose role is to ensure the business 'upholds the core principles of the Partnership'. This is supposed to be done through three activities: assurance, influence, and support.

The 'critical side' such as it is, also extends down into the operational parts of the Partnership. A series of registrars hold appointments at branch level in the JL department stores (one per branch or one shared between a couple of branches), and at an area level for Waitrose where a number of supermarket outlets are represented. The registrars were introduced by Spedan Lewis to help ensure that the far-flung branches were seen to be duly abiding by Partnership principles. They were also seen as guardians of individual partners. They reported to the chief registrar and even felt they had direct access to the Chairman if they had a local concern to report. The chief registrar was supposed to be an independent person who could withstand pressure from senior directors and who reported direct to the Chairman. The registrars now report to the Partners' Counsellor.

The Registrars

The registrar role is interesting and revealing as an emblematic symbol of the Partnership. In many ways registrars represent what is different about the

Partnership. They have no precise equivalent in any other organization. They play a quasi-welfare-officer role but with additional features. When we reviewed the role in 2008 there were twenty-eight registrars: fourteen in JL plus a divisional registrar and twelve in Waitrose plus a divisional registrar. The registrars were meant to be of high status—broadly equivalent to a managing director of a branch. In addition, there were a total of forty-four assistant registrars: thirty-six in JL and eight in Waitrose. These latter posts were of Departmental Manager status. There were seventy-two posts in total plus some other supporting posts. This represented a very significant investment in what was essentially a guardianship role. The estimated total cost of the function at that time was approximately £5.2m.

There had been a review of the registrars in 2003. This endorsed the place of registrars in the Partnership and led to a number of changes in the JL division—most notably—twinning of branches so that each JL registrar covered two branches rather than one, resulting in a reduction in the numbers of registrars in that division but there were relatively few significant changes in Waitrose.

In 2008/9 we were asked to review the role of the registrars more thoroughly. A considerable number of managers—at all levels—had started to question the value of the role. We found that a significant proportion of the registrars themselves judged that the ambiguities of their role required some resolution. The most unqualified support came from the non-management partners. They tended to lend instinctive support for the existence of such a role even when they were not sure what the registrars actually did.

The job description of the branch registrars stated that the main line of reporting was to the divisional registrar but the 'main working relationship was with the Head of Branch'. The 'client' is the branch. Registrars are expected to 'work with management to create a high performance culture', whilst ensuring that this is in accord with 'behaviour that is consistent with our principles and values' and to help deliver 'outstanding commercial results'. This is interesting as it encapsulates the overall ideology of the safeguarding of the Partnership Difference yet using this not to compromise commercial viability, but to enhance it.

The job was described as 'to work with management to identify the best ways to implement all aspects of the Partnership's objectives and the Branch Business Plan and to ensure the values of the Partnership are converted into practical and commercial operating principles and processes'. So here, in stark form, is the expression of the dual logics of commerciality and Partnership values. Further, the role was stated as 'To energise and support the development of initiatives within the branch which enhance Partners' understanding of their responsibilities as co-owners, and to take specific responsibility for their implementation as agreed with management'. (Note 'branch' here is

> **Box 2.1** JOB DESCRIPTION OF REGISTRARS
>
> Working with management, to help provide innovative solutions to internal communication.
>
> To ensure that the branch is a leading example of co-ownership and employee involvement.
>
> To take specific responsibility to drive high performance in this area from councillors and committee members. As a result, all democratic structures and processes in the branch will become increasingly relevant and rewarding to partners. Where appropriate, to manage the council administration team.
>
> To ensure that management has effective feedback mechanisms to provide an independent awareness of Partners' opinions views and suggestions.
>
> To provide independent and impartial support, coaching and advice for Partners in the branch/group. To act as 'honest broker' in resolving disputes informally.
>
> To lead the Registry function within the branch ensuring that it reinforces the 'main purpose' above. To ensure that the registry service provides value and look for all opportunities to improve cost effectiveness.
>
> In Waitrose, to chair committees for communication as agreed with the Partners' Counsellor. In John Lewis, to be the primary communication link with the Chairmen of Committees for Communication.
>
> In John Lewis and Corporate, to manage the Chronicle team.

the unit relevant to the John Lewis department stores; in the case of Waitrose the supermarkets were grouped into localities for registrar and other purposes.) Other key aspects of the job description for registrars are displayed in Box 2.1.

Based on a wide number of interviews with managers, non-management partners and the registrars themselves, we found that the role was beset with six main problems: it lacked clarity, duplicated other roles and caused confusion and expense; it had been overtaken by events, and was viewed by some as anachronistic; it was seen as impossible to achieve in the entirety of its description and thus raised expectations which could not be met; it required a calibre and competence which few incumbents could match; the registrars lacked accountability; the role was enacted in different ways in the two divisions and even varied within the divisions; the exercise of the role risked feeding cynicism about the 'Partnership Difference' as a whole.

However, the defence of the role was based on four arguments: without registrars the Partnership Difference would erode; the registrars were valued by non-management partners; they saved the Partnership trouble and expense because they informally quell discontent; and registrars offer managers an independent source of advice.

Some of the functions were being delivered by assistant registrars or other members of the steering group in the stores. Moreover, it was felt that the personnel function had grown and that this function had taken-on many of the roles previously undertaken by the registrars. Individual staff files, for example, were originally held by registrars but as the personnel function grew and as legislation increased, these files were increasingly owned by personnel.

So what is the essential nature of the role? Following a move away from one registrar for each and every branch to a sharing of a registrar across more than one branch, it could no longer be regarded as the one-to-one friend for all partners. Non-management partners did, however, look to their registrar for support. They did expect the registrar to offer a sympathetic ear and to understand and defend the owner-partner interests.

But there was much debate about whether the registrar could be the person who had special insight into partner opinion. The Partner Survey has introduced a more systematic approach to gathering partner opinion and managers at all levels suggested that they themselves were much closer to this than a registrar who was scarcely known to most partners.

Some registrars liked to maintain that they had a unique role as special strategic adviser to heads of branch. But few line managers and directors were willing to accept that registrars had this superior knowledge.

But, there was a role which *did* require and deserve emphasis and which offered clarity for registrars. This is the guardian/guarantor of the Partnership Difference and the source of expertise on what this means in practice *and how it can be operationalized*. This recasting of the role requires individuals in the role who are committed to, and passionate about, the Partnership element—and able to offer expert and, credible, and convincing advice to heads of branch about *how to enact that Partnership element and make it real*. This, as a number of managers were keen to emphasize, is 'not just a person sitting at the end of the table who occasionally asks: "what about the Partners?"'

There were various sub-aspects to this role as guarantor of the 'Partnership Difference'. One is the work registrars can undertake in the future to support the revised democratic processes. This entails explaining and promoting the democratic bodies. Another is the opportunity to play a new distinctive part with respect to potential grievances. A further aspect is the need for registrars, in special circumstances to play a whistle-blowing role so that instances where business units depart from good practice are brought to the corporate attention in a timely manner. Additionally, they advise those managers who need this advice, about the best way to conduct themselves in a Partnership way.

A subsequent change programme affecting this area was called 'Driving the Difference' (DTD). This broke down Registry's role into three parts: Partnership assurance, democratic engagement, and partner support. Previously, these three things were mixed together in the registrar role and this resulted in some confusion for managers, partners, and the job-holders alike. The DTD programme resulted in a new organizational structure with new roles:

Partnership Assurance Leads, who work with local management to assure the business is being run in the best interests of partners as co-owners and that balanced business decisions are being made; Democratic Engagement roles that help ensure partners' voices are heard through their elected representatives, through Partner Survey results, and Partnership journalism; a centralized partner support team that provides individual personal support by phone or face to face, as and when required.

Sharing Knowledge

Information and knowledge is shared through journalism, through line management-led communication, and through committees. The *Gazette* is a business-wide company magazine which contains detailed information about performance including weekly branch performance. These results show weekly performance compared to the previous week and compared to the equivalent week a year before.

The *Gazette* is a journal of record and disseminates key decisions and new developments. As noted, it also publishes anonymous letters from partners which take individual directors to task and publicly challenge their decisions. The *Gazette* has long employed professional journalists. The Director of Communications, who is ultimately responsible for the *Gazette*, commented that he didn't believe that any journalism is independent and he certainly didn't want to be publishing stories which are negative. While he accepted the idea about the critical side, his instincts were to present the Partnership in as positive a light as can be. In the past, there were serious reports and verbatim reports of key committees. But, in more recent times, the *Gazette* is seen as closer to a more typical in-house magazine with good news stories.

But the anonymous letters are seen by some as a corrective. It is argued that this public voice means that directors take care to think things through very carefully before making changes.

In addition, each larger JL branch has its own magazine called *The Chronicle*, while Waitrose has a divisional one. Typically, the local registrar acts as editor.

At director level, there are three Registry roles: a Partners' Counsellor who has a seat on the JLP Board, and Partnership Registrars on the JL and Waitrose management boards. The Partnership Registrar roles report to the Partners' Counsellor. The Partners' Counsellor reports to the Chairman. Notably, it is the Chairman who appoints this person and also conducts their appraisal. It is arguably a significant problem if that role is intended to be the main focus and representation of an independent critical side. Perhaps in recognition of this issue, a rule change in 2012 means that the Partners' Counsellor cannot be dismissed without the specific agreement of the Trustees of the Constitution. But since the job-holder is appointed and managed by the Chairman and is a member of the senor management team, and given the definition of the role, it is unlikely that this provision will be required.

The Partners' Counsellor 'appoints registrars to work as colleagues of senior management in all the partnership operations.... They have independent status within the partnership and are responsible, through the Partners' Counsellor, to the chairman for ensuring that the partnership principles and policies are applied consistently in the branches where they work' (The Constitution 2015, rule 89).

Voice and Power

Partner voice is based on a series of elections to representative bodies. The elected directors on the Partnership Board are supplemented with directors appointed by the Chairman from the executive team. There have been attempts to equip elected board members with skills and knowledge to help them discharge their responsibilities. In practice, the elected member representatives have increasingly tended to be mainly managers rather than shopfloor workers.

The Partnership Council is an assembly—with members elected by the branches. There are seventy plus members in total: twenty-nine from JL, thirty-nine from Waitrose and two from corporate (the central offices branch) and a growing number from Partnership (shared) services. In addition to the Partnership Council, the two main businesses—John Lewis and Waitrose—both have their own divisional councils. They are supposed to hold their respective management to account. They meet four times a year. The MDs present the results and answer questions. In the past, council meetings tended to be more formal, complete with a debating style with formal proposals and votes akin to Parliamentary debates. Nowadays, the style has changed and has become more informal with managers providing information and encouraging conjoint problem-solving.

Within the branches there used to be branch-wide 'forums' (called Partner-Voice) for discussion, and at the next level there are also departmental forums. In 2007, the forums replaced the erstwhile branch councils. In the previous format, partners could meet in a 'committee for communication' without managers being present. Throughout its history, and even into present times, the Partnership has invested in and maintained an elaborate infrastructure of partner representation. There is ongoing active internal debate about the vitality and meaningfulness of the democracy. Some managers argued that there were too many partners who were not engaged with the democratic processes. But others argued that even if a significant proportion of partners did not actively participate in the democratic bodies, the very presence of these bodies provided a reassurance that was crucially important. It is the presence (even if only in the background) and actuality of the democratic bodies and their continued operation that is important to the everyday operation of and viability of the model. These issues are explored in detail in Chapter 7.

Conclusions

The Partnership is an unusual and in many respects a laudable institution. It is not hard to see why it has been so highly regarded and indeed put forward as a 'model' for others to follow. To some extent, the 'Partnership Difference' is best understood when comparisons are made with some other large retailers. Retail can be a turbulent arena. Outlets can be opened and closed at a remarkable rate; ownership transferred and carved-up as financial gain dictates. For example, department stores such as Debenhams and House of Fraser and store groups such as Arcadia, owned briefly by Sir Philip Green and then by his wife, are bought and sold like commodities. They move in and out of the Stock Exchange and are periodically acquired by private buyers and consortia of private equity firms. Often, significant parts fall into foreign ownership and stores are closed down with little ceremony. The collapse of BHS in 2016 is a case in point. Notably, House of Fraser had its origins more than a century and half ago and Fraser family members retained key positions until around 1980. But its recent fortunes are telling: it has since been bought and sold by private consortia of investors including the Al Fayed family and more recently by Chinese investors. Likewise, Debenhams department stores has a long history, its origins indeed can be traced to the eighteenth century. It was acquired by the Burton Group in 1985 and sold in 1998. It was acquired by a private consortium which included Merrill Lynch and Texas Pacific Group in 2003 and eventually relisted on the stock exchange. A tranche of shares was bought by Sports Direct, the company owned by Mike Ashley.

In comparison with the volatile and often precarious nature of such competitors, JLP is a haven of stability. But key questions nonetheless remain. For example, is it really an industrial democracy? Is there any evidence that the model results in higher performance? Are the managers really being held to account? How, in practice, do managers handle the unusual array of competing objectives and principles? Most important of all, what does the practical enactment of this model tell us about the operability of a 'trustee corporation'? These are the questions examined in the following chapters.

3

Lessons from Employee-owned Businesses

What type of firm is the John Lewis Partnership? As noted, commentaries in the press and elsewhere invariably insist its success is attributable to its 'co-ownership' and 'mutual' status. Positive news reports about the commercial success of these retail businesses are customarily accompanied by reference to the 'employee-owned' nature of JLP and the manner in which 'partners' share the profits. There is a clear implication that an 'explanation' has been offered for the successful performance. And, as we have noted, there have been numerous calls to move towards a 'John Lewis economy' or, on a less grand scale, to transition individual firms to be more like John Lewis. Such exhortations and counsels suggest a shift from the conventional shareholder-owned firm to some *alternative form*. But just what is this alternative? Exactly what is being advocated? Presumably advocates are not calling for a precise replication of all aspects of John Lewis but rather a shift to something of this type of business. But what type is JLP? Is it a cooperative, a mutual, a co-owned firm, an employee-owned firm, a corporate trusteeship, or something else? Each of these types has operated in the past and can be found in various locations internationally. So it is sensible to seek lessons from these forms: lessons which may reveal opportunities and threats for the JLP, and which may also be relevant for the wider debate about alternative forms based loosely on the idea of a wider stakeholder model. In addition, the JLP may carry useful lessons for other employee-owned firms which have generally been less successful in exploiting the full potential of the partner–customer–profit cycle that John Lewis has been so effective in understanding and utilizing.

With JLP apparently riding high while many conventional firms remain in the doldrums, the ideas of co-ownership, partnership, and associated notions have enjoyed a revival as a point of focal interest. Yet these ideas have a long history and they have not always been so highly regarded in the public estimation. Indeed, only a few decades ago, 'de-mutualization' was the popular theme. In boom times, following the de-regulation of the City, the mutuality model was depicted as old fashioned and restrictive. The pressure to 'de-mutualize' overtook most of the Building Societies and, for a time, John Lewis itself was not immune and there was talk about the de-mutualization of the Partnership. Times have certainly changed. Now, the twin attributes of 'principled business' and 'financial success' in a landscape strewn with organizations which appear to exhibit neither of these, make the John Lewis model look attractive. As a flag bearer for the idea, John Lewis in the current climate has unwittingly re-ignited interest in the ideas of co-ownership, mutualization, and cooperation.

So there is a need for a wider analysis of employee ownership in other settings and to draw lessons from these cases. Worker cooperatives, mutuals, and employee-owned businesses are normally considered to be characterized by at least three features: they are owned by their members, they are democratically controlled and they are often seen to have a wider social purpose.

As we will see, the nature and extent of ownership may vary—from total ownership by worker members through to forms where ownership resides in a trust fund or with some mix of worker ownership and conventional shareholder ownership. Likewise, the degree and nature of democratic control may vary from a one-member-one-vote form of decision making, through to various forms of elected representation of those who make decisions. The third element, the notion of a wider social purpose, is even more variable but it is an important consideration. For example, the UN Secretary General, Ban Ki-moon, has stated that 'Co-operatives are a reminder to the international community that it is possible to pursue both economic viability and social responsibility' (cited on the ICA website and the UN International Year of Cooperatives website).[1] This dual theme of social responsibility allied to 'economic viability' runs through much of the discussion of cooperatives and partnerships.

Many advantageous outcomes are said to stem from these forms of enterprise—and these gains are usually associated with high levels of employee engagement. They include gains in better health and well-being, enhanced innovation, and reduced absenteeism. Employee ownership is regarded as a pathway to 'unlocking growth' in the wider economy.

The purpose of this chapter is to explore the phenomenon of employee ownership in order to draw out their potential, the common tensions they face, and the wider lessons for the kind of corporate trusteeship model as advocated by Mayer and others.

There are multiple dimensions to the phenomenon. There is a historical dimension (the cooperative idea and cooperative practice in the UK goes back at the very least to the mid nineteenth century); an international comparative

---

[1] For the UN International Year of Cooperatives website, see http://social.un.org/coopsyear/, accessed 22 January 2016. For the International Co-operative Alliance, see http://ica.coop/sites/default/files/media_items/ICA%20Factsheet%20-International%20Year%20of%20Co-operatives.pdf, accessed 14 February 2016.

dimension (worker cooperatives are currently highly influential in many European countries); and a conceptual dimension (there are a number of related concepts to disentangle including partnership, co-ownership, employee ownership, social enterprise, mutualism, and employee engagement). There is also a political dimension. Spedan Lewis subtitled his book *Fairer Shares* (1954) 'A Possible Advance in Civilisation and Perhaps the Only Alternative to Communism' (Spedan Lewis 1954). From a different political stance, the idea of 'workers control' was pressed by others with an alternative rationale (Coates 1976). In very general terms, the ideas of partnership, mutualism, and employee ownership currently tend to attract support across all political parties, but what they are championing—and why—tends to be less clear. A report by The Smith Institute on various forms of employee ownership concluded that the evidence of the impact of shared ownership on productivity and commitment is ambiguous (Coats 2013).

In the 1970s, under the Labour Government led by Harold Wilson, there was a strong interest in advancing the idea of Industrial Democracy. This was prompted in part by high levels of industrial conflict and in part by developments in areas of Europe where worker representation was enshrined in law. The Wilson government appointed a Committee of Inquiry led by Lord Bullock. The subsequent report (Bullock 1977) recommended that in large companies there would be a legal right for democratically elected worker representatives to sit on the main board. Indeed, they would be equal in number to shareholder representatives with a government appointee as the balancing vote—known as the 2x + y formula. This formula appears to reflect many of the principles and ideas found in recent discussions of corporate trusteeship. The way the ideas were received is therefore of some considerable interest in the present context. The business representatives on the inquiry refused to sign the majority report and produced their own minority report which sought to temper the proposal. They wanted to see worker representatives only on a supervisory board and not on the main board; they said that these representatives should be in a minority; they would be elected by all employees, and would not be dependent on trade union channels, and the supervisory board should not be able to drive policy. Reactions to the main report from a number of quarters was critical and even hostile. Employers' organizations were opposed to it and a group of City lawyers wrote a response which restated the case for the underlying principles of the joint stock company system. This, they maintained, is 'a system based on the concept that the ultimate authority and control over a company rests with those who provide the capital (i.e. the shareholders) in general meeting. It is they who, at the outset, come together to incorporate the company as a legal entity and it is they who by the contract of incorporation embodied in the company's original constitution agree between themselves what the company's business and objects shall be and in what way the company shall be organised and managed' (City Company Law Committee 1977). The Bullock proposals even split the trade union movement. Many trade union leaders were critical and a number of them expressed a preference for the retention and extension of the collective bargaining system in place of the prospective complications of shared decision making. There were some experiments with workers on the boards of British Steel and the Post Office but these did not survive.

This is the wider backcloth against which our analysis of JLP takes place. In the first section we set the scene with an examination of the policy context which promotes the ideas of employee ownership and mutualism; in the second section we delve more deeply into the meanings of the various terms such as 'mutuals', 'co-operative', 'employee ownership', and 'partnership'; in the third and final section we look at the history of such enterprises both in the UK and in other countries and seek to draw lessons from their experience.

The Policy Context

In this section we review government policy, the stance of various political parties, and the infrastructure of support bodies which seek to promote mutualism and cooperatives.

The 2010–15 Coalition Government (consisting of Conservatives and Social Democrats) championed the notion of 'mutualism'—most especially in areas of the public services. The New Labour administrations before them likewise tended to promote the idea of 'social enterprises'—most notably as part of the mix of models for delivering public services. Conservatives, Liberal Democrats, and Labour have all supported related ideas based around employee ownership of one kind or another.

The policy agenda has been pursued along two channels—with a focus on the public and on the private sector. The first strand of the agenda was led by the Cabinet Office. The talk was of an aspiration to see one million of the approximately six million public sector workers moving into John Lewis style mutuals.

The strand of the employee ownership agenda which focused on the private sector, and on enterprise more generally, was led by the Liberal Democrats and the then Minister for Employment Relations, Norman Lamb, who commissioned Graham Nuttall to undertake a review of employee ownership in 2011. Nuttall's report *Sharing Success: The Nuttall Review on Employee Ownership*, was published in July 2012 (Nuttall 2012). Nuttall set the scene as follows:

> Everyone in the employee ownership sector applauds the Government's announcement that it wishes to see employee ownership in the mainstream of the British economy. There has been all party support for decades, and successive

governments have encouraged employees to acquire shares through tax advantaged share plans but this Government is the first to promote the *wider concept of employee ownership*. (Nuttall 2012: 5–6, emphasis added)

And the Nuttall Review of 'employee ownership' also noted:

The Government's stated ambition is to promote employee ownership so that it plays a bigger part in the economy. The Deputy Prime Minister has set a challenge to move employee ownership 'into the bloodstream of the British economy'. Promoting employee ownership also offers the chance to increase the diversity of ownership models in the economy. The Ownership Commission argued that a plurality of ownership models makes for better ownership, increases the resilience of the economy, and provides greater choice for investors, savers and consumers. The Ownership Commission named employee ownership as one such ownership model that should be promoted further. (Nuttall 2012: 14)

So employee ownership is envisaged not as a uniform solution appropriate for all circumstances but as part of a 'plurality of ownership models' in a mixed economy. Thus, once again the intent to try to escape from the singularity and the shortcomings of an over-reliance on the shareholder-dominated model is evident, if implicit.

The Nuttall Review was directed at offering ideas for how employee ownership could be encouraged. This included greater awareness, simplified structures, a right to request, a new institute to support nascent formations and other similar ideas. But it was not a review of how employee-owned firms actually operate in practice. The review works from the assumption that employee owned firms are a good thing. It offers a range of ideas, templates, and toolkits for employee buy-outs and ideas for raising capital.

In parallel, the Cabinet Office established and commissioned work from a 'Mutuals Taskforce'. This was chaired by LSE Professor Julian Le Grand, and its work was very much focused on public sector services. This built on a previous evidence paper, *Our Mutual Friends: The Case for Mutuals* (Cabinet Office 2011b). The government's White Paper 'Open Public Services' (Cabinet Office 2011a) refers to empowering public sector staff by giving them 'new rights to form mutuals and bid to take over the services they deliver'. The White Paper also states that 'We will not dictate the precise form of these mutuals; rather, this should be driven by what is best for the users of services and by employees as *co-owners of the business*' (emphasis added). The first Civil Service mutual, the agency My Civil Service Pension (MyCSP), was spun out from the civil service in 2011. This has itself been controversial: proponents claim it was employee led, but the PCS union claim it was imposed from above. Hence, the drivers for mutualism are seen as a source of controversy. This can be illustrated, for example, by the Department for Health's 'Right to Provide' policy. As Nuttall (2012: 39–40) notes, this 'allows NHS and public sector social care workers to make a request to take ownership of a public sector service and run it in the private sector. This Right to Provide is now integrated in the Cabinet Office's mutuals programme which is working with individual Government departments to develop and implement other Rights to Provide'. But the implication of this strand of work is that the problem to be tackled is not so much private share ownership distortions but problems stemming from public ownership.

Separating out the public sector aspect from the private sector element is, however, difficult. Hence, for example, in July 2012 the government announced that it was pressing ahead with a 'Mutuals Post Office'. It claimed enthusiasm amongst sub-postmasters, staff, and the wider public for a stake in the Post Office. Post Office trade unions were more guarded. In the privatization of the Royal Mail, a proportion of the shares were reserved for employees. This was based on the notion that a sense of commitment would be inculcated as a result of some co-ownership.

There have been non-governmental bodies which have actively pursued a similar agenda. For example, Co-operatives UK is a national trade association which seeks to promote the cooperative alternative across all sectors of the economy 'from High Street consumer-owned co-operatives to pubs and football clubs, healthcare to agriculture, credit unions to community owned shops' (Co-operatives UK 2012).[2]

Taking a very broad interpretation indeed (for example, including consumer cooperatives as well as producer ones) it claims that there are more than 5,900 cooperative businesses (i.e. owned and controlled by members and not by shareholders) in the UK. These organizations are said to have a grand total of 13.5 million members and to operate across all business sectors and contribute £35.6 billion to the UK economy. Co-operatives UK further suggests that 'For the past four years, the sector has outperformed the UK economy, demonstrating resilience in difficult economic times and proving that values and principles go hand in hand with commercial performance' (Co-operatives UK 2012). Subsequent problems in the Cooperative Bank and the Cooperative Group more generally, rather dented this claim.

Co-operatives UK continued: 'Co-operative businesses are owned and run by and for their members, whether they are customers, employees or residents. As well as giving members an equal say and share of the profits, co-operatives act together to build a better world' (2012). These are bold claims. The state of employee ownership is by no means as buoyant as these claims tend to suggest but there is a range of bodies which exist to promote it. Bodies such as Mutuo and the Employee Ownership Association[3] promote enterprises owned by employees as well as by customers. Specialist advice focusing on the

---

[2] http://www.uk.coop/about/about-co-operatives-uk, accessed 14 February 2016.
[3] http://employeeownership.co.uk/, accessed 14 February 2016.

technicalities of employee share ownership schemes is offered by a division of the Institute of Financial Services.

Other initiatives have sought to promote cooperatives and employee-owned businesses in Scotland, Wales, and Northern Ireland. Co-operative Development Scotland (CDS) working under the aegis of Scottish Enterprise offers support and advice for those interested in setting up employee ownership enterprises in Scotland. This agency offers advice on different models of cooperation including community cooperatives and mutuals as well as the model based on a transfer of assets from a private owner to employees. CDS says that it is seeks to create a 'John Lewis Economy' in Scotland. The Wales Co-operative Centre is a cooperative development agency. It supports the development of social entrepreneurship, social enterprises, and cooperatives in Wales. It offers advice on employee share ownership schemes and on the range of options for arranging employee buy-outs at the point of business succession. There are also a number of bodies at the international level which exist in order to advance the cause of cooperation and mutualism.

So it is clear that political support for the idea of mutualism and cooperation is widespread and it is equally clear that there are a number of support bodies which have as their mission the development and promotion of cooperatives and mutuals. But, in reviewing the government policy initiatives and the bodies which have been established to promote and support mutuals and cooperatives, it is also evident that there are significant variations and differences in ultimate purposes and aims. To address these issues more directly, the next section reviews the range of concepts and the associated range of objectives.

The Variety of Concepts and their Associated Meanings

A number of terms are often used in overlapping ways. Some of the distinctions can be important and interesting because they reveal alternative choices and options as well as tensions and controversies. The key ones include ideas about employee engagement, involvement and participation, and worker cooperatives, social responsibility, social mission, and the sharing of power, knowledge and rewards, and of course industrial democracy. Many recent discussions of such terms echo Spedan Lewis' ideas about a more 'responsible' mode of capitalism: ideas which presciently addressed the kind of concerns about modern corporations described in the first chapter of this book.

There are overlaps and connections between the various terms. As the Nuttall Review (2012: 15) observed, 'The concepts of employee ownership and employee engagement are interlinked and mutually reinforcing: employee owners are more likely to be engaged with their company, whilst employee ownership can enshrine employee engagement into a company, for example, by providing management structures allowing the employee voice to be heard'.

But, while the ownership and employee engagement ideas are acknowledged to interlink, Nuttall questions the (necessary) association with wider social purpose: 'The connection with social enterprise... causes confusion. Whilst many employee owned companies consider themselves socially responsible, and some employee owned companies are social enterprises, this review's contention is that employee ownership must be seen as a *business model* in its own right with its own benefits. It is a business model characterised by who owns a company not what the company does' (Nuttall 2012: 34, emphasis added). By implication, social enterprises and employee owned businesses are not necessarily imbued with a deeper social purpose than other forms of enterprise. The same might be said for worker cooperatives and not-for-profit enterprises although these terms are often used by enterprises which declare some kind of social purpose. Nuttall says that his review 'considers that employee ownership is best understood as a business model [which] can be just as effective in achieving growth and profit maximisation as other models'.

It is evident from these comments that there can be confusion about whether the different terms signal not only different ownership types and business models but also potentially *different purposes*. Profit maximization is often—arguably normally—understood as the prime objective of conventional private sector shareholder businesses; but the introduction of alternative forms such as cooperative, partnership, social enterprise, or mutual, tends to open-up the possibility that not only is ownership and decision making different but that significantly different ends are also being being pursued. This, as we will see in later chapters, is at the heart of many of the important controversies and tensions within the John Lewis Partnership. Much of this comes back to the core question of what an enterprise is for.

In order to assist the process of clarification of terms, Table 3.1 lists the key terms along with some brief characteristics normally associated with each of the terms.

Partnership

The term 'partnership' is one of the most widely used and yet one of the most diffuse of concepts. Such an ostensibly non-adversarial mode of employee relations has long been persuasively articulated and urged by Kochan and Osterman in the USA (Kochan and Osterman 1994). In essence, it refers to a joint commitment between an employer and workers and their representatives to work cooperatively in pursuit of objectives which will yield mutual gain. In the UK, the idea was promoted by the Involvement & Participation Association (IPA) in its influential document *Towards Industrial Partnership:*

Table 3.1. Towards a clarification of terms

Concept	Typified features
Partnerships	This may or may not imply ownership or a share in ownership. Arguably, Circle, the healthcare organization, is more appropriately located here rather than as a worker cooperative because Circle employees own shares in a Trust which account for 49 per cent of the total shares—the largest part is owned by a group of funding consultant partners and private equity.
Employee ownership; worker cooperatives	Where employees own the majority of shares.
Mutuals	A wide term embracing a number of types of enterprise; often used to include building societies.
Consumer cooperatives	Customer owned (e.g. the Cooperative Society) or member owned organizations (e.g. the Nationwide Building Society).
Social enterprises	Organizations with a social purpose.
Industrial democracy	Balance of power based on rights and enshrined in law.
Workers' control	Capture of power–historic political-economic philosophy popular in Soviet Russia post 1917, and Germany and Italy 1918–20.

A New Approach to Relations at Work (IPA 1992). Following this, a public policy approach supportive of partnership between employers, trade unions, and employees saw the introduction of the Partnership at Work Fund which supported a series of projects to improve employer–employee relations (ACAS 2011).

But the idea has proved controversial both from an employer and trade union perspective. Some researchers have pointed to the instability of partnership arrangements (Martinez Lucio 2005; Jenkins 2007). One indicator of relative success is that 248 'partnership agreements' were signed between 1990 and 2007 covering almost 10 per cent of all British employees in 2007 and one-third of public sector employees (Bacon and Samuel 2009). Such agreements indicate a formal declaration of intent to work together constructively. However, analysis of the contents of these agreements shows fairly modest aims and progress. Some have seen partnership as a strategy to preserve some role for trade unions(Ackers 1998). Crucially, trust and managerial skill are shown as necessary for partnerships to weather recession. The JLP model extends more widely and deeply than many of the partnership agreements. There has, at times, been an explicit attempt to leverage the partner advantage by linking it to the partner–customer service–profit/value chain idea (Heskett et al. 1997), an approach pursued at Sears (Rucci et al. 1998).

Employee Ownership and Worker Cooperatives

What counts as 'employee ownership'? The Employee Ownership Association (EOA) talks about an employee-owned stake of 50 per cent or more, but the

Nuttall review is less demanding and states: 'In this review, employee ownership means a significant and meaningful stake in a business for all its employees. Over 25 per cent is substantial from a company law perspective. This review heard evidence that the full benefits of employee ownership can be achieved at lower percentages' (Nuttall 2012: 21). What counts as 'meaningful' is evidently the issue; it may not depend on simply the proportion of shares owned. Influence and voice may also stem from other factors.

Employee ownership may take different forms:

- *direct employee ownership*—using one or more tax-advantaged and other share plans, employees become individual owners of shares in their company;
- *indirect employee ownership*—shares are held collectively on behalf of employees, normally through an employee benefit trust; and
- *combined direct and indirect ownership*—a combination of individual and collective share ownership.

Employee ownership can be accomplished in multiple ways: employees can buy stock directly, be given it as a bonus, can receive stock options, or obtain stock through a profit sharing plan. Employee-owned firms and employee cooperatives could potentially be viewed as an extreme form of Employee Share Ownership Plans (ESOPs). But the most common form of employee ownership is the employee stock ownership plan which offers part-ownership of a firm's capital. In the United States about 11,000 companies have plans of this kind and they include over 13 million employees.

Worker Cooperatives

The International Organisation of Industrial, Artisanal and Service Producers' Cooperatives (IOIASP) and the International Cooperative Alliance (ICA) have declared the basic characteristics of workers' cooperatives to comprise a number of key elements (ICA 2005).[4] Cooperatives have the objectives of: creating and maintaining sustainable jobs and generating wealth; improving the quality of life of the worker-members; dignifying human work; allowing workers' democratic self-management; and promoting community and local development. As a general rule, work shall be carried out by the members—that is not by employees of the members. This implies that the majority of the workers in a given worker cooperative enterprise are members. The worker-members' relation with their cooperative shall be considered as different to that of

---

[4] http://ica.coop/sites/default/files/media_items/ICA%20Factsheet%20-International%20Year%20of%20Co-operatives.pdf, accessed 15 February 2016.

conventional wage-based labour and to that of autonomous individual work. Their internal regulation is formally defined by regimes that are democratically agreed upon and accepted by the worker-members. They shall be autonomous and independent, before the State and third parties, in their labour relations and management, and in the usage and management of the means of production.

Mutuals

The term 'mutuals' tends to be used more loosely than the term employee ownership to refer to consumer mutuals such as building societies as well as to work organizations where employees are in some way perceived as 'owners' of the enterprise or as controllers of its fortunes.

There are two determining features. The first is about a form of joint ownership by stakeholders (whether these be consumers or workers), so it is about a defined 'membership' (distinct from an open market in stocks and shares). The second feature relates to purpose. In the case of a mutual the purpose is the joint interests of the members, whereas, in a conventional shareholder business the purpose is the profitability of the enterprise.

ACAS argues that, 'Unlike charities, mutuals seek to make profits. But unlike PLCs, the motivation for making profits is not to deliver financial returns to investors, but rather to deliver on the corporate purpose of the organisation with profits reinvested and returned to members whether through lower prices or improved services, as well as possibly through cash payments' (Mitchie 2012). Here, 'purpose' becomes central. It is suggested that the core reason for people coming together in some form of assemblage is to pursue a common purpose which goes beyond the instrumentality of turning a profit—even though that purpose may still essentially be monetary and pecuniary in nature. Whether or not this is a 'higher' purpose is a difficult assessment.

Other Terms

In addition to the terms already discussed, there are a number of others that have been used which are relevant to the theme of this discussion—too many indeed to describe fully here. Noted in the table, for example, are 'Social Enterprises', 'Industrial Democracy', and 'Workers' Control'. Such terms tend to be associated with specific social and political moments. The term 'social enterprises' became popular in the late 1990s under New Labour. It denotes work enterprises established with goals other than profit maximization; social purposes are brought into focus as a prime purpose. 'Industrial Democracy' also had its historic moments. In the 1970s it was seen as an answer to industrial relations problems through trade union representaion on company boards.

'Workers Control' has had more radical connotations and has been associated with political movements which offer alternatives to capitalist or state solutions. The idea has flourished at different times including, for example, in the 1930s. Trotsky was a notable advocate.

In summary, the range of terms reflects the multiplicity of ideas and aspirations and motives associated with these 'alternative forms'. In varying ways, these forms seek to depart from the conventional shareholder model with its overriding focus on profit maximization and the primacy of shareholder interests with all of the unintended consequences that this entails as outlined earlier. The alternative forms, though different from each other, generally aspire towards some degree of sharing of power, sharing of rewards, and a widening of purpose.

Employee Ownership: History and Practical Experience

In this section we turn to a consideration of actual practice in order to attend to the cumulative experience and lessons from past and current examples of employee-owned firms.

The practice of worker ownership has been traced to antiquity (Adams et al. 1993). But in its more modern form its roots can be directly traced to enterprises established in Chatham and Woolwich in the 1760s and the 1800s as reactions to the industrial revolution. In 1828, a monthly paper titled *The Cooperator* was being published in Brighton. Robert Owen, the social reformer and mill-owner, established a number of cooperatives in the UK and in the USA but all of these cooperative communities failed (Adams et al. 1993: 12). Around the same time similar ideas were being propounded and tried in France.

One of the most notable historical landmarks in cooperation was the formation of the Rochdale Society of Equitable Pioneers (usually known as the Rochdale Pioneers) which was founded in 1844. This was distinctive in that it formalized a set of principles which have been adopted and adapted worldwide. These principles included democratic control, membership open without restriction to race, creed, and social class, surpluses to be distributed among members, products sold to be pure and measured in full, and funds to be set aside from surpluses for the purposes of member education. This list exemplifies the aims of the Rochdale Society which acted as a catalyst to the formation of many hundreds of other cooperatives in the UK in the first decade following its formation. Their principles expressed far-sighted social purposes which were adopted by the International Cooperative Alliance in 1937 and which in modified form persist to this day. However, while the consumer arm flourished, the producer cooperatives did not.

The history of worker cooperation in the United States can be traced to experiments in the late 1790s and early 1800s. One of these experiments started during a strike in Philadelphia where boot- and shoe-makers opened premises to sell products made by their members. It was in the 1830s that a significant number of worker cooperatives were started. The National Trades Union resolved to raise funds to help start cooperatives so that 'producers of wealth may also be its possessors' (cited in Adams et al. 1993: 15). Numerous worker cooperatives were launched in a variety of trades over the ensuing fifty years.

Internationally, the worker cooperative idea has waxed and waned. It found particularly fertile ground in the Basque Country of northern Spain. The Mondragon worker cooperatives have attracted a great deal of international attention and as a result the movement is probably the best documented case study of a thriving worker cooperative. The Mondragon version of worker cooperation is notable for a number of reasons—sheer scale and success are high among these—but also because it has taken the notion of cooperation beyond mere participation in the decision making of a single unit and has extended the concept to include wider social responsibility to create new cooperative businesses in the wider community.

A thorough analysis of Mondragon was conducted by a team from Cornell (Whyte 1991). Overall, this team gave it a positive evaluation. Bradley and Gelb (1983) compared the Mondragon cooperatives with other businesses in the region and noted the merits of the model in both economic and social terms. However, a more critical appraisal followed (Kasmir 1996). These studies took place many years ago and the world and the Mondragon cooperatives have changed a great deal in the meantime. These Basque cooperatives enjoyed successful international growth until 2007/8, but since then they have seen a reduction of employment from 103,731 in 2007 to 74,117 in 2014. Fagor, its most emblematic industrial firm, went into bankruptcy in November 2013. Even during the growth period up to 2008, the Mondragon cooperatives employed very large numbers of staff who were not members of the cooperative.

UK Worker Cooperatives of the Early 1970s

In the UK in the early 1970s there was a period of de-industrialization and industrial conflict. As companies sought to rationalize their assets through factory closures, a number of workforces responded by occupying their workplaces. In some of these instances they called for state injection of funds to enable the launch of worker-run cooperative ventures using the existing sites, plant, and machinery. Three cases from that time (often referred to as the 'Benn cooperatives') illustrate this phenomenon: Meriden Motorcycles, the *Scottish Daily News*, and Kirby Manufacturing Engineering. Each was given state financial support—often in the form of 'loans' and each failed.

The story of the Triumph Motorcycle factory at Meriden in Coventry in the 1970s is instructive. The saga reveals numerous critical tensions in the worker cooperative idea. Meriden motorcycles inherited the remains of Norton Villers Triumph after that merged company faced bankruptcy in the early 1970s. In 1974, supported by government money of £4.95 million, the new co-op was started. In subsequent years the government put in additional money as loans and waived interest payments. In 1980, £9 million of debts to the government were wiped out. The business collapsed in 1983 having struggled for a decade and the factory was demolished in 1984.

The phenomenon of the anti-redundancy cooperative was not unique to Britain but sponsorship by the state was, and this is attributed to the determination of Tony Benn. Some local union officials argued that the worker cooperative idea was merely a negotiating ploy to keep the plant open.

Kirby Manufacturing and Engineering (KME) was located in Kirby, Liverpool. It was a manufacturing plant making, among other things, central heating radiators. Born from the ruins of Fisher Bendix, it started trading in January 1975 with around 950 employees. It was entirely funded by a government grant of £3.9 million, a further grant of £860,000 was made in 1977. The money ran out towards the end of 1978. Following a favourable report from PA Management Consultants, the co-op applied for government money but was refused. Efforts to find a private buyer failed and the Conservative election victory in 1979 effectively ensured the end of this worker co-op.

One assessment of these three cases drew these vital lessons:

> They all started business seriously undercapitalised. They all started in very risky businesses. And they all started without clear ideas of how to resolve the conflict between management and workers—which is so effectively institutionalised in the industrial relations set-up of conventional companies. These failings were a direct result of the circumstances surrounding the co-operatives birth.
>
> It is difficult to read too much into the viability of worker cooperatives from these particular high-profile and highly politicised cases. All three cases after all had also witnessed failure under conventional private ownership models. Market conditions in each case were highly adverse. The kind of lessons that could be drawn were of a rather different order and these related to the tensions played-out and the relative lack of direct employee-decision making while under cooperative ownership—which in many ways amounted to a kind of public ownership but with a drip-feed contingent financing arrangements. (Hird 1981)

Challenges and Controversies

The main areas of controversy relate to suspicions about the motivations behind the promotion of employee-ownership and mutualization, the extent and method of employee involvement in decision making, power and influence, and the financing of employee-owned firms. We examine each of these points in turn.

It was notable under the Benn cooperatives that most workers sought public ownership and not employee ownership. It was the Minister, Tony Benn who wanted to experiment with the cooperative idea. Likewise, in more recent times, one source of scepticism is represented by a trade union perspective which viewed the Conservative–Liberal Democratic Coalition's agenda for the promotion of mutualization of the public sector as a device to reduce state services and to undermine trade union organization of the public sector. This critique is advanced most notably by the Public and Commercial Services union, the PCS. The PCS tend to view mutualization as a form of privatization.

One of the potential challenges is to work out how managers should conduct themselves in businesses where workers are also the owners. The conventional 'boss' role is arguably ill-suited to an employee-owned organization. In John Lewis there is sometimes discussion and even fascination about the way in which mid-career external recruits in management will cope with this challenge. A highly participative and consultative approach is expected while maintaining an ability to manage.

One dimension is showing appropriate 'respect' to all co-working partners. Of course, respect ought to be a feature of all work organizations; but employee-owned businesses can be expected to place greater emphasis on managers showing respect for the dignity of work and the worker. Hence, meaning and variety in work and the opportunity for growth and development may be expected. In John Lewis, provision for cultural activities outside work is an added dimension. Another, is managers' ability to communicate and to be 'held accountable' by representative bodies. This means being willing to share information and to be able to explain convincingly the rationale behind decisions. Another aspect is the positive encouragement of participation in decision making by as many partners as possible. This is an unusual skill set for many managers.

Our evidence from John Lewis suggests there can be challenges at all levels of management. The extent to which workers are able to exercise a different kind and degree of influence on decision making in employee-owned enterprises is one of the central themes in the literature on this topic.

A concern is that employee influence will be so strong that it will slow down decision making, make it less effectual, and thus threaten commercial viability; a different concern is that it will be so weakened that professional managers will be able to steal the show.

Managers of cooperative firms, it is argued, face a distinct challenge unlike that experienced by managers in conventional companies. They are expected to submit to continuous and critical internal scrutiny and control by cooperative members. This, together with controlled differential salaries between workers and managers, may make recruitment into the managerial cadre of worker cooperatives problematic (Morales 2004). It has also been suggested that managers coming from investor-owned firms find it difficult to adapt to the culture and values of the cooperatives. As a consequence, they may experience difficulties in their relations with employees and, perhaps most of all, with the cooperatives' governing councils (Bataille-Chedotel and Huntzinger 2004). Such external managerial recruits have a greater tendency towards short tenure. Some authors also suggest these managers may have difficulties with worker participation and that they may undermine the influence of worker-owners and are an impediment to cooperative success (Meek and Woodworth 1990). Thus, managers themselves may be a potent source of the degenerative effect and they have been identified by some as the main cause of cooperative failures (Münkner 2000).

Issues of access to information, representational structures, seats on boards, capability, and a culture of accountability tend to arise. Underlying each of these is an often unspoken perceived tension between favourable terms and conditions on the one hand and commercial drive and expansion on the other. In one regard, this could simply be seen as the same kind of tension found in, say, a family-owned firm or indeed a shareholder firm where there are different priorities and pulls towards long-term or short-term gain.

Whether or not there is a role for trade unions in an employee-owned firm is a further question (McCarthy et al. 2011). Enterprises transferred out from the public sector will be subject to transfer of undertakings (TUPE) regulations, but trade union recognition is not a necessary requirement. One line of argument is that without proper safeguards for effective employee voice then representation may atrophy, or, when severe difficulties are faced representation may be ignored. Some argue that trade unionism is incompatible or unnecessary in an employee-owned enterprise but there is evidence that such organizations work more effectively when there is representation (McCarthy et al. 2011). Representational modes can be ambiguous and disconcerting under such new ownership arrangements (Davies 2009).

In employee-owned enterprises, senior managers may expect everyone to put their shoulder to the wheel and make sacrifices in their commitment to the social purpose and this may lead to breaches of employment rights. This tends to be a danger in charities and voluntary organizations where employees and volunteers may be treated less well than in conventional businesses. It seems possible that something similar may happen in employee-owned businesses where higher values rather than instrumentalism are given priority.

On the positive side, employee-owned enterprises may encourage shared commitment which in turn may yield flexibility and innovation.

Another area of controversy relates to power and influence. According to agency theory (Berle and Means 1967), in a conventional PLC, there is a well-tried model for handling relationships between Principals and Agents. Private shareholders (Principals) whether they be private individuals or institutional investors set up institutional governance arrangements backed by state regulation to ensure their interests are protected and that company directors (Agents) act in the interests of shareholders. While such shareholder power and institutional arrangements do not always work to offset the power of managers (Agents) there is some reason to question whether this relationship might be even more problematic in employee-owned firms where these institutional constraints do not exist.

There are also concerns that the ideals of common ownership may be exploited and then betrayed by an opportunistic sale of assets. To counter this risk there are ideas for devices such as an 'asset lock-in' to prevent assets being sold to benefit current employees or other stakeholders.

The literature points to a number of limitations and challenges facing cooperatives including problems in accessing capital (Van der Krogt et al. 2007), risk aversion (Park et al. 2004), time horizon problems, and common property problems (Spear 2004). In other words, the literature tends to suggest a host of reasons why commercial success might not be expected in cooperatives.

One lesson from the history of employee-owned firms and worker cooperatives is the difficulty they have often encountered in raising capital. Sources of capital for employee-owned enterprises tend to be limited. It has been noted that 'Employee ownership is normally associated with debt finance insofar as employee owners are reluctant to have their ownership interest diluted by seeking out equity capital. Closing off equity finance limits the options available to finance employee ownership' (Nuttall 2012: 15).

Employee-owned companies face a number of technical complexities concerning legal issues, financing, tax, and governance. These can serve as obstacles to the establishment of worker cooperatives. For example, evidence presented to a UK Parliament inquiry stated that a concern was 'a lack of access to genuinely expert support and advice, and a budget to cover the cost of that advice' (All Party Parliamentary Group on Employee Ownership 2011: 10).

Likewise, the 'legal, tax and other regulatory complexities of employee ownership were cited as barriers to its adoption, or as burdens facing existing employee owned companies. Setting up an employee owned company necessarily raises several questions of corporate governance and structure, and has tax implications. . . . the complexity of these arrangements could burden and discourage those interested in employee ownership' (Nuttall 2012: 16).

Managing to Counter 'Degeneration' in Employee-owned Organizations

The literature on employee-owned firms has been dominated for more than a century by the 'degeneration thesis' (Potter 1891; Webb and Webb 1920; Meister 1974). According to this view, mutuality is always a transient phase on a deterministic trajectory either away from mutuality as commercialism takes the upper hand, or towards commercial failure as democracy takes the upper hand. Such a view posits an opposition between employee-owned firms and effective management, suggesting that any constraint on managers' ability or authority to manage reduces management efficiency, and thus the firm's performance.

This line of critique might be considered as managerialist. It consists of two mutually supportive and potentially fallacious components: that if the power of employees is strong, management will be weak and performance poor; conversely, if performance is strong then management must be strong and employee power diminished and the would-be alternative firms become less distinguishable from conventional capitalist firms as they make compromises with their principles.

Analysing the evolution of different cooperative production societies in Great Britain during the nineteenth century, the Webbs (1920) and others found a record of commercial disaster and repeated failure; the few organizations that did survive quickly 'degenerated' by moving away from their democratic roots in different ways. These ways included employing a growing percentage of outside labour; concentrating power in managers' hands; selling parts of the company to outside shareholders; and disqualifying members from taking part in decision making and governing bodies. This view that cooperatives are bound to fail or to degenerate into capitalist forms of business has been a prevailing view in the literature on employee owned firms (Meister 1974, 1984; Ben-Ner 1984; Miyazaki 1984).

The cooperative degeneration process has also been traceable in the Basque cooperatives mainly because of the nature of the growth strategy followed in recent years and the consequent increase of non-members in the workforce. The level of member participation in the Mondragon group has reduced sharply from 86 per cent in 1991 to 29.5 per cent in 2007 (Altuna 2008).

In line with authors who contend that degeneration is not inevitable and who argue that cooperative 'regeneration' can take place, recent research on Mondragon suggests that a cooperative regeneration process could be slowly reversing the degeneration. In JLP there have been periods when the democratic experiment lost momentum, and episodes when there seems to have been efforts to breathe new life into the representational forms (Flanders et al. 1968; Bradley and Taylor 1992; Cox 2010).

Degeneration may result from different dynamics. Some cooperatives start to deny membership status to parts of the workforce. This may occur as cooperatives take on temporary staff without membership rights, or they outsource certain activities such as cleaning and IT, or they acquire conventional capitalist firms (overseas or locally) with working conditions and working arrangements very different to those of an employee-owned parent company. Another type of erosion of the cooperative ideal stems from what has been termed 'goal degeneration'. Cooperatives may increasingly prioritize profits or growth as their prime purpose. Additionally, there may be 'organizational degeneration' when power and control are increasingly concentrated in a few oligarchic hands.

According to the degeneration literature, cooperatives and other democratic associations often have a 'life cycle' within which degeneration progressively takes place. Meister (1984) describes this degeneration process as occurring in four stages. At first (the Conquest phase) enthusiasm, idealism; and commitment are high, decisions are made in the assembly, but economic activity is badly established; second (the Consolidation phase) there is a period of transition in which, if the cooperative survives, conventional principles of organization are adopted, initial idealism slowly gives way to indifference and the power of management is reinforced; in the third phase (the Coexistence phase) degeneration signs are many: democracy becomes restricted to a representative board, the proportion of members attending meetings and participating in assemblies is lower, cooperative values are subordinated to economic ones and the growing complexity of the economic activity makes it difficult for members to effectively control important decisions made by managers; and finally (the Management Power phase), members and their representatives lose power and managers assume total control.

However, some authors (Batstone 1983; Hernandez 2006) have argued that cooperative degeneration is not inevitable. Cooperatives can also regenerate. These authors stress that regeneration takes place in cooperatives with a culture of open criticism and discussion and where there is an active and explicit commitment among members to change their organization. Using data from sixty French cooperatives, Batstone (1983) found that besides surviving in market terms, these cooperatives maintained a high degree of democracy. This suggests that Meister's life cycle model is too pessimistic.

A new life cycle model of three stages was suggested by Batstone. The first step corresponds to the beginnings of most cooperatives, where the majority of the initial workforce are members and democracy and commitment are high. In a second stage, there is a progressive decline of primitive democracy, non-member workers are increasingly recruited and there is an widening gap between managers and members. If the cooperative survives, Batstone suggests that total degeneration is not necessarily the next step, and a stage of a 'resurgence of democracy' is also feasible. This resurgence of democracy takes the form of 'an increase in membership, a decline in the dominance of professional management and a re-emphasis upon the interests of labour as compared with those of capital' (Batstone, 1983: 152). Similar results are found by Estrin and Jones (1992) using panel data for 283 producer cooperatives in France throughout the period 1970–79. Estrin and Jones found that cooperatives had a low mortality rate, many of them survived for more than thirty years and some indicators such as growth rate, labour productivity, and the capital intensity of production did not fit with the view that cooperatives are bound to fail. Furthermore, their study showed evidence against the degeneration predictions of surviving cooperatives: productive efficiency was higher in cooperatives where the membership rate was high.

Hernandez (2006) suggests that cooperatives are neither fully democratic nor oligarchic, and should be understood as 'a site of unresolvable contestation between oligarchic and democratic forces'. From this point of view, the internal contradictions and tensions described by the degeneration and regeneration literatures do not necessarily lead to resolution, but instead tend to be everlasting.

On the basis of this analysis, it cannot of course be claimed that there are no tensions between commerciality and the principles of employee-ownership; there clearly are. But, what can be claimed is that this tension can be managed so that it is shifted from a zero-sum relationship to a mutually supportive relationship with positive linkages between structures and processes of accountability, participation and consultation, and commercial success. Conversely, while the co-owned model can be a source of competitive advantage, it is by no means an automatic causal connection.

This approach, while it is always precarious and undoubtedly prone to possible excess, seems to be associated with a means of escape from the perceived or actual limitations of employee ownership. In managing this co-existence, members of the dominant coalitions also have to carry with them not only workers at all levels but also a number of their senior managerial colleagues who themselves continue to conceptualize the task as one of maintaining balance and who worry that the emphasis had tipped too far in one direction or the other. Facilitation of debate appears to be a positive feature. Cornforth (1995) found that openness to criticism and discussion was a feature of successful cooperatives.

New challenges present themselves. Commercial success and growth add to organizational complexity. This in turn requires ever more sophisticated management input and hence heightens the vigilance required to engage non-management partners/members.

The balance required is dynamic. Following the paradoxical perspective proposed by Hernandez (2006), we hypothesize that JLP will be found to be neither fully democratic nor oligarchic. Rather, we expect to find a site of continuous and unresolved contestation between oligarchic and democratic tensions and a playing-out of competing institutional logics.

Conclusions

In this chapter we have reviewed the policy context; the range of meanings which surround debate about employee ownership and related concepts; the history of practical examples of worker cooperatives; and we have summarized the key issues and controversies.

The different interpretations of the potential meanings of cooperatives—whether they are improved versions of capitalism or alternatives to it—are represented by the body of work presented in this chapter. Each of the works introduced here has something to add to the analysis we are attempting, though none of them precisely meets the needs of our project which focuses strongly on the intertwining of sustained commercial success and partnership working.

The review also reveals a number of challenges that tend to confront employee-owned enterprises. The failure of the Benn cooperatives of the 1970s—Triumph Meriden, KME, and the *Scottish Daily News*—tended to blight the concept for many years. The main problems afflicting these particular examples of worker co-ops were the difficulties of raising sufficient capital, the legacy of commercial failure which they inherited, and the difficulties they encountered in resolving managerial issues.

On a wider front, the history of employee ownership more generally reveals questions about purpose—this includes the question of whether co-ownership and engagement are ends in themselves or means to other ends.

There are also persistent questions about influence and control—in the language of corporate governance, who are the principals and who the agents, and how effectively in a co-ownership company can the principals (the employee-owners) control the agents (the managers)?

The issues raised in this chapter highlight the kinds of challenges which an employee-owned business such as the John Lewis Partnership can expect to face (finance, accountability, degeneration, unusual managerial challenges, and so on). The issues documented here summarize the kinds of challenges which any alternative form of corporation based on wider stakeholder principles would be likely to encounter. In the ensuing chapters of this book, we describe and analyse how the JLP, the largest, enduring, and most renowned of these alternative forms, has handled these challenges.

4

The Way the Business was Managed: 1990–2009

To put flesh on the practical problems faced in managing JLP as an employee-owned business, this chapter and the next describe and assess the happenings and development of the two main JLP divisions—John Lewis and Waitrose—over the past twenty- five years (1990–2015). This chapter focuses particularly on the years 1990–2009. The idea is to draw out the nature and the operation of the business principles by examining the practical leadership and management of the Partnership over an extended period of time in some detail. During this quarter-century period, the Partnership had to cope with renewal, growth, recession, and redundancy, with diversification, intense commercial competition in the marketplace, with the online revolution in retail, with calls for and experiments in international expansion, and with collaboration with commercial partners—to name but some of the many significant challenges. The ways in which these threats and opportunities were handled help reveal the 'true nature' of management priorities and the Partnership.

We draw upon internal documents, most centrally upon the business plans at both corporate level and at business unit level, and these documents are supplemented by insights drawn from interviews and observations across the Partnership during the years of our involvement. A timeline of initiatives and developments over this extended period reveals the JLP in action: describing and exploring how managers made sense of the fluctuating competitive environments they faced and how they ordered their responses. A key focus is on strategies and business planning. It is evident that handling the dual elements—some would say tensions—of commercial viability and partner well-being—was a significant and abiding concern.

1990–1999: 'Stagnation' to Awakening

The following passage is an analysis made by one corporate director when reflecting on the condition of the JLP at the start of the period in question:

> I think there was a time in the 1990s when, in John Lewis in particular, the business had stagnated. The leadership at the time needs to take responsibility. We rather just kept turning the handle on the same way of doing things. There should have been a point in the mid-1990s when somebody said: 'Actually we can't go on like this for much longer: we've got to start to change this business'. But that didn't happen until around the turn of the century when both businesses went through an accelerated period of modernisation. We had to catch up with the competition. During that period there was certainly some strain placed on the model because of this need to think a lot more about profits and commercial matters. (JLP director interviewed 2009)

Doubts about the performance of the business were not new. There had been difficulties before (for example, in 1952, JLP profitability was less than 1 per cent of sales). But by the mid–late 1990s concern about the sustainability of the JLP were growing. Towards the beginning of our period (August 1999) a business journalist assessed the JLP as follows:

> There is little doubt that John Lewis must adapt. The stores' unwillingness to take credit cards and their short opening hours (the department stores all close on Sundays and Mondays) conveys the impression that the outlets are there for the benefit of staff rather than customers. Several branches have started to look tired and run-down. The last set of results showed a 17 per cent profit fall and the next figures in September will be grim too. (*The Independent*, 7 August 1999)

Some saw the issue in terms of the qualities of managers and the level (or type) of professionalism. A senior manager suggested to us:

> Until Stuart's time [Stuart Hampson, the Chairman] the business was run principally by people who had a particular traditional way of thinking and a particular way of managing. When that generation moved out, a generation of retailers who'd been in the business for a long time were put into positions where they could say, 'Well if we want to be successful retailers there are some things we have to do'. I think a much greater degree of professionalism began to be called upon at that time. (Senior manager interviewed 2010)

Stuart Hampson was appointed Chairman in 1993. He was a key figure in the period under discussion and in leading the change. But he was cautious and it took him some considerable time (more than seven years) to feel confident enough to support significant change. During the 1990s, the JLP business experienced some modernizing changes. In 1992 Waitrose opened its one hundredth food shop. In the next year electronic scanning of purchases was introduced in Waitrose and Waitrose Winedirect—an early online venture—was launched. The following year, as a result of legal changes, eighteen Waitrose branches began trading on Sundays and the first Waitrose Food and Home was launched. In 1995 the first professional Public Relations officer was appointed—indicating the beginning of a shift away from the gentlemanly modesty that had characterized JLP's earlier stance on publicity issues.

But these developments were not a natural or automatic outcome of the JLP model. Democracy, co-ownership, shared values, and unusual objectives in and of themselves did not guarantee business success. Senior management became convinced that the success, possibly even the very survival, of the Partnership was dependent on management action which would significantly alter key elements of the business model. Management had to become responsible for ensuring business success and this would involve the maintenance and mobilization of the potential benefits of distinctive features of the JLP model towards the achievement of performance targets. There was general agreement among the managers interviewed that JLP was under-invested in the 1990s and that too little had been done to keep pace with the competition. The business was starting to look dated.

2000–2005: The Introduction of Business Planning

Business planning was first introduced in 2001. It began somewhat hesitantly and apologetically, as 'a new approach which aims to establish a closer alignment of the Partnership's business plans and activities with the principles set out in the Constitution'. Reference to the Constitution in JLP is an established and historic way to claim legitimacy within JLP. The 2001 Business Plan preamble notably sought to reassure everyone that the process would not be too onerous or demanding. The move from the previous management epoch to the new would be gradual: 'No one wants the objective-setting exercise and monitoring of performance to become an industry in its own right.' The communication continues with the assurance that producing the required performance data was not going to be arduous: 'Wherever possible, (performance) measures have been suggested that are already reported in some way, are easily available or can be derived from existing or planned divisional initiatives.'

In accord with these sorts of assurances that not a lot would change, the Partnership Business Plan in 2001 comprised just seventeen pages. Ten years later, the Summary Financial Impacts for the 2011 Business Plan, on its own, ran to sixty-four pages.

Early in the new decade, John Lewis moved from one style of management to another and from one style of retail to another. Many people (including JLP management) saw the change as a move to a more modern, professional approach. The business strategy was labelled 'Compete to Win'. This change project consisted of three phases. The first phase: 'Catch-Up' (2000–02) consisted of new shops, modernizations and refurbishments of existing stores, changes to trading hours, changes in corporate branding and identity, and investment in distribution. Phase 2, 'Consolidate' took place in 2003 and consisted of cost control, a focus on the supply chain, and a focus on stock availability and service. Phase 3, 'Compete' covered 2003–04 and focused on branding initiatives, supplier and inventory management, and a drive for what was described as a high performance culture.

The 2003/4 business plan concluded that as a result of phases 1 and 2, JLP profits had 'turned around'. However, despite this improvement, 'the current trajectory will not deliver sufficient profits to meet our commercial objectives. Significant top line growth is essential—we cannot deliver our objectives through cost cutting alone' (JL Business Plan, 2003/4–2007/8: 23). This phenomenon—that strategies succeed but, with changing environmental context, the success proves insufficient—proved to be a familiar one over the next ten years.

The transformations included changes to the direction and focus of the business as well as performance. During the period when the JLP businesses were being changed radically, the world of retail itself began to change. While the JLP businesses were modernizing through a range of strategies and policies aimed at achieving growth, increasing margins, achieving efficiencies and improved organization, and investing in new and refurbished stores, retailing became increasingly a matter of clicks rather than bricks. The period under review reveals attempts to modernize and improve in terms of the old model while increasingly trying to adapt to and adopt the new business model.

Business plans early in the period identified familiar objectives and one can see the beginnings of themes which ten or so years later would assume major proportions. Intriguingly, the 2001 business plan starts with an insistence that the plan represents no possible conflict between the development of the business and the Constitution. On the contrary, it seeks to establish a '*closer alignment* of the partnership's business plans and activities with the principles set out in the Constitution' (2001: 1). To argue this implies that the linkage between the development of the businesses and the values and principles of the JLP can vary (if the plan makes the alignment closer, presumably earlier it was looser); it acknowledges in effect that either through accident or design, through purposeful action or inertia and neglect, the direction of the businesses *could be* contrary to the intentions and principles of the Constitution.

The 2001 plan asserted: 'The Partnership will aim to increase profits from £154M in 2001/2 to £334M in 2005'—that is, a doubling. Later in the period, as competition increased, this emphasis on the urgent need to improve the performance of the JLP business by growing revenue and reducing costs and achieving performance improvements became increasingly marked.

Throughout the period, there is evidently a shared commitment to a broadly similar set of initiatives. Overall financial objectives are stated so that success or failure will be clear. Key commercial rivals and their competitive advantages are identified: success is not to be viewed relative to JLP's history but to current competitors' performance. Then the core JL customer proposition is clarified: quality, service, and honesty. But the rigour of the planning process developed slowly and gradually over the period. In 2005 we were told, for example, that despite formal business planning:

> There were no proper targets, so the divisions were not targeted to deliver anything. The Chairman would meet with a crowd of Waitrose managers and a crowd from John Lewis and he would say something like 'We've got enough cash in the bank to afford the capital, so off you go and do your best'. (JLP director interviewed 2005)

JLP as a whole, and JL department stores especially, struggled to identify a response to the e-commerce threat which did not undermine its existing businesses and their business model. This resulted in a symbiotic model whereby the physical and virtual stores coexisted to mutual advantage. A hybrid approach was developed in which the stores justify their cost base and online sales not only benefited from the existence of physical stores, but also contributed to their performance. Click and collect was just one part of this.

Loyal customers were recognized as the key to success. Waitrose, for example, identified customers in terms of levels of loyalty and sought to retain 'gold' customers, defined as those who spend more than 50 per cent of their grocery bill at Waitrose. They constitute 9 per cent of customers but account for 55 per cent of sales. Waitrose planned to grow 'silver' customers—those who make 10–50 per cent of their grocery purchases at Waitrose. JL too developed a sophisticated categorization of different types of customer and identified 'deepening emotional affinity' with customers as critical. Not surprisingly, JLP seeks not only to protect but also to deepen and strengthen the emotional links with customers:

> They're expanding all of their PR, the marketing, the community involvement, this foundation, that foundation, all that sort of thing, and it's really an attempt to attach the customer to the brand . . . you've got to have the customer in the palm of your hand, and then you can sell to them whichever way you like . . . that's the piece they're working on. (Manager level 2, interviewed 2005)

Managers saw the major threats to internal reputation with partners as arising from declining performance. They were less concerned about blows to reputation that may arise from business decisions intended to boost performance, which could be seen to indicate a deviation from historic JLP values and principles. A major component of JLP's reputation—among partners and customers—is described by JLP managers in terms of 'trust'. Trust is necessary to underpin confidence in JLP's honesty and thus its core proposition (plus service and quality).

But trust must also characterize partners' attitudes towards management and towards the democratic institutions and processes through which partners and management relate. Management argued that partners' confidence would reflect the Partnership's performance. If profits failed to recover, adverse comments to the effect that the Partnership was in decline could undermine the confidence of customers and result in partners losing confidence in management.

So, improved performance is necessary not only for competitive success but also to sustain the basis of the Partnership itself: that the JLP stands for a better way of doing business and a better way of treating staff, and that these differences are noted and valued by customers. The Chairman, Stuart Hampson, described to us what he saw as the differentiating proposition of the JLP businesses:

> We talk about relationships, others talk about transactions. They aim to maximize transactions; we aim to build relationships. In the end, the business that focuses on relationships will beat the one that focuses on transactions.

This conviction offers a neat way of conceptualizing the link between the components of the JLP model and the performance of the businesses. Partners' responses to their membership of JLP should be for the good of the businesses and for the benefit of the performance of the business. An internal statement from 2006 argued:

> For our business to be successful, we need to ensure that partners, as owners, are motivated and encouraged to view their membership as more than just a job. Every partner has rights as an 'owner'—rights to share in knowledge, power and profit. And with those rights come responsibility. To maintain the Partnership's competitiveness we need to ensure the incentive of ownership is reflected in partners' great motivation to improve their individual and the Partnership's overall performance. . . . Our ambition . . . is to refresh and strengthen the unique psychological contract of rights and responsibilities of ownership, which is what motivates and binds the Partnership. (JLP, An Enterprising Partnership, 1996: 3)

But it is difficult to realize this potential. The 2001 department stores business plan starts with a major worry: 'Sales and profit growth in the past three years have come largely from new shops. This growth has disguised underlying weaknesses in the performance of the more established department stores. Branch trading profit for branches opened before Kingston has declined over 4 per cent over the last four years despite an 11 per cent increase in sales' (Business Plan, 2001: 6).

The reasons for this decline in performance are given as: lack of a strategy to grow market share or to change the underlying cost structures of the business; under-investment in shops, the cost structure and speed of the supply chain, and in some areas, 'stagnation' which could damage the long-term competitiveness of the Partnership. These are unusually frank statements of self-assessment and critique.

Responses to the named problems included: changes to opening hours which were underway in 2001; an emphasis on the John Lewis corporate brand; investment in store simplification and cost control on the shop floor; attention to the supply chain; and finally, at the end of the list initiatives, 'develop John Lewis Direct'.

In 2001, Waitrose senior managers were worried. Between 1997/98 and 2001/01 Waitrose was successful in driving sales. However, the sales increases did not flow through to profits. Sales grew 25 per cent but profits stayed the same and 'increased central cost allocations meant an actual fall in profit by 21 per cent compared to 1997/8. All this occurred at a time when increasing competition was arising from competitors moving to new formats and direct channels, Sainsburys and Tesco rolling out convenience stores with some of these in tie-ups with major petrol retailers.

Something was wrong. Waitrose's response at this stage focused mostly on refurbishment and new stores (and Waitrose Direct) to generate growth which would enable greater buying scale, reduce costs and increase margins. Personnel costs at head office would be reduced but at this stage the Waitrose employment model in the stores was not directly addressed. Nevertheless the plan envisaged an increase in profit margin from 5.1 per cent to 6.9 per cent and 100 per cent increase in profit over the ensuing five years (Business Plan 2001: 10).

By the time of the top managers' conference, held at the JLP facility on Brownsea Island in Poole Harbour in 2004, an overview of JLP performance identified some worrying trends. Over the next ten years, the emphasis on growth was to be mirrored by an equal emphasis on efficiency and cost control.

Revenues and profits are only achieved because of the appeal of the products to customers. In each of the Business Plans of the early 2000s, the crucial importance of improving and sharpening JL's and Waitrose's distinctive appeal to customers is stressed. Partnership objectives for 2002 emphasized the importance of partners' satisfaction derived from secure and fulfilling employment, but also noted that co-ownership '*must become* increasingly relevant and vital in relation to partners' sense of responsibility to, among other things, our reputation among customers'.

Other objectives from this period also identified issues which would grow in importance: that profit was essential, that customer loyalty and satisfaction with value, choice, service, and honesty were critical, and that continuous improvement, change, and innovation were vital.

The JLP model was already being regarded as a source of strengths *and* weaknesses: the model could instill complacency and resistance to change: '...management recognizes the importance of creating a culture which is more receptive to change, which encourages all partners to think about ways of improving their own methods of working and to recognise channels for pursuing improvements outside their own competence'.

In 2002, the Partnership Business Plan stated that co-ownership and the overall purpose of 'the happiness of all its members' must be 'relevant' and vital—that is, should engender partners' sense of 'responsibility' to each other, to the democratic processes and to enhance the Partnership's reputation among customers and more widely. At that time this argument was relatively under-developed. But over the next ten years later it became the prevailing theme.

One director, in late 2002, explained the emerging consensus on the nature of contemporary competitive advantage as follows:

> The partnership way of doing business gives us a competitive advantage which is sustainable, difficult to copy, difficult to replicate, defensible, and is a true point of distinction. On the basis that it is a better way of doing business, that should translate into an economically more advantageous model. I would say, at the moment, it doesn't, and hasn't for a long time. Then you got to say why? I think there are a number of reasons for that, some of which are bizarrely bound up in the model. I think at worst sometimes the partnership model is used as an excuse to not do those difficult things which would generate that additional return. So I'm in a place where, at the moment, I would say it should give us the most fantastic advantage, but we struggle to turn that into an economic advantage. (JLP senior manager, interviewed 2002)

JLP management became concerned with an issue which was to grow in strength: the importance of creating a culture which is more receptive to change. At this stage implicitly, but later increasingly explicitly, the view emerges that aspects of the JLP model could generate not improved business performance but obstacles to business performance by encouraging complacency and resistance to change:

> I think the downside of any co-owned business is that you deal with all the legacy issues of complacency and managing change.... You could argue the model makes us risk averse. (JLP director, December 2002)

The experience of trying to get partner support for changes to opening hours possibly generated this assessment. The change of its traditional five-day opening took over a year. The proposal had to go through individual branches of the elected councils—twenty-six, in total. Luke Mayhew, the MD of JL remarked, 'I wouldn't have done it any other way.'

Once again, it is seen as managers' responsibility to address this issue. Management must ensure that the potential benefits of the Partnership model are translated into business success. 'I just think we're sitting on a heritage and a gold mine...the gold mine of ready engagement that other businesses pay a lot of money to get, but we don't know how to use it.' This concern about complacency became a widespread part of the management narrative. The following quote is typical of many similar statements that we heard at that time:

> I don't think we do a good enough job of it. I think historically we celebrated good effort rather than good achievement. One of the things I'm working on at the moment is how we re-calibrate in all departments an understanding of what good performance looks like. We rightly come under pressure over pay, and pay badly for the last couple of years. As partners say we are not delivering there, but actually, the truth of it is that we could deliver more individual as well as more collective reward for partners if the top 10 per cent of performance was replicated further down the organization. So, for me, it's about defining what good looks like and going after it, and enabling leaders to be more robust in their feedback. We have a very poor culture of feedback, it is polite and consensual. (JLP director, 2003)

The JLP model was recognized as inevitably associated with greater employment costs.

> If you believe in the model you've got to believe that the investment you make in all the other stuff does pay back. There are still areas, *sleepy areas*, who *think the business owes them a living* and need tackling, and there's still a lot of people who do not get the co-operation piece. That's part of the legacy we have to work through. (JLP director, January 2003, emphasis added)

This assessment, with its pointed reference to 'sleepy areas' and a 'sense of entitlement' reflects the concerns about the dangers of 'complacency' that we heard a number of times during this period. It was not always clear whether this was a danger perceived as inherent in the model itself, or whether it was a charge laid at the door of managers and partners during a specific period. The fact that the concern was raised at different time periods might suggest that the danger was more inherent and enduring rather than bound by time, place, and regime.

Increased revenues were to be achieved through a number of initiatives (many of which remain important several years later). These included: an assortment review; improved product offer especially in relation to own brand goods; buyer development and attention to special promotions; service and presentation improvements; the modernisation of selling floors—plus supply chain changes; increasing the percentage of time that partners spend with customers. Finally there was to be improved marketing, 'to increase brand awareness and change perceptions of the brand among non-shoppers'.

Cost would be reduced by simplification across a range of projects, controlling staffing levels, reducing the number of managers and centralizing aspects of purchasing. The longer-term strategic agenda included reviewing own brand possibilities, reviewing costs especially in supply chain, reviewing growth opportunities, and, crucially, taking advantage of synergies from multi-channelling.

But the focus was not solely on efficiencies; it was also on investment and growth. The Chairman commented: 'it would be possible to run this business in a way that produced higher levels of profit and, if we were driven by short-term considerations, that is precisely what we would do. We would employ fewer people, halt investment in new shops, systems and refurbishments and ignore e-commerce' (interview with the Chairman, 2002).

While managers try to direct the destiny of the businesses and convert the potential of the model into revenue and profitability, they are also managing impressions—worrying that the aura around the Partnership is safe and intact and untarnished—the Partnership's 'reputation'. The JLP image has many constituents but revolves around notions of decency, fairness, and honesty. Senior managers emphasized management's role in sustaining these values, and management's performance itself as a source of trust and confidence. This concern presages a major focus of later business planning: the attempt to create, through marketing strategies, a strong self-sustaining image of the JLP among both customers and partners, each confirming and sustaining the other.

2003–2004: The 'Compete to Win' Programme and the Launch of the Partner Survey

For management, the launch of the partner survey was an important way to monitor the internal 'reputation' of the brand and more specifically, of partners' confidence and trust in senior management. It was used as a critical barometer by management, a way of testing partners' responses to the search for greater efficiencies and to a range of organizational and commercial developments. The partner survey was launched in 2004. The then MD of JL remarked of the survey:

It was excellent that so many partners took the opportunity to express their views on how they feel we are doing against our objectives of offering 'worth-while and satisfying employment.' Messages and lessons were quick to emerge, and have been relatively consistent across branches. Despite the changes and uncertainty that many partners faced, the division's results were not signifi-cantly different from the rest of the partnership. But partners across all branches made it clear that we had significant improvements to make in leadership, management and communication. . . . it is clear we are not engaging and involv-ing partners fully.

It was recognized early on that the Partnership had, and still has, two of the strongest retail brands in the UK, but this was achieved through strong positioning and reputation not through dominant market share. The 2003 business plan recognizes that the JLP businesses face intense competition and identified five strategic priorities:

- drive 4 per cent like-for-like sales;
- capture 3 per cent margin improvements;
- hold front-line headcount, drive efficiencies in selling support;
- build a culture of high performance leadership;
- build scale through new shops and multi-channel operation.

Growth was a key element of JLP business strategy. It is regarded as essential to enhancing the vitality and competitive scale of the two businesses. This emphasis on growth continues, indeed has probably become more dominant.

But operational efficiency and organizational capability are also important. In 2003, senior managers identified the targets necessary for business success: a minimum return on invested capital (ROIC) of 8 per cent, to meet funding needs including the need to support pensions and the partner bonus. There was also an expressed intent to 'reshape the psychological contract with partners', shifting this from a perception of a 'job for life' to one of security of employment in exchange for a commitment to development and initiative, stressing the *responsibilities* as well as the privileges of co-ownership (emphasis added).

Both businesses were committed to improving profitability and to growth. John Lewis managers in particular recognized that their profit objectives could not be achieved through cost cutting alone: revenues must grow. The 'Compete To Win Programme', based on the Bain consultancy initiated by Luke Mayhew when MD of JL, consisted of a number of mutually supportive initiatives as reflected in the business plan of that time:

> We shall be clarifying and focusing our customer proposition; we are looking to build scale through growth via new shops and Direct; we are pursuing greater operational profitability through enhanced efficiency; we are aiming to improve organizational capability by developing a high performance culture; and co-ownership underlies the whole strategy by, for example, using it to drive the Partner/Customer/Profit value chain and improving Partner understanding of our business by communicating our strategy. (Business Plan, 2004: 27)

Increasing profitability is a constant priority. Although towards the end of the transition period the JLP model was being claimed as a source of improved business performance, earlier on it was seen in some sense as an historic liability (in performance terms), especially in JL. The five-year plan (2003–08) stated the dual principal aims as to 'improve the profitability of our department stores and to grow scale'.

Modernizing the JLP meant addressing the employment model. Managers were aware of the risks:

In pursuing greater operational efficiency we shall be continuing to change the way we work in a number of areas, principally through simplification of administrative processes and streamlining the supply chain. This will mean reducing the number of Partners in those areas. It is our firm intention to achieve these reductions through natural wastage where possible. However the cumulative effect may mean in some branches that posts will need to be made redundant. We are looking to make decisions in 2004 on initiatives which, between them, would reduce partner numbers by 600 but allowing for natural wastage the number of posts made redundant is expected to be much lower than this'. (Business Plan, 2004: 30)

Thus, despite the co-owned character, redundancy was most certainly considered an acceptable tool if circumstances required.

Waitrose at this time was recognizing that its historic trajectory could not provide a sustainable platform for continued growth and increased profitability. The historic dependency on increases in mark-up was not sustainable. The operating model—and cost base—had to change. The Waitrose board agreed a strategy to improve long-term sustainable competitiveness by modifying prices and modifying costs. Once again the strategy was for growth supported by cost reduction and improving the capability and performance of partners. Waitrose's strategic response was to focus on product quality and range, customer service, modernizing the stores and reducing its cost base.

In late 2004, JLP senior management presented a wide-ranging and comprehensive internal review of the progress and performance of the businesses. The review, entitled 'How are we doing?' was refreshingly honest. The review indicated that over the period 1994–2004 Partnerships sales increased from £2,322m to £4,500m but profits had fallen over the period from £300m to around £250m—a change in profit margin from 6 per cent to 4.5 per cent. Costs had risen faster than sales (sales increased by 106 per cent, overall operating costs by 123 per cent (and pension costs by 306 per cent). Falling profits resulted in falling levels of return on capital invested. Indeed, return on invested capital actually fell from 7 per cent in 1990 to 6.7 per cent in 2004. Over this period, JLP invested heavily, averaging £240m a year.

Over a number of years from 2004, Waitrose expanded through a series of acquisitions. First, there was the acquisition of nineteen Safeway branches in 2004. This took the Waitrose brand outside its previously confined geographical area. Six stores were purchased from Morrison's in autumn 2005. Then, in March 2006, Waitrose announced the purchase of five stores from Somerfield. In July 2006, Waitrose announced the purchase of six more stores and a distribution centre from Morrison's. The then Waitrose MD, Steve Esom,

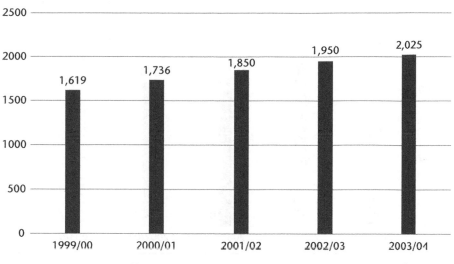

Figure 4.1. JL sales (£m), 1999–2004

always maintained to us that the concentrated work required of partners at all levels to convert these stores into 'proper' Waitrose branches motivated and energized his colleagues more than any other measure.

However, there were challenges. Legal requirements relating to the transfer of undertakings (TUPE regulations) meant that Waitrose was legally obliged to take on all the staff, including branch managers. There were concerns that the acquired managers may have become accustomed to different leadership accountabilities and might find managing in a JLP way problematical.

While capital expenditure was heavily focused on acquisition in the case of Waitrose, for the JL department stores the money was spent primarily on refurbishments. For example, £107m was spent on the prestigious Peter Jones store in Knightsbridge. There were also four new JL stores built in this period. This level of investment could not be funded by profits alone: additional borrowing was required to cover the shortfall.

By the time of the 2004 review, performance in the department stores suggested some underlying flaws in the business model (and possibly in the underlying employment model). Sales during this period increased from £1,619m in 1999 to £2,025m in 2004 (Figure 4.1). This reflected a considerable achievement with sales increasing each year.

But the problem was that profit levels were falling during this whole period. They declined from £149m in 1999 to £100m in 2004 (Figure 4.2). The net profit margin fell form 9.2 per cent in 1999 to 4.9 per cent in 2004. And there was also a declining return on invested capital (from 8.3 per cent in 1999–2000 to 5.6 per cent in 2003–04 (Figure 4.3).

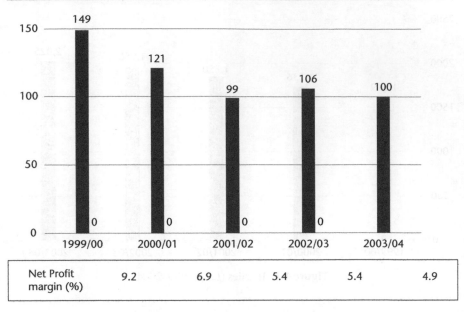

| Net Profit margin (%) | 9.2 | 6.9 | 5.4 | 5.4 | 4.9 |

Figure 4.2. JL profits (£m), 1999–2004

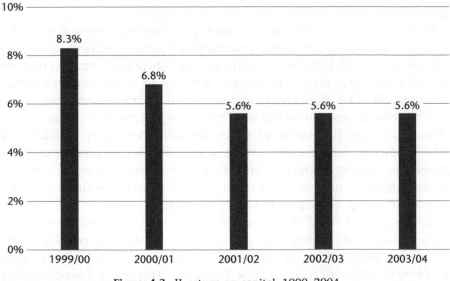

Figure 4.3. JL return on capital, 1999–2004

The problems were caused by JL's high levels of staffing which was not matched by high levels of productivity (i.e. sales). In a comparison with four other retailers, JL was second highest in sales densities but lowest in sales productivity (sales per full time equivalent). And JL's sales growth was not impressive either, coming fifth against a group of retailers.

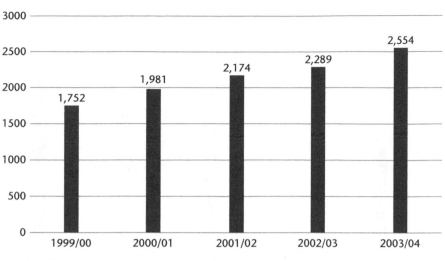

Figure 4.4. Waitrose sales (£m), 1999–2004

The conclusion is stark: in the year 2003–04, against a group of similar retailers, JL was highest by a considerable margin on employment costs (as a percentage of sales), with costs of 22 per cent, contrasting with the second highest, the fashion and homeware store, Next, with 15 per cent. For some JLP managers, this stark contrast reveals the financial penalty of the JLP model. Clearly this gap was unsustainable: either the cost of the model (and therefore presumably the model itself) had to be changed, or the model had to be made to work and the other part of the equation, sales, would have to increase.

The relatively poor profitability resulted from high employment costs alongside high levels of spend on refurbishments and new stores. This combination resulted in returns on capital that were less than those achieved by competitors. For example, in 2003–04, Next secured a return on invested capital of 17.3 per cent, while JL achieved 5.6 per cent.

During the period 1999–2004, Waitrose's performance was more positive. Its sales increased from £1,752m in 1999 to £2,554m in 2003–04 (Figure 4.4) Sales growth remained consistent at around 5 per cent per annum over this period. Profits also increased: from £64m in 1999 to £116m in 2003–04. This represented an increase in profit margin from 3.7 per cent in 1999 to 4.5 per cent in 2004 (see Figure 4.5). Its return on invested capital (ROIC) was 6.7 per cent in 1998–99 and this grew to 8.1 per cent in 2003–04 (see Figure 4.6).

However, despite this impressive performance, Waitrose ROIC was half that of its strongest competitor, Morrison's, which secured 16.1 per cent during this period. Market share for Waitrose moved from 1.8 per cent to 2.3 per cent. Over the five-year period, its space grew by the same percentage as Tesco's (although from a very different base).

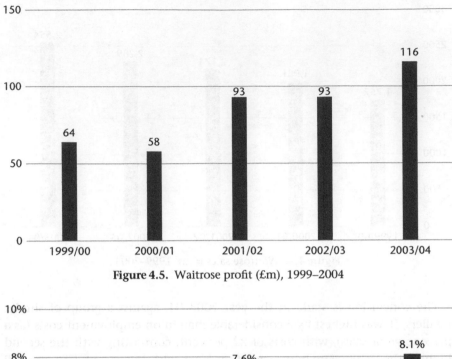

Figure 4.5. Waitrose profit (£m), 1999–2004

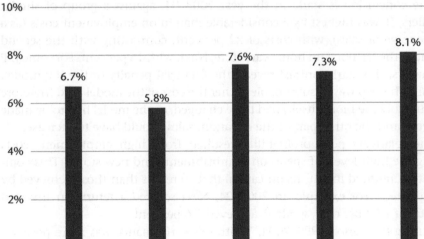

Figure 4.6. Waitrose return on capital, 1999–2004

Employment costs at Waitrose were higher than most, and sales densities higher too, but productivity lagged behind the competition. There was concern at this period that the profitability of Waitrose was too dependent on mark-up and that this was, ultimately, non-sustainable.

Waitrose, it was acknowledged, had reached a critical stage in its development and faced a major decision: whether to continue as a south of England-based niche retailer or to expand the geographical coverage and strengthen the format offer. The decision of the Waitrose board was to choose the latter option. This decision recognized the strengths of the brand and the Partnership culture but also acknowledged the vulnerability that came from an historically high cost base (the JLP staffing model) and uncompetitive prices. The reliance of profitability on increases in mark-up and an inflexible operating model were major worries. The objective of Waitrose was clarified as: 'to be the best quality food retailer for our target customers'.

So, both JLP businesses developed strategies to address the issues facing them. John Lewis' strategy included driving growth, controlling costs, improving performance and investing not only in new shops but also in multi-channel operations. The latter reflected a conundrum. If the historic business model underpinning retail was beginning to change radically but one was deeply committed to the bricks and mortar of the historic model, how to adapt to the new while being committed to the old? A way had to be found to link the two types of business. It was.

2005–2009: Revitalizing the Partnership Spirit

Work on the 'Partnership spirit' started in 2005. This aimed to 'reinvigorate and communicate the Partnership's fundamental values and behaviours and the motivation Partners draw from the partnership' (Partnership Business Plan 2005). Attempts to exploit the potential of partners' commitment had to be balanced with the need to restrict costs. The JL business plan included 457 job redundancies.

By early 2005, these strategies were beginning to have a positive effect: a 7 per cent improvement in productivity (sales per full time staff equivalent). The Partnership Strategy for that year stated that the 'We have hardly begun to tap the potential for the employer brand: a better place to shop and a better place to work' (Partnership Strategy, 2005: 2). Managers also added the related point about suppliers: 'You only get quality through the relationships you have with your suppliers. This is about being long term, from being decent, and only come from people that really care, buyers that care, there's always that extra 10 per cent they do where they just get something slightly better. And then you have suppliers that love what they do and the combination is very enticing'.

The JLP businesses and the JLP as a whole were not only trying to be clear about what customers wanted and could expect from JL and Waitrose but were also trying to be clear themselves about the nature and implications of the underlying core JLP dynamic. During this period this dynamic became clearly defined and the definition more dominant, offering a way not only to understand how the core components of the JLP model worked together but how they reinforced each other and generated potential competitor advantage. By 2008, the 'Partner–Customer–Profit' cycle concept was firmly enshrined as 'at the heart of our strategy (JL), enabling us to deliver a unique customer proposition whilst rewarding our Partners with the benefit of a great profit delivery' (Partnership Business Plan, 2008: 4).

This view of 'the heart of the strategy', whilst not a distortion of the founder's original conception of the Partnership's purpose, does represent a rebalancing of this purpose in terms of a claimed causal linkage between the experience of partners *qua* partners, and the experience of customers and the resultant level of profit (which flows to partners) generated by the appeal to customers of the various different ways partners behave in their work.

The partner–customer–profit cycle suggests that happy partners exist to serve the Partnership—through the way they behave with customers. The Constitution argues that the Partnership exists to ensure the work-based happiness of the partners. Of course, because the partner–customer–profit cycle is a cycle it can be claimed that the result of this sequence is, through the impact on profitability (which is shared with partners), partners' happiness. But something has been changed, if only in emphasis; a change which is probably indicative of the greater focus on commerciality.

This is not to suggest that current management in JLP have 'betrayed' or distorted the Constitution. What is significant about the cycle and its increasing use during the period is the way it posits and emphasizes a causal relationship between its components rather than the looser linkages suggested by the formula in the Constitution ('happiness *in* a successful business').

For JLP managers in this period, who saw themselves as responsible for improving the profitability of the businesses and who were all too aware of the threats posed by the businesses' poor margins, ensuring partners' happiness was dependent on the survival and success of the businesses and that required that the JLP model and its associated expense, be made to work. Not surprising then that managers were keen to stress the 'success' on which partners' happiness was dependent. These worries were to reappear with a vengeance in 2008.

The 2008 Waitrose business plan continued the established customer strategy—'dominate on food', 'differentiate on service'. It sought to be competitive on key lines and to support premium pricing where quality differential existed. It also sought a distinct and consistent store environment with effective customer communication to drive sales growth. But it was recognized that a strategy review was required to ensure that Waitrose developed a long-term sustainable business model with reference to the price/product quality/service offer in the face of intensifying competitive pressure. There was also recognition that the increasing move to new format stores and to multi-channel strategies raised questions about the adequacy of existing staff and organization structures.

In 2008, despite the planned improvements in the performance of both businesses, they were likely to remain near the bottom of the list of competitors on financial performance because competitors were also improving performance. In terms of ROIC, Waitrose was predicted to be in the bottom ranks of the competitor set over the four years starting in 2008, and JL margins were predicted to be significantly lower than competitors because of the high costs of the service model (despite lower rental costs).

2008–2012: Coping with the Financial Crisis

The plans went seriously awry. In 2008 a dramatic deterioration in the economic environment created a very challenging context for both JLP businesses. Growth stalled; inflation hit a 16-year high; consumer confidence collapsed. The housing sector collapsed, banks experienced a liquidity crisis and consumer spending suffered in consequence. In JL this occasioned a serious problem: falling sales with an inflexible cost base created a stark and unavoidable challenge—something had to go.

The effects for the JL businesses were serious. In the third quarter of 2008, Partnership sales were 6.9 per cent lower than budget, and profit fell by £32m against a forecast of £229m. JL Direct remained a positive source of growth but this was not enough to make up for the decline in the profitability of the established stores. The crisis of the economy revealed underlying deficiencies in the JL business model. A review of the business plans in 2009 stated clearly: 'The rapid worsening in economic outlook has exposed the vulnerability of our operating model' (Business Plan Review, 2009: 6).

JLP's strategic response was to move to a divisional rather than store-centred operating model and to reform head office to offer shared services for both divisions. Ultimately, the strategy was to grow sales and improve margins, but *prima facie* there could seem to be a contradiction between the two components of the determination to increase sales: 'through more shops and direct selling'. Was this a case of JL's historic pattern of being a fast follower rather than an innovator? Did it reveal some limitations to the JL Board's strategic thinking—limited by historic 'success recipes'? Or, more likely, was it simply a reflection of the realities facing JL? Although someone starting large-scale retailing in the first decade of the twenty-first century would probably not invest billions in expensive prime location department stores, nevertheless, JL was where it was as a result of its history: the owner of numerous flag-ship stores. If it was to move more vigorously towards direct e-commerce retail, it had to do so in a way which found some intellectually, and commercially viable way of using each means of selling to support the other. The solution was for JL to become *multi-channel*, using the JL brand to create a powerful direct selling offer that reinforced and built on the JL brand. This required not only the development of a multi-channel organization and supporting systems, but also the creation of a genuinely cross-channel experience. These initiatives were accompanied by changes to the selling support functions and the move to a semi-automatic distribution centre both of which have implications for the numbers of partners required: the former through job losses (100 per department store) the latter though job losses and the use of non-partner staff. This was an interesting, and for some, troubling development.

By the second quarter of 2008, Waitrose sales continued to fall as customers spent less and the business suffered a decline in market share for the first time for many years. Operating profit for 2008/9 was considerably less than budget. The issue was pricing: competitors were focusing on value. Waitrose had to develop a new customer strategy which would identify different types of customer and their different needs and allow a pricing structure to ensure an increase in sales. They had to strengthen the offer to customers and become truly multi-channel through Waitrose Deliver, and Waitrose Wine Direct.

During the period 2007–11, the economy remained weak with very low GDP growth. Throughout this period unemployment was high and disposable income growth low, mortgage approvals halved, and consumer confidence hardly rose above the historic low of 2008. These circumstances hit retailers hard: twenty-six retailers left the FTSE during the period and there was a 40 per cent average drop in the share price of the survivors. However, over the period, online and multi-channel retailers have performed better and food retailers have maintained their share value. Yet, even during these hard times, JLP businesses managed to grow sales by 29 per cent, with both businesses outperforming their respective markets. Waitrose was the fastest growing supermarket in 2009 and in 2010. And the John Lewis department stores division outperformed the British Retail Consortium (BRC) index for 42 out of the 60 months (2007–11) on a like-for-like basis by an average 2.7 per cent. The index-beating performance was especially marked from 2009 onwards as JL emerged from the recession far better than most other retailers.

Although management had still not found the magic formula that would unleash the potential of the Partnership, hopes remained high. Partners were still seen as critical not simply to the delivery of the strategy but to the strategy itself: 'Partners are not only at the heart of the mission of the business they are also key to our distinctiveness, the essential resource in delivering our strategy'. But also central to Waitrose and JL's business plan is the central decision to refresh the democratic character of the Partnership. No doubt this intention to revitalize the democracy was sincere, and the purpose, far from diluting the democracy, was to ensure that there is 'constructive challenge to the partnership on the definition and delivery of our Partner and Customer objectives' (Partnership Business Plan, 2009: 12).

Conclusions

The nineteen years from 1990 to 2009, took the Partnership on a remarkable journey. At the start of the period it was widely regarded as a venerable institution, stuck in its ways and with a rather dusty and increasingly dated estate. It was perceived to lack vigour and was being overtaken by new, contemporary, outlets. From around 2000, there was a concerted and sustained effort to modernize. This included longer opening hours, growth through acquisition in the case of Waitrose, a major programme of investment to refurbish the JL department stores, and investment in advertising. These business strategies were underpinned by the launch of business planning; a significant investment in online service; the recruitment of external talent—often at very senior levels; the introduction of an annual Partner Survey; the launch of shared services to rationalize costs across the businesses; and a far more rigorous form of managerial leadership.

The ways in which the Partnership was managed during this period reveals a far more focused attention to the exercise of professional management. The necessity for commercial success was made more evident. At the same time, Partnership values were not neglected; but they were reinterpreted. Taken together, these measures were harbingers of new times. Patterns of behaviour began to reveal the new ways of operationalizing the model. The ways in which the dilemmas were debated and decided upon offer useful insights into how this version of the 'alternative' trusteeship corporations operated in practice and by extension offers clues about how trusteeship bodies in general might fare.

5

The Way the Business was Managed: 2010–2015

From around 2009/10, there were growing signs that the existing business and operating models were not sustainable. Incremental strategies aimed at increasing the scale and efficiencies of the business (termed 'Fit for the Future') were no longer fit for the new future; something new was required. The old strategy had been to do the core things better; now the strategy was to do new things. These new things were to extend existing businesses with new products, new format, and services through new distribution channels to new places, and to explore new multi-channel offerings. Waitrose remained committed to being Britain's leading food supplier, trusted by customers and partners through an emphasis on quality, service, ethics, and environment. Partners were seen as a major priority. Volumes were still a problem, especially in mature stores and costs needed to be controlled. Waitrose would move into new types of stores (for example, convenience stores of various type), it would also launch a series of joint ventures with other retailers and would press on with an emphasis on e-commerce.

These initiatives, for example, the tie-up with Shell, raised troublesome issues of reputational risk. They also raised questions about the compatibility of these partnerships with the JLP model. For example, with regard to the decision about the status of employees in these hybrid situations: would they be partners or not, and would they be managed by partners? Waitrose planned and developed a range of possibilities in which the degree of Partnership control varied depending on conditions, such as the extent of JLP responsibility for the operation, and whether or not employees were partners. In one option, the store would be owned and run by Waitrose with the company taking full responsibility and with the employees as partners; on another model, an outside business might supply the space and services for a rent, but the store 'within a store' would be run by Waitrose.

Then there were franchise options. Waitrose could provide the name and brand, the franchisee might provide the capital investment and run the business day to day. There are variants on this proposition. In one type, the employees are partners and in other types they are not. Or Waitrose may grant a license to the franchisee which imposes quality control in relation to the manner in which the goods are to be sold, but does not control how the licensee operates it business; in these instances the staff are not partners. However, Waitrose specified that as well as being 'leaders in their field', those operating licensing/franchise relationships must 'share our customer values'. This range of variants triggered debate about the inherent meanings of the Partnership for they started to open up multiple ways in which the concept could be stretched or even compromised.

Many senior Waitrose managers argued that these initiatives required no special justification since they would not be contrary to the JLP Constitution or the principles of the Partnership because they would be undertaken with the objective of 'unlocking value for [the core] Partners by driving volume and efficiency in our core business, while improving access to the brand through new channels and formats that meet the evolving needs of our customers'. This justification is seen as giving *carte blanche* legitimacy with respect to the JLP Constitution—which, *prima facie*, seems odd, especially given the preoccupation with reputational risk which clearly increases the more arm's length the operation. Waitrose managers recognized that these initiatives would raise questions from partners. And in order to prepare for these or to forestall them, they attempted to anticipate them. But the list included (with one exception) a series of mainly *practical* issues of implementation. The possibility of any conflict between these new ventures and the goals and principles of the JLP was not considered. The background documents included such questions as: 'Do we have the right skills for future requirements? Will our current organization structure support our future business? How can we unlock efficiencies to prevent additional business models requiring incremental costs?' The only question which approaches any concern about the possible impact of these developments on the JLP employment model was: 'How can we retain the democratic nature of the business through a period of significant growth in scale and complexity?' This imbalance in the nature of the questions and concerns may be indicative of some underlying thinking at this time.

Waitrose senior managers continued to stress their commitment to the ultimate goal of the JLP: 'to deliver worthwhile and satisfying employment in a successful co-owned business'. There was a subtle shift in emphasis from stressing that the Partnership's purpose is the happiness of all its members *through* their worthwhile and satisfying employment in a successful business, to arguing, in effect, that achieving a successful business must, *ipso facto*, ensure members' happiness. This latter formulation potentially allows any sort of business venture to be defined as legitimate so long as it succeeds (and the profits shared with partners through the bonus). Would such a formula sit happily with the distinct values and principles of the JLP? To put it another way, what sorts of business ventures and partnerships would *not* be palatable or consistent and why? As we have seen, some options entailed partners acting in effect as employers of non-partner staff. As we noted in Chapter 3, this kind of departure could be regarded as problematical for a co-ownership business.

Most Waitrose senior management were unapologetic. One Waitrose director made the case to us as follows:

> You have to have strategies that allow you to compete and grow. If you didn't there would be no future. It [JLP] only exists because your customers, in one way or another, believe it delivers to them great value, and if they don't they won't shop with you or they won't trade with you. (Waitrose director 2012)

So, again the argument comes back to how you use the model to gain some kind of competitive advantage and where the model might be less good in getting competitive advantage. With respect to the new initiatives and the implications for staffing, the same Waitrose director argued:

> We operate two models. One is the straight supply model where we let people have Waitrose goods. Here Waitrose isn't just a retail brand. It is also a FMCG [fast-moving consumer goods] brand. Hence, in effect we run two models. We run a FMCG model—no reason why it can't be co-owned. And we run a retail model. The retail model is wholly owned with one exception. (Waitrose director, 2012)

However, while some senior managers remained concerned that new types of business relationships *could* represent significant change to the original JLP principles; others refute this:

> He (Spedan Lewis) came up with a mechanism that made people feel as though they had a real stake in the business. He gave them the profits, he gave them knowledge of how he worked, through a whole host of systems and he gave them a degree of power over the way in which their business runs . . . the core of the work is done. The management need to be true to those three fundamentals: that we will continue to share the profits, that we will continue to share knowledge as widely as possible with partners and not be afraid of doing that and that when it comes to running the business we will engage as best we can with partners. Now, provided we do that, our task is to say, okay, commercially what should we be doing? (JLP manager, 2013)

This argument justifying management's right to manage overlooks the key role allocated to (and the competitive benefit that accrues from) partners' commitment and discretionary effort that is a consequence not only of their status as co-owners and their involvement in knowledge and power, but also of their overall experience as a partner in JLP.

But justifying new types of business ventures by virtue of their contribution to partner happiness by virtue of their profitability (profitability = partner happiness = sufficient justification) also runs the potential risk that the ways in which profit is achieved could have adverse implications for partner happiness. Yet the notion of 'worthwhile and satisfying employment' explicitly identifies work experience as central to the objectives of JL businesses. Waitrose is aware that the Partnership has explicit responsibilities towards partners in their work and that the Partner Survey measures partners' satisfaction with some aspects of their work. However, not all potentially important aspects of work are measured by the survey, for example, the provision of career/promotion opportunities; and the survey itself shows that (at least in late 2010) partners were far from impressed with some features of their work. Low scores were achieved for the question 'We have enough Partners to get the job done', and low-ish scores for 'My ideas to improve our business are welcomed', and also for 'I can have a say in what happens in my branch'. Nor did the survey measure partner responses to the new ventures in all of their complexity and their allowance of non-partner status.

New Ambitions, 2010–2014

Despite the difficult economic conditions, the Partnership business plan for 2010–2013 was ambitious, forecasting a growth in sales of £2.5bn by the end of the period. At the start of this timeframe things were certainly difficult: GDP was negative, and unemployment at its highest for many years. Nevertheless, JLP forecast slow growth over the plan period in the markets in which the JLP businesses operated. The plan argued that the economic downturn simply underlined long-term industry trends to which the businesses had to respond: the importance of multi-channel operating and online, market consolidation, the importance of price, and more demanding customers.

The JLP business plan showed both divisions improving their financial metrics considerably by 2013. JL improved its return on capital invested from 6.6 per cent to 9.5 per cent. Waitrose raised its return from 7.9 per cent to 8.9 per cent. By the end of the planning period, JLP divisions would begin to look quite different: with a larger number of small branches and new formats, a range of commercial arrangements, and a larger online presence. The balance between JL and Waitrose which had been shifting steadily in Waitrose's favour continued, and by 2013 Waitrose was expected to contribute 65 per cent of JLP sales.

In the department stores, a change programme called 'Branch of the Future' was designed to rebalance the proportions of customer-facing and non-customer-facing staff. Three years were spent systematically going through all aspects of back of house in the stores with a view to rationalization. In the main, customer contact-handling was moved from each of the stores to just two national centres, one in Manchester and one in Glasgow.

In 2011, senior JLP managers remained clear that commercial success was essential to the survival of the JLP and that growth and improved financial performance, by industry-established metrics, were essential to success. But *if* the objectives of the business are unequivocal and undeniable (commercial success within two highly competitive market places) it does not necessarily follow that success *alone* (or success at any price) is *sufficient* to ensure partner happiness. The methods used to achieve success could be contrary to partners' happiness and well-being.

The business plans of 2011 showed an awareness of the risks raised by the nature and degree of change across JLP divisions. The potentially adverse effects on partners were recognized. This part of the story is important because it is by JLP's own admission that the fundamental distinctiveness of the JLP customer proposition and business success arises not from IT or structures or capital investment, but ultimately, from the behaviour, attitudes, and commitment of partners. Hence, if there were a risk of partner disengagement or disillusion, this would strike at the heart of the JLP competitive differentiator.

The Partnership Business Plan for 2011–14 had six priorities reflecting the standard partner–customer–profit cycle. In the partner category were these priorities: 'develop a *clearer* direction for Partners which enables a consistent experience reflecting the commitments'; '*promote* the partnership model and *refresh* its democratic character'. 'Clearer', 'promote', 'refresh'—these terms all suggest that senior managers recognize that the P–C–P cycle describes a set of inter-connections which could work negatively or neutrally as well as positively and which require monitoring and management. The corporate plan consists of initiatives which are: 'developing and bringing to life the responsibility and rewards of co-ownership'.

Despite the context of a struggling economy, the JLP plan for 2011–14 was to more than double in size with respect to sales (£11,617m by 2014). Waitrose was to invest £269m in thirty new stores, driving £461m of new sales. In food, the convenience market was growing at double the rate of the traditional food shopping market and online grocery was growing even faster. The four major convenience players were expected to open over 300 new convenience shops in 2011 and the same number in 2012. As the Waitrose plan notes, the pressures of changing customer behaviour and changing competition to meet (and create) these demands are developments that Waitrose could not ignore unless it was happy to lose market share. This is a clear example of the pressure both businesses were under to maintain commercial success: as they saw it *the status quo* was not an option: it was change and grow—or atrophy.

The move to smaller formats in both divisions presented a challenge to the principle of 'consistent Partner experience'. This kind of concept might not be so important in a conventional business but it is of concern in a partnership. To give one example, in the smaller format stores space is limited for staff catering facilities. Traditionally perceived as an indicator of JLP's difference, the 'Partners' Dining Room', where partners can obtain a subsidised main meal every lunchtime has been substituted in these settings with self-catering arrangements such as buying food off the shop floor at a discounted rate. As most of these partners are part-time, they do not necessarily want a main meal, but the lack of a consistent experience was a source of anxiety among some partners. Such developments seemed to signal an erosion of dearly-held distinctive privileges.

The JLP plan also shows a continuing struggle to achieve forecast and planned levels of margin and of ROIC. Sales in 2010/11 showed levels beyond the range expected, an increase of over 10 per cent and this level of sales growth was expected to continue through the plan period—margins were just within the expected range at less than 5 per cent and they did not show improvement until the end of the period.

The growing online channel had a key role to play not only in sales (which were expected to rise to over £1bn by the end of the planning period) but in profit: in 2010/11 over 20 per cent of JL profit came from the online channel.

JL's experience reflects that of both JLP divisions over the period under discussion. Initially at the beginning of the period the pressure was to modernize, to upgrade stores, to review the assortment, to modify opening hours, etc.—to do more or less the same things but better. Very soon the businesses were hit by two new pressures. First, the gradual emergence of a new form of retail—online—a transformation of the retail business and operating model. So simply improving the original historic model was not enough. JL also had to adapt to meet the online challenge and indeed to develop a major online capacity which could exist symbiotically with the core business—a complex juggling act which led to significant innovations.

In 2011, Waitrose opened four stores in the Channel Islands. Overseas experience had previously been limited; there had earlier been a franchise arrangement in Dubai. In the UK, there was a marked growth in small format stores, that is, the small convenience stores of under 3,000 sq feet. These were were termed 'Little Waitrose' (Figure 5.1). There were four in 2010 increasing to forty-nine in 2015.

The second problem to hit the JLP businesses during the period was the serious global economic downturn which increased the pressure on margins and drove the search for improved margins and increased efficiencies.

Improving efficiency was a dominant theme of all the business plans throughout the period. A paradox for JLP is that the major source of strategic

Figure 5.1. A Little Waitrose store

advantage—partners—is also a major source of increased costs. Reducing costs often means reducing the number of partners, reducing the income of partners, finding ways of making partners work more effectively and efficiently or more intensively, or replacing partners with cheaper employees. None of these possibilities is taken lightly in the JLP and all of them raise concerns about their impact on partner attitudes. Partner Surveys revealed that partners had felt the pressure of change.

The Chairman shared such worries. In his commentary on the 2011 Business Plan he identified five areas of concern, two of which were: partners' 'confidence in the balance being struck between Partner, Customer and Profit'; and 'will the Partnership's reputation be enhanced through the plans?'. (The other three questions concern practical and financial aspects of the plans.)

These are important questions and it is interesting that the Chairman raises them. Clearly there had been signs of disquiet and discontent. And equally clearly they had been picked up. With respect to the first question, the Chairman is referring to a series of initiatives which may reduce anxiety about partners' responses: a range of communications media which will explain the JLP's partner commitments, a better calibrated partner survey which would supply better quality data on partner attitudes; some reform of pay policy; and divisional activity aimed at improving management feedback to partners and implementing the partner commitments.

The 2012 plan continues this concern for partner well-being commitment and capability. As ever, the recurring motif and ambition were emphasized—the perennial JLP dream: 'unlocking the competitive advantage of Partners'.

Customers believe that the way partners are treated within the JLP affects how they behave towards customers, and the 'narrative' of JLP, its distinctiveness and difference, brings comfort to customers as it does to partners themselves.

But by what management alchemy can this JLP 'difference' be turned into the long-sought-for gold of competitive advantage? And is there a risk that the two joint components of all JLP partner initiatives: enhanced efficiency and increased commitment/capability, may conflict? JLP managers worry about this possibility. The 2012 plan offered a range of initiatives: 'to focus more on creating meaningful work, being a more inclusive organisation, creating and embedding contribution, productivity and flexibility into our cultural DNA... provide real clarity and understanding about what we stand for as an employer and communicate and embed this...'. The desired outcome of these activities? To allow partners to fully contribute to the business by being the best they can be, where they are rewarded for their performance and have more meaningful work and careers: 'bringing to life the rewards and respon-sibilities of co-ownership'.

And the JLP's objectives for customers reflect its commitment to partners in that this relationship too is seen as a *moral relationship*, not simply a transac-tional or contractual one; a relationship based not simply on commercial exchange but characterized by customers having trust and confidence in JLP's reputation for 'value, choice, service, honesty and our behaviour as good citizens'.

But in some respects, the Partnership and efficiency are at odds and efforts to improve efficiency—for customers and for partners—can also risk damaging the engagement of partners. As one senior director contended:

> One of the things I think many customers would say about John Lewis is that they trust the organization, and that trust is born out of a sense of order, a sense of exquisite service, allied with good product knowledge. So you've got people there that understand the stock, deliver the service really well, and that in itself builds that trust. Where we let ourselves down on some of our processes is we didn't deliver to partners in the way that we would be proud to deliver to customers, and so the two jarred. Having said that, I think we're back on track again. But I do see that as we gain aspirations for large process changes in the organization which we're going to need to make, that that won't be an isolated incident, it'll be something that will become a more regular occurrence, and the damage there of course is that, although everyone may hold the model close to their heart, as soon as you start damaging trust, then you start to damage people's faith in the model, and the discretionary effort we get from partners at the moment—which is greater than other organizations—could be lost. (JLP director, interviewed 2012)

The year 2012 saw further specification of, and emphasis on, 'tying our partner agenda even more tightly into delivering our customer and profit goals'. This was to be achieved by enabling and requiring leaders to drive continuous improvement from leaders, addressing roles and systems to ensure they are designed in ways that enable and encourage partner engagement; and ensuring partners can develop the skills they need.

However, one curious and notable feature of these plans is that despite the democratic aspects and structures/processes of the JLP, and despite the infrastructure of consultation, representation, and communication, these activities designed to engage partners seem somewhat managerial and hierarchic: top down, expert initiatives designed to refresh democratic institutions or processes of consultation and representation. Given the frequency of reference to the need to improve partner contribution, and the variety of devices devised to achieve this goal, it is reasonable to assume that these plans are not so far sufficiently successful. If this is the case, the reason possibly lies not in the quality of the proposal but in the means whereby they are developed. Maybe partners themselves should play a bigger role in the discussions about how to upgrade their contribution?

Between 2012 to 2014, Waitrose sales outperformed the industry—for the sixty-two consecutive months; market share increased to 5 per cent, total online services gross sales of £161m, with online grocery gross sales up 54 per cent, but operating profit was impacted by substantial levels of investment across the business and the market sales slowdown. But fifteen new branches opened, eleven more than in the previous year. There were 670,000 more weekly customer transactions and membership of the loyalty scheme 'myWaitrose' rose to 4.8 million.

Between 2006 and 2011, despite the very difficult trading circumstances which had seen a number of familiar retailers go out of business, and witnessed the survivors struggling (on average suffering a 40 per cent drop in share value), JLP managed to grow sales by 29 per cent. Both divisions outperformed the market. Waitrose was the fastest growing supermarket in 2009 and 2010 and JL outperformed the retailers in the British Retail Consortium (BRC) for forty-two out of the sixty months on a like-for-like basis by an average of 2.7 per cent. These results were the consequence of management strategies and associated investment (which grew during this period by 38 per cent to £543m in 2012). This performance and the strong balance sheet it generated enabled JLP to maintain its investment status and to pay partner bonuses of an average of 16.5 per cent over the period. The businesses' strategies—value, innovation, service, multi-channel offerings (including click and collect), and trust were consistent not only with the historic customer propositions of the divisions but also reflected the distinctive and familiar and broadly recognized and celebrated JLP values, practices, and reputation—the JLP narrative. And they were clearly attractive to customers. It does seem that there is indeed something in the maxim: 'a better way to do business'.

By late 2012, both JL and Waitrose had been gaining market share over the previous three years. Partnership sales in 2010/11 were £7,464m, and in 2012/2013 were £7,864m. As usual over recent years, Waitrose made nearly two-thirds of these gains. Waitrose had been growing faster than JL for some time. The Partnership planned to continue to open new stores over the coming years, including new format stores, and would invest in supply chain and IT to support the more complex operational model necessitated by the expansion of multi-channel offering. In 2012 John Lewis launched a new flexible format store. This new format was a store between a full-sized department store and an 'At Home' model. The 'At Home' version is usually around 30 per cent of a full-sized store and carries furnishing and electronics. There are plans to increase the number of At Home stores to fifty; four were opened in 2012. The first JL store outside the UK opened in Dublin in 2012. John Lewis began delivering to France and Ireland to service its online business in 2011. The plan is to extend this to eleven other European countries and to the USA and Australia.

But despite these innovations and their impressive impacts on financial performance as measured by revenue, there was concern among some senior managers about the ability of the Partnership to turn this performance into profit. Could it be that the model was simply too expensive to operate? Table 5.1 shows financial performance measures during the eight-year period between 2007/8 and 2014/15.

The message from Table 5.1 is clear: despite a substantial increase in sales, retained profits remained more or less static. In 2007 they were £108m (1.9 per cent of revenue), and in 2014 just £102m (1.1 per cent of revenue). By 2015, there had been some improvement on this measure. Retained profits were £144m which was 1.5 per cent of revenue for that financial year—still below the ratio for 2007. Notably, if the bonus had not been cut back in that year, the retained profit would have been only around £100m. One interpretation of this could be that this indicates a stable, mature, business; that the profit figures are a reflection of the sector more than the firm itself. But that interpretation is belied by the revenue/sales figures. For these show a dramatic increase—by roughly 60 per cent over the period. (And it is the sales figures, not the profit figures which attract so much comment.) The 'Retained Profits' figures of course are what is left after the bonus has been paid, and the bonus increases over the period from 2007 not because the per cent paid varies greatly—it hovers around the same area during the period—but presumably because the number of partners has increased. It is also true that the 2014 figures are affected by an exceptional item—the £47.3m payment to staff due to an historic error in calculating holiday pay. But this was a cost incurred as part of operations, albeit a cost that would have been spread over a longer period.

Table 5.1. JLP: Nine-year performance summary[1]

Financial year ending 31 January	2015	2014	2013	2012	2011	2010	2009	2008	2007
Sales (£m)	10943	10172	9541	8730	8206	7422	6968	6763	6362
Sales growth over previous year (%)	5.7 (2)	6.6	9.3	6.4	10.6	6.5	3.0	6.3	10.4
Revenue (£m)[3]	9701	9028	8466	7759	7362	6735	6267	6052	5686
Revenue growth over previous year (%)	5.6[2]	6.6	9.1	5.4	9.3	7.5	3.6	6.4	10.4
Net (post-tax) profits (£m)[4]	300	304[5]	312	301	322	258	359[6]	320	263
Profit margin (%)[7]	3.5	4.2	4.1	4.6	5.0	4.6	4.5	6.3	5.6
Return on invested capital (ROIC) (%)[8]	7.6	8.3	8.0	7.0	7.9	7.7	6.8	8.5	7.9
Partnership bonus (£m)	156	203	211	165	195	151	125	181	154
Bonus (% of salaries)	11	15	17	14	18	15	13	20	18
Retained profits ('profit for year') (£m)	144	102	101	136	127	107	234	130	108
Retained profits as % of revenue	1.5	1.1	1.2	1.8	1.7	1.6	3.7	2.1	1.9

Notes
[1] Based on the most recent financial returns for each year, including retrospective accounting adjustments and restatements.
[2] Figures adjusted to 52-week basis as the 2014/15 financial year comprised 53 weeks.
[3] Revenue equals sales less VAT and 'sale-or-return' sales.
[4] Profits after tax but prior to partnership bonus (i.e. profits available for distribution to partners or retention in the JLP business).
[5] Profits affected by material exceptional cost.
[6] Profits boosted by material exceptional gain.
[7] Profit before partnership bonus, tax, and exceptional items expressed as a percentage of revenue. [Note that the decline in the year to 31 January 2015 was mainly due to the decline in the operating margin at Waitrose as a result of intense competition in the UK grocery market.]
[8] Defined by JLP as: 'Post tax profit, adjusted for non-operating and exceptional items, as a proportion of average operating net assets, adjusted to reflect a deemed capital value for property lease rentals'.

These figures confirm what we know from the analysis of the JLP business plans—that the firm is operating in a very competitive business environment where the cost of sales is being squeezed aggressively—a trend which is especially difficult for the JLP with their historic employment model. But it also shows us something about management priorities: despite the static profits, management continues to pay a healthy bonus. This may be because of JLP values and their emphasis on partners' happiness. But it may also have something to do with the various benefits that accrue to management from the continuing prevalence of the JLP narrative: that the JLP model (and management) works.

An assessment of JLP's performance cannot be gained only by an analysis of JLP over time—which shows how deeply entrenched and intractable are both the positives of the model (sales) and problems of the model (costs and reduced margins)—it also requires sectoral comparisons. The point is not only that JLP shows its mastery of its efficiency challenges but also that it demonstrates its superiority vis-à-vis its competitors—a *better* way to do business—that is, better than its competitors. But is this aspect of its claim supported by the data?

The Partnership's 'outperformance', its 'bucking of the trend', is apparent from the revenue growth figures: hard evidence of the JLP success, under harsh competitive pressure including the rise of e-commerce, at holding its customer base and building market share. This is a testament to management stewardship.

But, despite its reputation for success, the profit figures show that relatively, in terms of profitability or return on sales (key efficiency measures), the Partnership is lagging behind its main competitors. Marks and Spencer, for example, widely regarded as having lost direction recently, at least in comparison to the JLP success story, generates more profit and achieves more than twice JLP's levels of profitability.

Secondly, despite superior profitability (and profits) M&S (and most competitors) paid a lower percentage of profits in dividend/bonus than JLP: a further indication of JLP's emphasis on partner happiness, or maintaining the crucially important narrative of JLP success.

Table 5.2 summarizes JLP's performance versus that of certain of its competitors in 2014/15.

Table 5.2 shows a good performance record on growth of revenue compared with its major competitors. It also shows return on sales (calculated as operating profit × 100 per cent/revenue) tends to be lower than its competitors. We argue in this chapter that this may reflect an appropriate set of judgements by the Partnerships' management in recognition of the stakeholder nature of this firm.

In JLP, as we have seen, the strategic focus is on growth, but implicitly it is also on building and maintaining reputation partly, at least, by maintaining the level of bonus and pension payments. Because they are free of market

Table 5.2. JLP: 2014/15 performance relative to competitors

	JLP	M&S	Debenhams	Next	House of Fraser (Highland)
Financial year-end	31 Jan 2015[1]	31 March 2015	31 August 2014	24 Jan 2015	31 Jan 2015[1]
Revenue (£m)	9701	10311	2313	4000	785
Revenue growth versus previous year (%)	5.6	0.0	1.3	6.9	5.8
Operating profits (£m)	450	701	129	812	26[3]
Net (post-tax) profits (£m)[2]	300	482	87	635	
Partner bonus (JLP) or share dividends attributable to the year (£m)	156	296	42	222	0
Bonus or share dividends as % of net profits	52	61	48	35	0
Return on Capital Employed (ROCE) (%)[3]	10.8	11.5	9.3	58.2	4.7
Return on Sales (ROS) (%)[4]	4.6	6.8	5.6	20.3	3.3[3]
Net profits minus JLP bonus or dividends (£m) (retained profits)	144	186	46	413	
Net profits minus JLP bonus or dividends as % of revenue	1.5	1.8	2.0	10.3	(0.4)

Notes
[1] Revenue growth figures for JLP and Highland are adjusted to 52-week basis given that their 2014/15 financial years comprised 53 weeks.
[2] This profit line is post-tax but prior to dividend payments or, in the case of JLP, its partnership bonus. It sets out the profits available for distribution to partners or shareholders and for retention in the businesses.
[3] ROCE equation used is (operating profit × 100%)/(long-term liabilities plus equity).
[4] ROS equation used is (operating profit × 100%)/revenue.

pressures, they can make decisions, with less challenge or fear of market-based sanctions, which may explain the level of bonus payments. JLP managers are immune from take-over and are largely independent of capital market discipline—so the firm lacks an attribute conventionally considered by many to be important for successful performance.

The priority given to the bonus probably also reflects senior management's genuine commitment to ensuring the happiness of partners. But with competition increasing and the threat from e-commerce increasing, with efficiencies proving intractable, and profit levels proving hard to shift, JLP is or soon will be under pressure to satisfy all the budgets that require funding. The recent decision to change the pension scheme was entirely predictable and reflects the pressure on the JLP to square the circle of static profits combined with ambitious commitments to pensions, bonus, investment, and interest cover.[1]

JLP's retained profits are too slim to be able to continue indefinitely to fund current levels of planned expenditure on bonus, pension, capital expenditure, and interest cover.

Once again the downward trend (albeit modest, particularly after exceptional items) in return on sales (ROS) reflects the story we have already identified of flat-ish profits versus growing sales (and sales revenue) in recent years. In order to fund the various demands on JLP's profits, the businesses need to make and retain more profits than they are currently doing. Table 5.3 shows JLP's financial performance between 2007 to 2015, based on return on capital employed, return on sales, and interest cover.

The falling trend in interest cover (in a period when interest rates have been very low) is the consequence of flat-ish profits versus growing debt. At 2008, borrowings were £463m; in 2014 they were £804m. With debt nearly doubling over that period whilst profits have been flat-ish, it is no surprise that the interest cover ratio has halved. And during this period the pension fund was under sourced, a deficit which now has to be restored, thus adding to the demands on JLP profits. This is why the pension changes were entirely predictable, apart from increases in longevity.

Conventional retailers faced with these challenges (and of course they wouldn't be faced by the pension liability to the same degree or the emphasis on bonus/dividends) would respond with a limited number of classic

---

[1] From April 2015, John Lewis new partners will wait five years rather than the previous three to join the final salary pension scheme. And from 2016, after five years of employment, staff will build up a retirement income of *120th* of their final salary for every year they've worked without having to make a contribution, instead of a 60th. JLP will add contributions worth 3 per cent of basic pay to an investment-linked pension pot. JLP made a payment of roughly 10 per cent of the current pension fund deficit last year, on top of annual contributions of £44 million a year under a ten year plan to eliminate the deficit.

Table 5.3. JLP: Performance 2006/07 (2007)–2014/15 (2015)[1]

Financial year ended 31 January	2015	2014[5]	2013	2012	2011	2010	2009[6]	2008	2007
Return on Capital Employed (ROCE) (%)[2]	10.8	11.1 (12.3)	12.1	10.6	11.9	10.7	14.2 (10.2)	13.8	12.6
Return on Sales (ROS) (%)[3]	4.6	4.7 (5.2)	5.3	5.1	5.9	5.8	7.2 (5.2)	6.5	6.0
Interest cover[4]	4.4	4.3 (4.8)	4.0	5.4	6.2	4.4	8.2 (5.9)	9.9	8.3

Notes
[1] Based on the most recent financial returns for each year, including retrospective accounting adjustments and restatements.
[2] ROCE equation used is (operating profit × 100%)/(long-term liabilities plus equity).
[3] ROS equation used is (operating profit × 100%)/revenue.
[4] Interest cover equation used is operating profit/finance costs.
[5] Figures in parentheses show ratios excluding material exceptional item (£47.3m payment to staff due to historic error in calculating holiday pay in 2014.
[6] Figures in parentheses show ratios excluding exceptional item (£127.4m gain from the disposal of the investment in Ocado).

solutions: manage down costs using more efficient staffing ratios; downsize through natural wastage; use (cheaper) contract or outsource providers more; and be more aggressive in terms of suppliers' contracts (after all, others are doing this and so the prevailing wind is in the right direction).

And JLP managers may still be tempted to move in these directions, as we have seen in earlier chapters. They will be under pressure (from themselves and from the need to finance their liabilities) to improve the profit performance to keep up with sales. JLP may be a better way to do business but it is not (and should never claim to be) a better way to make money. The whole point about the JLP approach is that the model is not simply a means to improve performance; it is a means to redefine what performance is.

But JLP managers will find these responses difficult: partly because they can be seen to clash with the principles of the Partnership, partly because they risk reputational damage (especially since the reputation has been so energetically and deliberately enhanced), and partly because to the extent that the JLP management narrative—that treating people better makes for more committed partners and thus more satisfied customers—has an empirical basis, using non-partners or treating partners less well risks a reduction in the distinctive JLP competitive edge.

One illustration of the risk is indicated by reports in early 2015 of a series of customer complaints to a national newspaper about poor service. This criticism of 'Britain's best retailer' was traumatic. It transpired that the service problems related to deliveries from orders to the online service and that the delivery agents were sub-contractors. After care services had been outsourced and so too delivery. The reputational damage was high. Longstanding customers told of 'washing machines and fridges dumped in gardens, cancelled deliveries and failed orders' (Brignall 2015).

Despite such setbacks and the risks associated with growth through alliances with other businesses, growth remained a priority for most of the managers we interviewed.

Further Expansion, 2015–2020

New department stores were planned for Birmingham in 2015, the Victoria Gate area of Leeds for 2016, and Westfield London and Oxford for 2017. A new 'flexible format' shop is planned to open in Chelmsford in 2016. This format sits between the full-size department stores and the At Home shops. The shops, averaging 65,000 to 100,000 square feet, highlight fashion, home and consumer electronics products.

The At Home format focuses exclusively on the home sector including home and electrical and home technology assortments, with no fashion assortment.

The Partnership plans to open new At Home format shops in Basingstoke in 2015 and Worcester in 2016 as part of co-locations with Waitrose.

To support the expansion plans, a new very large distribution centre was opened in Milton Keynes in 2016. This is responsible for large furniture, electricals, and home furnishings. This is in addition to the existing distribution centres in Milton Keynes.

The Growth Imperative?

As the analysis demonstrates, growth of the JLP businesses is a basic, high priority strategic objective of current management, constantly reiterated, presented as beyond debate. Such an objective arguably presents a fundamental problem for stakeholder businesses with 'alternative' objectives to those of conventional shareholder businesses such as the fashion retailer, Next. This turns out to be a problematical issue.

JLP businesses have ambitious growth plans. Both MDs insist that growth is not only sensible, it is undeniable: not to grow would be to decline and to endanger the future of the businesses. There is, JLP partners are told, no alternative to growth. Investment in growth means spending resources which would otherwise go to partners now (in bonuses) or in the future (in pensions). So partners are funding and carrying the risks associated with growth. And the risks of growth are various—to reputation, performance, and core Partnership institutions and values.

The Chairman is clear that there is no point expanding an inefficient model and if there are difficulties in making the existing businesses efficient these difficulties will be compounded when the businesses are bigger and more complex. The Chairman, Charlie Mayfield, commented:

> Growth will continue to be important. But growth increases business complexity and impacts our costs. Focusing on efficiency is becoming more important and to achieve a balanced and profitable growth, whilst delivering enough profit to distribute to our Partners, we need to carefully prioritise our investments and further instil cost control discipline. (Charlie Mayfield, 2014)

John Lewis is once again preparing to almost double in size, launch a French website and open more stores outside of the UK. By 2023 the MD calculates that John Lewis is likely to have sixty-five stores, compared to forty-three at present, with annual revenues rising from approximately £4bn currently to £7bn. In 2014, John Lewis opened stores in York and at Heathrow airport. John Lewis will also expand its wholesale concessions network whereby other department stores offer John Lewis products. Online growth continues to outperform stores. Online continues to power John Lewis' total sales increases. The 'bricks and clicks' strategy is expected to stabilize at around 50/50 by 2020.

John Lewis is set to embark on its next phase of international expansion, considering entry to ten new Asian markets through shops within local department stores. The existing wholesale deal with the South Korean department store Shinsegae, as well as shops within four of its branches, including in Gangnam, is regarded as a success. This arrangement is set to expand. John Lewis managers are considering concessions in Asia, with possible locations including Kuala Lumpur and Tokyo. John Lewis has also expanded its international online business, shipping to thirty-three countries including France, Germany, Spain, Italy, the USA, and Australia.

Waitrose's growth plans are even more ambitious. It has been growing rapidly at around 6 per cent more than the market but still lags behind the big four who account for 75 per cent of market share. Waitrose aims to expand sales threefold over the next ten years, investing £300m every year to launch twenty new branches a year as well as increasing online sales, to become a £15 billion income a year business. Waitrose will take on 2,000 new staff as it looks to expand its footprint across the south east and parts of northern England and will open sixteen new stores from the spring 2015, seven of them smaller convenience outlets.

Waitrose online grocery service, Waitrose.com, is now available in over 150 branches. In 2014, online sales increased by 50 per cent. Waitrose opened a second dotcom fulfilment centre in Coulsdon, South London, in 2014, more than doubling the retailer's online capacity in the capital.

To support its continued expansion across the north of England and Scotland, Waitrose has opened a new regional distribution centre in Chorley, Lancashire. In January 2013 plans were announced to open a new cookery school and supermarket as part of the redevelopment of London's Kings Cross. The development opened in 2015.

Waitrose's expansion includes not only new formats but new organizational arrangements with other businesses and retailers which involve a range of employment and management models. In some cases Waitrose simply supplies product to other retailers. Waitrose first started exporting products in 1996 and now has a presence in forty-seven countries worldwide including Singapore, Canada, Hong Kong, Thailand, the Falkland Islands, New Zealand, Barbados, and India. In the past two years, Waitrose has rapidly grown its export business, with products available in Chile, Gibraltar, the Philippines, the Bahamas, the Turks and Caicos Islands, and Ibiza for the first time.

This is about the relative value and priority of the JLP and all its associated values, about partner happiness, and commercial performance, and the extent to which the latter should limit the former. But more fundamentally, it is about the basic issue: what is the JLP for? Is it to secure and increase benefits to existing partners or to increase the number of partners? We have seen that growth is a high priority for both John Lewis and Waitrose. But growth is defined in terms of market share, revenues, and numbers of stores. But what about growth of the JLP model? Is it part of JLP's growth plans to spread the JLP model so that more people are able to benefit from the model?

Current senior JLP management have tied the success—and possibly the survival—of the JLP and its businesses to the achievement of very ambitious and very expensive growth targets for both businesses. Of course not all investment is in growth. Investment is also required in refurbishments and in growing e-commerce operations. But the growth strategy is critical, especially at a time when it is clear that JLP profits are not sufficient to cover the demands of bonus, pension, and investment, so problems of 'affordability' require some form of adjustment between funding partners directly, through pensions or investing in the hope of future benefits. The wisdom of this strategy is important because the survival and success of the JLP depends on it, and because the strategy represents a statement of the relative importance, to senior management, of the competing claims on the JLP's funds.

But as important as growth is efficiency: there is limited value in growing a business model if it is not very efficient. One director echoed many:

> But you know, the truth of it is we can't afford to run the John Lewis model as it currently stands. It's too expensive. . . . You can do as many branches in the future as you like, it won't unlock the conundrum. You've got to work out in the value chain what you can afford to do really, really well and I think historically the Partnership has tried to do everything really, really well and we can't afford to do that going forward.

Lessons from the Pensions Fund Story

Following identification of a serious deficit in the pension scheme, a review was undertaken in 2013. There was a further review of its 'affordability', in 2015. In consequence, the Partnership announced important changes to the JLP pension scheme in 2015. The non-contributory final salary pension scheme was changed to a hybrid scheme partly based on staff contributions. The period staff must wait before they qualify to join the scheme was lengthened from three years to five years. The changes were supported by the Partnership Council.

These changes are important because they directly affect partners' benefits. But they are also significant for what they may indicate about management policies and priorities and even for our understanding of the performance of the JLP. The changes also reveal something about the fundamental tensions within the Partnership that arise from the way JLP profits (themselves under competitive pressure) are distributed between the various claimants and how, and how successfully, these tensions are managed by JLP management.

JLP's was one of the few remaining final salary schemes, and this, and the increase in average life span were stressed in explanation of and justifications for the proposed changes. But the need for change also arose as a result of internal decisions. The 2013 review identified a deficit in the pension fund of £840m. While it can of course be argued that factors entirely beyond the control of JLP management directly contributed to this deficit (the increase in funding levels required to support enlarged pension payments as a result of increased life spans), the deficit (a prime determinant of the need for changes to and reductions in, the benefits of the JLP scheme) was also a consequence of management decisions. These require attention for what they may reveal for an understanding of the dynamics of the JLP. JLP management describe the pension in terms which, given that the JLP is co-owned, could be questioned.

Within conventionally-owned businesses, it is entirely reasonable for managers to remark on the 'affordability' of the pension arrangement or to say things such as 'we reward our Partners for their efforts'. But comments like this could be seen to indicate a distinctive and challengeable conception of the agent/principal issue discussed in Chapter 3. In JLP the managers are the agents of the partners, not the other way around. The pension is often presented by management as a matter for self-congratulation. But although partners have a total interest in the profits (their profits, as owners) of JLP, unlike conventional shareholders who benefit from increases in share value, they cannot expect and will not derive benefit from retained profits except indirectly through the profits earned from investments. Therefore, pensions benefits could be seen as a right, a compensation for being excluded from benefiting from retained profits, and not as an indication of management generosity.

This makes the reduction of the pension benefits more than simply an adjustment to a pressing reality and a reflection of a possible distortion of the underlying principles of the Partnership.

The history of the pension could support this assessment. It was only in the 1970s that the pension fund stopped lending from the pension fund to the JLP businesses (a form of self-investment that was then common but is now discredited). But this may reveal the ways in which management saw the pension fund—as a business asset, not entirely separate from the business. This may explain the fact that until very recently the chair of the pension scheme was the finance director of JLP, an obvious potential conflict of interest.

This may also contribute to an explanation of the pension deficit which is partially a consequence of some critically important assumptions made by the pension scheme about the level of expected return of the funds and the level of increase of partners' salaries—two assumptions which significantly influence the assessment of funds necessary to support partners' pensions, and therefore the assessment of any possible deficit. We are not arguing that JLP management deliberately and knowingly pushed through over-optimistic recent valuations in order to enable management to divert profits to the partner bonus in order to keep the staff happy and to give a positive impression of the performance of the businesses. But, the governance arrangements permitted an acceptance of a view of the responsibilities of management and the role of the pension and some key valuational assumptions, which benefited the business at the expense of the pension.

It is possible also that management's understandable and often stated emphasis on ensuring the happiness of partners, and their concern to ensure investment in what they believed to be the necessary basis of improved performance (growth) coupled with their conception of their responsibilities as managers (and the permissive governance arrangements), encouraged a tendency to privilege the bonus and investment above the pension fund. But if this was the case, it reflects questions about the adequacy of JLP's governance arrangements especially the audit committee, which are raised in Chapter 7.

So the recent decisions on the JLP pensions may reflect JLP leadership priorities for the business and how these have changed over the period addressed by this book. It should be noted that this is an issue on which JLP managers, both current and recent, differ. As we have seen, current JLP leadership insists that there is a connection between growth (scale) and competitiveness and margin. They argue that without growth during the period the Partnership would be much weaker relative to the competition. And they see their responsibility as building the Partnership and so passing it on to future generations in as strong a position as possible.

Critics argue that starting in the 1990s and especially since 2000, senior management has subtly redefined the Partnership's objectives. Since partners have no prospects of capital growth that they can withdraw, their prime interest (in a relatively poorly paid sector where their wages are not significantly above industry norms) is in high rates of partner bonus and in the pension scheme and less interest in investment unless this generates high rates of return. Current management are also concerned with rates of return on investment and indeed use a 'return per Partner' measure to assess the wisdom and effectiveness of investment. Ultimately the disagreement boils down to the quality of leadership strategies and decision making and the risk, as with all businesses, that managers begin to agree too much and to share a set of assumptions and convictions, deviation from which is unlikely because it simply creates too much dissonance. This is why, as we argue, the vitality and independence of structures and processes of accountability within the Partnership are so important.

Overall Assessment

Analysis of the business plans over the past twenty-five years shows that JLP is well-managed. If it is true that a few years ago, business planning took the form of a general discussion between business MDs and the Chairman concluding with the admonition: 'Do your best', this informal approach is most decidedly no longer the case. Investment proposals are carefully prepared using formalized frameworks, and are scrutinized according to demanding financial metrics in attempts to assess risk and calculate rates of return. Recent finance directors recruited from outside the Partnership have revolutionized the business planning and capital expenditure processes. So one can assume, on good evidence, that the specific proposals within the growth strategy will be assessed in terms of the rigour of the business case.

But it is one thing to ensure that the growth strategy is properly implemented; another to question whether it is right in the first place. Hypothetically it is possible to do the wrong thing well.

Senior management offer two rationales for their insistence on growth: that growth brings economies of scale and that not to grow is to decline in terms of relative size or market share.

In what ways could growth be difficult for or even wrong for JLP? What are the challenges of growth for JLP managers? There are a number of separate but ultimately inter-related worries (all of which are apparent to JLP senior managers and discussed in the risk assessment associated with the business planning process). These are management and organizational risks, reputational and brand risks and Partnership risks.

In March 2011, the City Editor of the London *Evening Standard* headlined his analysis of JLP's growth plans 'Will being biggest really mean best for John Lewis? As Middle Britain's favourite store powers ahead, it risks losing the ethos that made it so loved in the first place' (Blackhurst 2011).

Blackhurst's piece catches some of the worries. Essentially, his analysis indicates concern about the nature of JLP strategic thinking. He is concerned about the emphasis on growth: 'One worrying aspect is the insistence on massive growth. Why? It's not as if John Lewis has investors whose ever-increasing demands need constant feeding' (Blackhurst 2011).

Blackhurst identifies some specific dangers—for example, the challenge of managing vastly increased scale and complexity. But underpinning his anxiety about the 'insistence' (interesting word) on growth is a suggestion that organizational success—as for example in Marks and Spencer, or Tesco a few years ago—can too easily lead to problems. Paradoxically in business life success can easily lead to failure because managers (in any organization) can begin to believe their own rhetoric and to assume that the strategic 'recipes' which delivered success in the past, and the strategy-making processes will continue to succeed in new types of business, a new scale of activities, new forms of business, and new geographical areas. 'Businesses, even ones that seem to be run on perfect lines, in the end are controlled by humans. That means despite the beauty of the model, no matter how well they stand up to examination by MBA students at business school, the (managers in general) are still prone to complacency, greed and hubris' (Blackhurst 2011).

Blackhurst's argument is important because it raises wider and more fundamental under-pinning issues—essentially suggesting the key to good strategy is the quality of the debate, challenge, critique, and accountability that underpins strategic thinking. JLP managers do indeed 'insist' on the wisdom of growth as an ambition, seeking, understandably to persuade partners and elected representatives and to build consensus. As an integral element of this consensus they claim that there is no alternative to growth and not to grow is to decline, so, lack of growth endangers JLP and the happiness of partners. Growth then is mandatory, a moral duty.

There is no doubt that JLP managers see themselves as equal to the management challenges this will raise. And their confidence will be boosted by recent successes in outperforming the markets in which they compete. Yet it is not churlish to point out that other UK retailers, famous brands that appeared invincible, and equally buoyed by successes, ran into problems.

With the growth programme—which means not just spectacularly more things but also new things in new places with new businesses—JLP will have to change and change well and efficiently. And this programme not only represents a number of major changes, it also represents a change in the way JLP has traditionally, changed. Blackhurst spotted this: 'Success (in JLP) did not happen overnight. It was built on decades of soft-slow, slow-slow expansion. It's only in recent times that former army officer Mayfield, and his predecessor Sir Stuart Hampson, and their colleagues, have pushed the management foot harder on the accelerator.'

A recent JLP change programme indicates some difficulties. The Branch of the Future programme reduced selling support roles in JL branches and directly impacted the jobs of 3,500 partners (out of a total of 27,000 selling support functions). Such disruptions and redundancies were a significant problem for an organization which was dedicated to partners' interests. One view was that the programme was not well–handled and that in a later, similar programme, Waitrose was able to learn from this and that they handled the changes in a more evolutionary manner thus enabling some transfer of employment as other outlets grew. In both instances, redundancies were at least not handled in the quick, sharp shock way that some companies have used. With change in both branch staffing composition and growth, Partnership leaders began to talk about the potential for 'life time employment' if partners were prepared to be flexible.

Change in JLP also represents two further challenges. First, managers must be able to show that the change is consistent with the history, values, and Constitution of the Partnership. Since these historic elements are many and varied and by no means entirely consistent, it is not too difficult to argue historic continuity and legitimacy especially since the core principle: 'the happiness of our partners and their satisfaction from being part of a successful business', can be seen to lay great stress on the achievement of a successful business within which partners can be happy, thus opening the door to arguments about the need for (and prerequisites of) measures necessary for business success.

The magic of the JLP took years to develop; but it would take less time to destroy and the worry is that it might only be clear that it was gone (or going) when it was too late to save. That the change programmes *could* threaten the source of the JLP success—the JLP essence—is apparent to senior managers.

Understandably, much is made of JLP being owned by its partners—the extraordinary historic fact, as one director described it of the 'complete insanity' of Spedan Lewis 'giving everything he had away'. This collective 'ownership' is—happily—institutionalized in a legal framework which rules out the possibility of the sort of carpet-bagger style demutualization which enriched members, but destroyed the uniqueness of many mutually-owned organizations, in the 1980s.

Partners' ownership of the JLP has important implications for the assessment of, and an analysis of, the implications of the growth strategy (or indeed any fundamental strategy). One director identified three components of the JLP model and insisted that the basis was the collective ownership but that this was not the whole story. Ownership gave commitment and engagement, but it also allowed trust because the business was not run on the basis of exploitation of one group by another. And shared ownership allows a different basis for investment decisions.

But the real challenge is less what investments to make (though this must always be a live issue when there is a choice to be made), but the ways in which and the extent to which the investment decision-making group, the Partnership Board, is held accountable for its investment decisions. In conventional PLCs the board spends shareholders' money and is held accountable by shareholders and their representatives on the board for how and how well this money is spent. In JLP the Board is spending whose money? Constitutionally the money may belong to the partners, or to the Partnership, but to whom is the Board accountable and through what mechanisms for its stewardship of these funds? And how effective are these mechanisms?

This raises a critical point. If the protection of the model and the monitoring of the balance between model and commercial initiatives, is, to some degree, left to the consciences and integrity of senior individuals, this is a potential source of vulnerability because it places great reliance on the processes whereby tomorrow's leaders are recruited, developed, promoted, and monitored.

Managing the strategy-making process in JLP may seem easier as a result of the ownership situation, and in many ways it is, most obviously the possibility to pursue longer-term projects with longer-term paybacks; but as so often with JLP's advantages, there are also drawbacks. This fundamental feature of the Partnership also generates potential problems which the Partnership Board must identify and manage successfully.

The Challenges of Growth: Reputational Issues

'Reputation' in JLP has two elements which are closely related and this inter-relationship constitutes in effect a theory: that the special and distinctive way in which partners are respected and treated creates a willingness to behave in ways which customers will enjoy and appreciate. The way partners are treated accounts for the quality of the customer experience and for the success of the JLP businesses. A key constituent of this thesis is that JL and Waitrose are distinctive and different because of the difference in ownership structures and employment practices of the JLP. Management's role in this narrative is, implicitly, relatively modest and neutral: to ensure the right direction of the businesses and the effective operation of the partner–customer–profit sequence: that is, to make it work.

The JLP reputation—or brand—is crucial. Certainly the realities of the products offered and the service offered in Waitrose and John Lewis are real and valuable and valued. Customer feedback as well as sales performance testify to this. But underpinning the realities of the shopping experiences in both businesses is a clear and powerful narrative which stresses the moral nature and the quality of the businesses and argues that the latter is a consequence of the former. This narrative powerfully shapes expectations and experience. This raises the possibility that certain growth strategies could have implications for the JLP brand and the Partnership itself.

Reputational damage may be relatively small scale, impacting on particular projects; or, it may be larger scale, incurring serious damage to the JLP brand as a result of organizational and employment policies developed as part of the growth programme or by the sheer scale of the programme.

The Middle East partnerships—Dubai and Bahrain—are different. These franchised stores look like Waitrose stores and sell Waitrose products, but the employees are not partners. The brand is licensed to the local firms. Waitrose checked how these firms treated their staff. This raises potential brand and model risk. If partners are critical to the Waitrose experience as the narrative and JLP managers claim, how can a Waitrose work properly without partners? And if it can, what does this mean for the argument that partners are critical?

The partnership with Welcome Break raises similar issues. Welcome Break, private equity owned, probably wanted Waitrose as part of the package of concessions in order to create a halo effect and upgrade the business with a view to enhancing the value of the business and perhaps ultimately to sell it. The attraction for Waitrose was that this deal gave them an entree to the convenience travel market. However, it raised issues about the model and the role and contribution of partners. The eventual solution, or as one manager described it to us, the 'fudge', was that while the staff of the Waitrose store in the Welcome Break are partners, the managers are not. Overall the usual mix of staff is around 50/50. Again this raises questions about the model and the brand. As one manager put it: ' . . . we have ended up with this fudge, which is very uncomfortable actually'. The reason why Welcome Break would not have accepted a deal with 100 per cent partner staffing is simple: Welcome Break employees are cheaper. They haven't got the Partnership package of benefits. It was argued by some that managers had to be Welcome Break employees in order to comply with licensing requirements. Interestingly, the Shell deal was to have been staffed by partners but if it had been rolled out in scale, this decision would have to have been reviewed and a different level of benefits created.

These new developments are financially marginal. And the issues of differentiation of the brand and the model can, to a degree, be resolved by the fact that in some of the new arrangements—for example, Welcome Break—customers will not get or require partner-level expertise, since they are by and large simply accessing some Waitrose products. The question is, how does the Partnership model make this a better experience for customers? If it doesn't improve the experience through service then it is probably through the availability of Waitrose products sourced by Waitrose from Waitrose farms and suppliers. One manager remarked: ' . . . I kept thinking you've got . . . somebody at the service station doing exactly the same job in a service-related capacity as you've got in a Waitrose branch ten miles away. So, why the hell would that be a franchise person and that couldn't, and if you could read that, we might as well franchise all our branches out. Why don't we do that?'

So some growth projects raise issues of brand and model: some of these developments could mean that people shopping in what looks like a Waitrose would not have the same experiences as they would in the classic, pure model. That's one danger. There are also issues around the model raised by these innovations in that either the model is simply too expensive or that its sales and performance benefits would not be enough to cover the level of margins required by the partner business. So in effect these developments not only cause some variation in the realities of the JLP model, they also generate debate among managers and partners about the nature and limitations and flexibility of the JLP model.

There is a fundamental point here: should the Partnership develop businesses which do not comply with, or even deviate from, the JLP model? Or, how much flexibility in the JLP model should be tolerated in the name of business and commercial benefit? How far is too far? The issue is not simply a matter of principle or morality; it is also a matter of the integrity and viability of the JLP model if we believe that the success of JLP arises from the unique JLP model. If JLP has businesses that lack this model then all other things being equal they are either going to be less successful, or if successful, suggest the model is not essential after all. For with managers energetically stressing that the distinctive quality and trustworthiness of the JLP experience is a result of the distinctive JLP model, any occasions when any part of this thesis is missing threatens the integrity of the narrative, and could tarnish the image.

It's also important to note that not all new ventures involve some degree of breach of the JLP model. John Lewis has a new sourcing operation in India staffed by partners. Indian staff recruited in India will be partners with their own ring-fenced profit-sharing mechanism.

Of course these recent Waitrose partnerships and deals are smallish stuff, unlikely to make a significant contribution. But, in a way, this makes them more puzzling: why endanger diluting the brand or undermining the core JLP narrative for marginal business benefit? And what does this tell us about the strength and effectiveness of the structures and processes which are intended to protect the JLP difference: if there is a struggle (and there is and there should be) between the values of the Partnership (and the integrity of the JLP brand) and commercial imperatives, do these developments signal the way this struggle will be resolved?

Part of the answer to this is the cost implications of employing staff as partners and this is discussed below.

The Challenges of Growth: Organization, Systems, and Leadership

Retailers pursuing growth and overseas expansion are not the only businesses that may encounter the paradox that when expanding and moving into new regions or activities, all too often success and reputation reach their limits, that success recipes run out of steam and that new activities in new places stretch management competence to breaking or require new competences beyond the established ones. But it is certainly common in retail. Marks and Spencer, Asda, and Tesco have all suffered severely from the hubris of failed expansion—expansion which was confidently planned and executed by senior management at the peak of their reputation after years of success.

Growth *may* be imperative; there *may* be no other option—these are debateable. But no firm can grow for ever. Ultimately growth must reach its limits: increased organizational complexity and scale, market saturation resulting in new stores taking customers from existing ones, declining marginal returns will reveal through metrics like declining revenue against assets that it is time to stop. If the JLP Board is open to challenge and critique, they will recognize this before they over-reach themselves, as their competitors Tesco have recently done.

This is not an abstract issue. The debate must be about how to achieve the right balance between growth and the risks and costs of growth. What are the risks of growth, to reputation, performance, or the Partnership? Are the JLP businesses' organizations, management, and processes capable of rising to and handling such dramatic growth and change?

On these questions, the successful expansion of the JLP businesses over the last twenty years is a major source of reassurance of course and should not be minimized; to be capable of running forty-one John Lewis and 322 Waitrose stores efficiently is an enormous achievement. But if the businesses are to grow and move into new formats and new types of stores and new employment/ franchise models in new geographical regions, organizational and system efficiency will be crucial.

The contribution to organizational performance made by the JLP model tends to stem from enhanced individual effort not system efficiency. Indeed, some managers even argued intriguingly that partners' commitment and system efficiency could be, perversely, *negatively* related.

Managers noted that if growth were inevitable it would bring not just increased scale but also increased complexity. This would require robust and efficient organization and systems: aspects which some argued were vulnerabilities in JLP.

The case for growth was stated succinctly as follows:

> We have to grow because if we don't grow, we shrink relatively; the competition are growing every year, or planning to grow every year, by the size that we are; therefore we have to grow. And if we don't grow, it will affect our performance longer-term. You're also, I would have to say, adding complexity to the model if we grow in different formats, and that is also working out what is already an inefficient competitive point. So there is definitely a tension for us. . . . .; it actually relied on process efficiency, which as I've said we're basically crap at. (Senior Manager, 2012)

So, JLP managers, even while insisting on growth, recognize that this will not only require improved efficiencies but also that increased scale and complexity will impose new, higher performance requirements in areas which are not historic strengths.

This argument actually suggests another intriguing perverse consequence of the model: that there could be a causal link between system weaknesses and virtuoso customer service—the 'hero culture'—in that partners spend more time on, and attach greater value to 'saving customers' than contributing to the less interesting and more complex system improvement: '. . . how do you create a positive out of process, when most people find it quite boring, and how do you get people to stop their default, which is I want to spend my time over here saving people and partners, as opposed to looking end to end and doing something which is quite dull and complicated?'

The pursuit of growth also places great pressure on JLP leadership. The increasing scale and complexity of the businesses would almost certainly exacerbate the tension between the components of the JL Partnership—performance linkage: the partner–customer–profit cycle. So, senior managers would need to be even more wary of this balance and even more assiduous in their stewardship of the Partnership. They know this of course: 'In this whole piece about the partner–customer–profit metrics, it is definitely my job to judge how hard we're going after all three at any one time. Now, there's a hole in my argument, because you should say to me, well, actually, you keep arguing they're reinforcing, but you can all see that, even if that might be so in the long-term, in the short-term there are trade-offs. And I absolutely see it as my job to judge the speed on all three' (Senior JL Director, 2014).

So leadership is defined, certainly by long service career JLP managers, in terms of stewardship—not simply of the Partnership, but of the balance between the three elements of the cycle, balancing Partnership and business performance.

But this raises a further question: how effective and sustainable are the processes that will ensure that future leaders, or the leaders being prepared in the pipeline, will take this view of their leadership roles, will be able and willing to fulfil this responsibility, or will define and locate 'balance' in the same way as current incumbents?

If so much of the responsibility for the protection and preservation of the JLP depends on the consciences, morality, and commitment of individual leaders (as managers argue in effect, it does) then how good is JLP at recruiting or creating leaders with the right qualities, bearing in mind that 'right' in the context of JLP means much more than simply high quality leadership and technical competence. It also includes a real understanding of, commitment to, and sympathy for, the JLP model principles and values.

Managers expressed concern about this. They felt that, so far, on the whole they had been lucky. Current senior management are mostly long time JLP people who had joined as graduate trainees (the MDs of both John Lewis and Waitrose). The next wave of management might have had less exposure to the

Partnership and its values. And the stakes were too high to have to rely on luck. As one long-standing JL director observed: 'I think they (the processes that recruit, develop, retain, monitor and performance manage the leadership group) might be better, and I think there's a recognition across the business they could be better. . . . So my sense would be that, we're still in the very early stage of making sure that we've got really outstanding processes in place to ensure we recruit, retain, and develop the right people, and then reward them in the correct way.'

Recent growth has already required, and planned growth would increase, the need for new technical skills at senior levels within the JLP: disciplines which had simply been missing earlier—like, surprisingly, marketing. But it also requires new attitudes, new approaches to business to augment the home-grown approaches of long-term JLP managers. But new senior level recruits not only bring new business attitudes and approaches and skills they also may come with different attitudes towards or different levels of understanding and commitment to, the core institutions and values of the JLP. As many interviewees noted, this potential problem was also a potential benefit. Some historic institutions might need challenge or refreshment; old hands might have become complacent, they certainly didn't have a monopoly of knowledge. On the other hand, a commitment to the core JLP values and principles was essential for the survival of the Partnership, and the introduction of significant numbers of senior people from outside who lacked long-term exposure to JLP values and principles could threaten dilution.

The introduction of external senior level recruits may have brought fresh ideas and approaches, but it has not always been successful. A number of star recruits have left the Partnership following adjustment difficulties. This could be a good sign, of course: it could show that the JLP remains distinctive and that a demonstrated sympathy for the JLP model remains important and that when it is lacking, the recruit leaves. But the fact of external senior level recruitment could also be seen as a potential worry in that if the outsiders stay in sufficient numbers, they might introduce assumptions and values which weaken the JLP model—a source of 'dilution'.

Long service JLP managers reject this possibility, arguing that while outsiders might bring business ideas and approaches from which JLP can learn, when it comes to JLP values and principles, the learning must go the other way. As one director argued:

> I am firmly in the camp which says that's [external senior recruitment] a positive thing, because the far bigger problem is complacency within the people who have been here for too long. [Names some senior managers] . . . aren't complacent people, but even so, we can't be arrogant enough to believe that we don't need some external input. So, it has been a huge add-on, actually, it's a cop-out saying 25 per cent of the people are external, because it's the responsibility of the 75 per cent

internal to get the best out of that without allowing dilution of the JLP principles. (JLP director, 2014)

But others took a less rosy view, seeing the introduction of specialist outsiders as a threat not only to careers (as a generalist background, historically the background of senior managers, gives way to demand for specialists) but also to the value-basis of the Partnership):

> Waitrose is not now what it was when I joined in 1982. I think that my job, as one who's been around for many years, is to ensure that our principles stay the same. I feel slightly under siege if I'm being honest. I'm a classic partnership generalist and the partnership did very well with generalists for many years. Now the partnership is bringing in specialists—people say 'I'm a marketer', or 'I'm a convenience format specialist', or 'I'm a merchandiser'. They bring their business experience with them but no sense of our values. (JLP director, 2014)

Tellingly,

> I see them all wanting to join a partnership which is suddenly successful and sexy. Yet in the 1980s and 1990s Sainsbury's was the sexy place to be. Now I see them having been made redundant and swimming to our lifeboat and I sort of wonder. (JLP director, 2014)

The Partnership has given thought to the leadership qualities required and there is a leadership framework of a number of key behaviours at different levels which is used for recruitment and also for performance assessment and thus for development. Recently, the MD of John Lewis has stressed that leadership is defined in terms of a number of qualities including honest and consistent communication, prompt, visible and considered action, emotional connection and reflective empathy with all partners, and the ability to inspire and give hope for the long term.

The identification of 'Partnership Leadership Behaviours' was introduced partly in response to the increasing growth of external senior hires who might not 'get' the JLP way. The leadership behaviours sought to balance strong commercial leadership ('drives performance' and 'takes decisive action') with working collaboratively in a co-owned business ('inspires ownership' and 'works across boundaries'). It provides a framework for use in recruitment, performance management, and development. The initiative was felt by some to be an improvement on relying on the 'hunches' of long standing JLP senior managers.

Growth and Impact on the Partnership

Growth of the JLP, and planned future growth, carry consequences for the JLP model. This is so regardless of the consequences of management initiatives to 'reform', 'modernize', or 'revitalize' the democratic institutions or other components of the model. Increase in size and the expansion into new employment models and new geographical regions in themselves generate change to the model. And the business strategies being pursued by the JLP businesses also carry implications for the model.

Size alone carries major implications, for, the greater the number of partners, the linkages between any individual partner and his/her representative in democratic bodies is attenuated. Greater size means that the real and psychological distance between senior management and senior management decisions, and shop-floor partners becomes greater. As one manager at Group argued:

> ... if you put yourself in the position of a partner on the selling floor in, say, Peterborough, you start to think, 'hang on a minute, the democracy isn't really working for me. It appears that business decisions are being taken out there on a commercial basis, where's my involvement with this, where's my engagement in this?'. (JLP manager, Group)

The challenge for management is to ensure growth is successfully achieved, that the Partnership model is protected and preserved and held in appropriate balance to commercial ambitions, and also that the Partnership is re-imagined. No one is naïve enough to wish for a return to a golden past; everyone—even those who may regret the changes that have occurred over the past twenty years—recognizes that the model must be 're-engineered' in ways which are true to the spirit and the intentions of the Founder but in ways which could vary considerably from the details of his vision. But what would this re-imagined JLP model be like? How can the spirit of an idea which started with one shop be re-applied to an organization with so many more partners?

> I think one of the big challenges for us . . . is that we started off as one shop . . . and a man with a huge idea, and that huge idea at that stage was not fully formed but it was being delivered to an organization that that man could get his arms around, metaphorically speaking, so that the people that worked for him in the building within which the model was being experimented, was all very here and now. It was geographically very easy to get to; it was very straightforward to know who everyone was . . . And then you add geographic diversity to that, and on top of that you add the conundrum that we face in the current economic world, which is that scale has to equal efficiency. (JLP director, 2014)

As this manager notes, the pressure of increased size is exacerbated when growth also involves new employment models and new geographical locations some far from the UK and the democratic institutions of the JLP.

> 'So, I think the appetite for scale, I understand it intellectually, but I think we don't apply the same kind of thing about how can we scale the partnership and the

partnership values in the same way. We put no emphasis or resource behind that.'
(JLP director, 2014)

The first test of the growth strategy is that it achieves its claimed objectives. Partners (and JLP managers) will be acutely aware that the decision to spend profits on growth diverts partners' funds which would otherwise be allocated to bonus or pensions. Partners are sacrificing direct personal benefits to finance investment in the future—investment which is justified in terms of the returns it will generate, if it generates them. While growth itself brings potential benefits (scale discounts and economies, bargaining power) it also raises risks. Some of these risks are commercial risks—namely the truism that, in retail, size is crucial. JLP managers are fond of saying, as an irrefutable and undeniable fact of corporate life that 'if you don't grow you die'.

Yet some argue that with respect to food retailers:

The supermarket sector is in meltdown. An overstatement? Hardly. In the cool-headed assessment of the *Grocer* magazine, the most authoritative voice on UK food retail, 'consumers are abandoning supermarkets in their droves'. Tesco, once the darling of the stock market, the government's pet performing British company, is in the most acute distress. From January to June this year, its profits crashed by 92 per cent. Investigators have yet to plumb the depths of the big black hole in its books. Morrison's is also in a bad way—its pre-tax profit for the six months to August was halved. Sainsbury's share price has dropped. Even the supposedly trend-bucking Waitrose cannot be complacent: its profits for the first half of this year slumped by 9.4 per cent. (Joanna Blythman, *The Observer*, Sunday 26 October 2014)

The Tesco case could suggest the opposite: that if you grow you die. 'Empires', writes Felicity Lawrence, with reference to food supermarkets, 'often seem at their most indomitable shortly before they fall. The march of the supermarket giants across our food and shopping landscape has, until very recently, felt inexorable. . . . Yet suddenly here they are in precipitate decline in the UK: Tesco, Sainsbury's, Morrisons' (Lawrence 2014). Lawrence describes the current problems of Big Retail: food supermarkets face commodity inflation and rising energy prices, but the real problem is a business model predicated on assumptions—about the good sense of global just-in-time supply chains or the customer-appeal of out-of town shopping, or the power of rewarded customer loyalty. Changes in customer behaviour have driven the rush to smaller, high street formats which have higher overheads. But, argues Lawrence, the main point is that, 'the fall of empire, when it does come tends to be fast, the seeds of decline obvious in retrospect'.

Under these difficult conditions JLP managers will be acutely aware that their strategy of ambitious growth must be able to demonstrate through its success that partners' funds were well spent and have achieved the required levels of return if they are to retain the confidence and trust of partners.

Growth and Who is a Member

New ventures require choices about whether or not work activity is to be performed by partners or by non-partner staff, or by third-party contractors. Growth in size is associated with the move to new formats, possibly geographically distant, with new employment, management, and ownership models. It also associated with business strategies which themselves raise questions of who is, or should be, a partner? And of course, growth requires improved efficiencies. For example, the growth of e-commerce is likely to result in the expansion of non-partner, contract staff (IT people, warehouse staff, logistics, couriers) and to require expansion into new skill areas and the decline of conventional competences—with implications for historic partners, 5,000 of whom have been made redundant in JL over the last five years.

New strategies (for example click and collect) also mean new jobs in new areas (for example, IT and distribution) which are less likely to be staffed by partners. There may be other organizational and business developments—for example centralization of call centres, expansion of IT, or increased professionalization in the supply chain or other aspects of the business—all of which can mean a growing use of non-partners.

Non-partners can be employed because the nature of the work—variable, seasonal, new skills—makes it necessary to hire and lay-off; or because the skills required are not required permanently, or because the outside contractor brings scope, expertise, and organization not available to JLP. There is also a cost consideration: if JLP staff cost, say, 25 per cent more, can this extra cost be justified especially when whatever commitment might be associated with being a partner (and thus costing more) is possibly unrealizable because of the nature of the work. It was argued, for example, that drivers who are partners cannot drive 25 per cent faster than non-partners. But a counter argument was that the drivers who interface directly with customers can make a huge difference to customer perceptions. (The complaints about outsourced deliveries noted earlier illustrate this point.)

The recent growth of the Partnership businesses has resulted in an increase in the number of non-partner staff—especially in IT and logistics. Typically, the Partnership has a process and a policy to handle decisions on this matter; and it is clear that the significance of the issue for the Partnership is understood. Yet the attempt to manage this tension, to find a balance between Partnership principles and commercial pressures, we suggest, actually reveals an underlying ambivalence and uncertainty at the heart of the Partnership: 'solving' this tension merely serves to stress a troubling uncertainty of purpose and priority.

JLP's policy dilemma arises from the claim that 'we create discretionary value from partners'. This, by implication, introduces a qualification: suggesting not only that the presumption might be flexible in practice, for example, when discretionary value *cannot* be achieved for one reason or another; or possibly when extra value might actually be gained by employing non-partners.

This impression of a pragmatic basis for the 'principle' is supported by the five considerations which should inform decisions on whether or not people involved in work activity should be partners. These include (i) capability (what is required and can we do it?), (ii) readiness, (iii) speed, (iv) commercial viability, (v) implications of the decision for customers and partners—all very sensible, pragmatic, and practical considerations.

In practice, decisions to use third parties or contract (non-partner) staff can be taken for a number of reasons:

> Sometimes it's because we don't want to train people up to have that particular skill because it might not be long lasting and so we use a third party while we need that skill and then when we don't need it anymore we break the contracts... Sometimes we use it for a spike in work, so it's a big bulge of work and you don't want to recruit a whole load of people, make them partners and then maybe have to not make them partners, make them redundant when tough times come. (JLP director, 2013)

Sometimes third parties bring scale and experience and scope way beyond what the Partnership could offer, and in these cases it makes perfect sense to use outsiders, for example specialist logistics, IT support, etc.

But there is also a cost consideration ('commercial viability'). There are two issues here; first the additional costs of partners, and secondly the extent to which the type of work involved is likely to permit or require 'discretionary effort'. Some work simply does not allow much opportunity for such extra effort, especially when it is not customer facing.

Waitrose has warehouses run by partners and by third parties. The opening of the Chorley RDC was the occasion for much discussion as to whether it should be run by partners or a third party. Partners are more expensive. Could partners produce 25 per cent greater productivity in a non-customer-facing business? The conclusion was probably not, although even here the commitment of partners was seen as adding real value—especially around absenteeism—but not to the extent of 25 per cent.

While there are business reasons for using third party contractors, including their much greater skills, global reach, scale, and expertise (Waitrose's third party logistic company is seen as 'best in class from a global retailer's perspective' (Director, Waitrose, 2011)), there are still pragmatic instrumental arguments for using partners in such situations, one of which is the reluctance to outsource a critical business process. As one manager said, 'Fundamentally supply chain is absolutely caught in your success as your business and would you want to outsource that totally?'

It is hard to escape the conclusion that this issue is still unclear. The priorities and principles by which the decision should be taken are not established. Although the policy states that there is a *presumption* that employees will be partners and work will be done by partners, this is justified in terms of partners' capacity for discretionary effort. So, when this capacity is limited and the role and value of discretionary effort limited, the implication could be that the presumption is weakened. Also the conditions under which exceptions to this presumption are seen as reasonable include a number of pragmatic reasons, so it is not entirely clear what the presumption adds up to. On the other hand, the fact that high level authority is required when large numbers are involved suggests some residual unease on the issue. Yet, the manager involved in the decision on the staffing of the new depot described how he was under 'huge pressure' to 'throw it across the fence to be contractor-run'. No wonder a number of managers suggested that the issue was unclear.

In the UK, John Lewis and Waitrose use non-partners in cleaning services, in some parts of the warehousing and delivery service, in electrical after-sales service, and in customer handling by telephone. Outside the UK, as we have noted, non-partners are also used for IT and related outsourcing. The case of the staff who clean John Lewis shops and premises highlights the dilemmas. John Lewis uses contract cleaners, hence they are not paid directly by John Lewis nor does the partnership determine their wage levels. There has been a campaign, so far resisted, to bring them back in-house. Further, this is publicly contentious—and publicly damaging—because the cleaners receive less than the 'living wage'. A petition calling on JL to pay cleaners the living wage attracted over 120,000 signatures. This issue shows that the JLP businesses, because of their reputation, are held to higher standards of conduct than other retailers. It also reveals the fundamental tensions about the attitude of the Partnership towards the issue of 'who is a member'. Neil Spring, group senior external communications manager at John Lewis Partnership, defended the stance thus: 'Like all retailers, we work with many different contractors of various kinds throughout our supply chain. We could not operate effectively if all our contractors were partners'. But if effectiveness were the key business priority how much of the JLP model would survive?

These instances of non-partner employment raise important questions of principle. As one director suggested to us:

> We have a number of third parties that I think we'll be using for year after year. And, for me, there's a question mark about that (er ...) well, if you really believe in the partnership model, if you really believe that being a partner means it's just a better way of doing things, you'll get a bigger return, then why aren't those people partners? And it ... at the moment it's a bit

confused. I don't think there's complete clarity in the company. It seems like we use 'the partner' bit when it suits us, but occasionally when the commercial imperative is so great we seem happier these days to park it. (Waitrose director, interviewed 2013)

The growth of the partnership will put more pressure on the use of non-partner staff, because growth in itself creates the conditions under which the use of contract staff or third party suppliers is encouraged or made possible or even necessary (through new employment models, business strategies, and the need for new skills and capability).

It is not clear how JLP will respond to this tendency. The policy states the 'presumption of membership'. But both the policy and the decisions implementing it, seem set around with a high degree of pragmatism suggesting that the tension between commercial priorities and the values and principles of the JLP model remains unresolved, and therefore that responses to these pressures will be hard to predict. A senior manager, with specific responsibilities for the stewardship of partners' interests commented on this matter. She argued that any decision about who is a member could be solved by referral to the 'commercial decisions' for the 'collective of the partnership'. But this argument could open the door to any decision so long as it was commercially productive, and supports the dominance of pragmatic considerations while not obviously assisting a clarification of the dilemma identified above which presumably will persist: is the priority to preserve and expand the partnership model (by creating more partners whose lives will be enhanced by employment within a business addressed to ensuring their well-being) or is it to drive as much dividend as possible for current partners?

Well, I do wonder. I wonder because I've got 450 people working in IT at Bracknell. 300 are partners and 150 aren't. That's a big chunk of my workforce. Some of those contractors have been with me now for two or three years. I can't tell the difference. As I wander around the floors of my function, they're all so familiar to me that the partners and the contractors look the same. They all know me by name, I don't treat them any differently, but actually they're on completely different terms and conditions. The contractors probably earn a bit more up front but don't have all the security and the bonus and the . . . and don't have access to all the facilities. (Waitrose director, 2013)

JLP managers' highly successful efforts to create a narrative of JLP which stresses the moral nature of the JLP/partners' relationship and, as a consequence, the moral nature of the JLP/customer linkage, works powerfully inside the Partnership and externally to sustain an impression (based on a reality) of distinctiveness and difference but this narrative, while it enthuses partners and customers, also acts as a restriction on business options and generates expectations which may be hard to sustain.

These chapters have identified a number of ways in which the commercial goals of the JLP raise challenges for the Partnership—challenges which in the main JLP managers are acutely aware of and insist they can handle. For JLP managers are responsible not only for the success of the business—for making the elements of the partnership 'work', but for protecting these elements—which contribute to the well-being and security of the Partners—who own the business.

Conclusions

A question that arises from the frequent attempts by senior JLP management to mobilize and focus and make more efficient the work of partners whose commitment and engagement is for the most part assured, is: why is all this management effort necessary? And why does it fall to managers to improve the work of partners? Surely in an organization like JLP with its apparent history of consultation, democracy, and communication, and with its partners as co-owners, it should not be necessary for management and specialist HR professionals constantly to take on the task of devising numerous techniques to encourage and focus the work of partners? Why don't they do this themselves? Why aren't the structures and processes of representation and consultation used to mobilize the partners to work in new and more effective ways for the businesses they co-own? Much is made within the JLP of the 'responsibilities' of co-ownership (in attempts to balance the historic emphasis on 'rewards') but why is it incumbent on management to identify and emphasize these responsibilities rather than the co-owners themselves?

Why does management have to be so active and so proactive in these endeavours? Why can't partners see what managers and their HR advisers see? It is possibly revealing that managers seem to care more about the dangers facing the JLP than the partners or the partners' representative structures. So there may be a possibility that with the increasingly dominant role played by management—for understandable reasons—over the twentyfive-year period as management increasingly took control of planning the future of the businesses (in the name of ensuring success to ensure partner happiness), an inadvertent consequence was that partners became dependent on management guidance and direction and less willing to or capable of taking responsibility themselves via the available institutions. Or are these institutions designed for consultation and commentary rather than for initiating proposals? Is this one of the reasons for the constant efforts to 'refresh' the democracy: efforts which however well-meant and sincere, since they are contrived and imposed by management, become not the solution but an exacerbation of the problem?

Central to the perennial goal of realizing in productivity the value of co-ownership—of transforming base metal into gold (though partners may see it the other way round)—is an emphasis on the potential contribution of managers who have, it is recognized, the greatest potential to influence partners' experience and behaviour. A variety of organizational developments and training and initiatives have been put in place with the designed effect of making managers more effective in engaging partners and unlocking the contribution of which they are individually capable. But the problem remains and increased competitive pressures exert pressure on this inherent issue.

6

Reflections on Managers and Managing in the Partnership

Like their colleagues in conventional businesses, JLP senior managers have two prime tasks: to plot an intelligent, profitable strategic direction for the business which identifies and acknowledges environmental challenges and opportunities and selects a profitable way forward; and to build the organizational capacity of the organization to deliver this strategic purpose.

JLP managers claim that the JLP model generates consequences which are attractive to customers and so add to the businesses' performance, thus implying a minimal role for management. But, in reality, management has a major role to play, if anything more, not less complex than in conventional businesses.

Managers have to deal with the implications and the constraints of the JLP model. As already noted, this has a number of elements including, for example, principles and values; and a series of historic practices, institutions, roles, and relationships. All policies and decisions must be, or must be presented as being, consistent with these historic constraints.

JLP managers must also balance, and live within, the pressures from the democratic constraints (these are discussed in Chapter 7). Management decisions must also be consistent with, and not breach, the moral expectations partners and customers have of JLP as a trustworthy, decent, business.

Chapters 4 and 5 showed how, over the past twenty-five years, senior managers have developed and implemented a range of business strategies and innovations but have struggled fully to 'release the potential' of the Partnership, to balance the costs of the Partnership difference by improved profitability, to realize the benefits that the JLP's distinctive and better way of doing business must—in their view—generate.

Management action to build capacity in JLP must address two major consequences of the JLP model: that it is a potential resource, and also potentially an obstacle which must be overcome. This accords with the manager we quoted earlier who worried about the Partnership model being 'used as an excuse' to avoid doing the 'difficult things which would generate that additional return'.

The Strategic Objectives of the JLP

Earlier chapters discussed and analysed the detailed business strategies of the JLP, especially the emphasis on growth, and other more detailed strategies including the omni-strategy: combining bricks *and* clicks to mutual benefit. Here we are concerned with a more fundamental question: what do JLP managers seek to achieve? What are their underpinning purposes?

Fundamental objectives are to achieve a balance between partner happiness and 'sufficient' profit. One way to solve this is to insist that in effect these are the same: the latter serving as a source and measure of the former. But 'sufficient' still requires attention. This can be solved pragmatically: 'sufficient' is defined as enough to enable the JLP to satisfy all the demands on JLP funds; or as much profit as can be achieved without serious or dramatic breach of the JLP model or constitutional principles. It is a trade-off or balance.

Profitability, managers argue, is what is necessary to meet the challenges the Partnership faces from five directions: supporting the pension fund, the costs of which are rising; increasing the efficiency of the businesses and changing the skills and capabilities base, which requires investment; funding growth— new stores and online; investing in technology and adapting the historic— 'shop-based'—model and the systems and processes which support it; and lowering the cost of existing branches. JLP businesses must meet these challenges; sufficient profit is the degree of profitability necessary to fund the divisions' reactions to these threats (Document source, 2013).

But, desired levels of profit remain contentious: a corporate level director remarked:

> You will hear partners at the Council ask 'Have we got too focused on profit? Is profit too much the king these days?' So, some see the partnership model as meaning we shouldn't always try to be as profitable as everybody else. I think it would be a huge mistake to take that way out. We need to be continually innovating and improving the business. (Director, Group, 2013)

A related question is how much to invest and when to take and use the profit. Another director observed:

> We undertook an experiment. Having developed our business model that showed the numbers we then constructed an alternative model that involved no refurbishments, so no money spent improving the stores we've already got, allowed for no new convenience stores, etc. What that exercise delivered was a massive hike in profit. In terms of our operating margin we would have been the industry leaders

by miles. We did it to show the board that it would be a silly thing to do. We'd deliver fantastic profit, industry-beating stuff, but for how many years will that last? (JL director, 2014)

But the target *level* of profitability remains contentious. It is hard to avoid the impression that levels of profitability have both real and symbolic significance: are regarded not only as means of ensuring funds for investment, pensions, bonus, debt interest (and maintaining credit status), but also as a symbolic and public indication of corporate performance—as a way of demonstrating internally and externally, the quality of corporate achievement and thus of the JLP model and of JLP management, and so of management legitimacy.

Senior JLP managers are clear on the performance targets. A senior finance manager argued, 'No, it's not about maximizing profit. What it's about, and what I do sense probably more strongly than I've worked anywhere else, that it's not about maximizing profit in any one year: it's about providing a *sustainable* return over many years'.

But still some managers worried that using conventional retailers and their metrics as benchmarks of performance might inadvertently import their standards and values into the JLP. One manager remarked:

Why have we got a ROIC which is the highest? Why have we measured against an operating margin which is the highest in the industry except for Tesco? Surely that's not right. Shouldn't we be looking for a lower operating margin because it's about the longevity of the business and it's about investment that comes as a consequence of it? If we're looking for a ROIC which is 8/9 per cent, that again is at the top end of the market place. . . . . . I think the creation of the target is driving a set of behaviours that will ultimately only lead to you to one answer, which is more and more commerciality being built into the business at the cost of other objectives. (JL Director, 2011)

Whereas, in conventional business, the key business performance metrics are—by now—accepted as beyond debate, as fixed and as 'facts of life', in JLP performance metrics remain to some limited degree as items of debate and discussion—even disagreement. A small number of managers expressed anxiety about the implications of the emphasis on conventional performance metrics for the Partnership's difference. This is an issue that has also been raised in the Partnership Council.

There is value—especially in the JLP—in maintaining this debate about key measures and purposes. In fact, these measures vary around the world in different forms of capitalism; they are not fixed. But there may be a risk that senior managements' efforts to persuade partners of the necessity for and legitimacy of, current key performance measures (and the efforts to improve them) has the effect of closing down debate, of ruling out alternatives, of suppressing challenge and opposition in the face of a corporate and moralized consensus. The focus on partners' happiness, the reference to 'sufficient' profit, the references to the JLP being 'different', raised questions for some in JLP about the necessity, legitimacy, and potential dangers of employing the same efficiency metrics which are used by conventional retailers. But the legitimacy of such worries was seen as problematic in the face of dominant management insistence.

With respect to business strategy, Michael Porter (1985) has argued that while performance differences arise from the activities and processes required to produce, move, sell, and deliver products—which generate costs—benefits arise from doing that more efficiently than others. But, while the advantages gained through increased efficiency may be *necessary* for competitive advantage, Porter suggests they are not *sufficient*, because these cannot be sustained because they can be quickly replicated. Competitive advantage, he contends, is built on differentiation: being different either in what the firm does or in how it does it or delivers it. Sustainable strategy relies on the creation of a unique, valued, and sustainable proposition. Porter argues that a business can out-perform its rivals only when it can establish a difference that it can preserve.

And this is precisely what John Lewis and Waitrose have managed to achieve—or to maintain—for the potential difference was bequeathed to current management. But as one manager put it: 'We tend to be forced down a route of becoming more and more similar to everybody else, just like Sainsbury's and Tesco's, but if we lose that difference then we've lost everything'.

So the possibility arises that a certain level of focus on operational efficiencies could damage JLP's distinctive source of differentiation which might jeopardize partner engagement or restrict the activities and routines which lie behind, and support, the richness and attractiveness of the customer experience.

However, in analysing the possible consequences of the JLP Board's use of metrics similar to those utilized by conventional retailers, it is necessary to recognize the nature of the relationship between the Partnership Board—where target figures for performance ratios on key metrics are generated—and the divisional boards where responses to such pressures are developed and to consider where and how and with what energy, independence, authority, and success the JLP model is 'protected' within the modern JLP through the strategies and responses of divisional boards. The responses of the divisional boards introduces the possibility that the level of the performance targets themselves, or divisional response to such targets, may reflect the need to protect the JLP difference.

Achieving sufficient profit is another balancing act, between the various demands on the JLP's funds: The Chairman comments in the Partnership Council meeting of 24 June 2009: 'We aimed to make sufficient profit, not as much as the most profitable companies in the sector nor as little as some of the least profitable ones. But enough to be able to fund our Pension Fund commitments, to be able to pay a reasonable bonus to Partners and to be able to fund the growth and vitality of the partnership as a whole so that we are able to invest in our business.'

So 'sufficient profit' incorporates a recognition of the balance that must be achieved between the model and performance. JLP managers insist that JLP is not about maximizing profit; the risks of seeking to maximize profit for the survival of the JLP 'difference' are obvious to everyone. It's about ensuring an adequate level of return to ensure the sustainability of the JLP in the future: to cover bonus, investment, and pension costs. And even that could be difficult.

In reality, JLP profitability is not at the same level as other retailers; this is not by design and it is regarded as a regrettable shortfall that must be addressed through efficiency and other initiatives. Furthermore, the relatively low level of profitability does make it difficult to fund the Partnership's various commitments, which is why in 2015 the pension arrangements were altered, the bonus was reduced and a bond for £3m issued to cover payments to the pension fund. But is a low level of profitability a success or a failure?

An important issue is the nature of the performance metrics and targets and their implications for the treatment of partners. Another, related, issue is debate about this fundamental question. Within JLP, discussion about the ends, by the businesses, is at times ruled as illegitimate because it is defined as unrealistic, un-worldly. The powerful and pervasive management narrative that 'there is no alternative' to current management priorities restricts debate about alternative futures. An organization that is renowned for its commitment to consultation and participation, the most important issue for debate (the purposes and direction of the businesses and the implications of these for decisions about how the businesses and the Partnership work) is at risk of being ruled out of bounds.

One senior critic, however, stood his ground thus:

> The Partnership Board is demanding that the businesses operate with a financial set of metrics that are common in the market place. You see the dynamics of the plan start to change and you see the partner agenda take second place. It's a difficult one to challenge because what you get thrown back is, well, we have to be competitive: we don't survive as an island; we are in a competitive environment that says we are on every high street, we are competing against Dixons, we are competing against Morrison's. But in my view the measurements that we impose should be measurements that we decide are the right ones for this business. (Director, Group, 2014)

The reference to Dixon's was perhaps telling as in 2014 it was forced to merge with Carphone Warehouse Group.

Managers also insisted that the JLP's ownership model had major strategic significance. During the period of Stuart Hampson's Chairmanship (1993–2007), JLP made a series of investments that might not have been taken if JLP was a conventional PLC, since the investments unquestionably hit the business's profits. £100 million was invested in the refurbishment of Peter Jones in London's Sloane Square ('the best department store in Europe'), JLP also invested in the refurbishment of the Edinburgh and Nottingham John Lewis stores and invested significantly in Ocado and John Lewis Direct. Hampson commented: 'They all had a negative impact on the P&L [profit and loss]. If I was a CEO driven by how the City sees me and my share options, it would have been advisable to duck-out on them.'

Building Capacity

Recent developments in the Co-operative Society confirm in a dramatic way that shared ownership in itself is no guarantee of business success. Both John Lewis and the Co-op are familiar names in UK retail, with a broadly similar range of products and services, both have been around since the nineteenth century, have turnovers of more than £10bn a year, and neither is owned by conventional shareholders but are owned by staff or members. But the two businesses have recently fared very differently. The Co-op unveiled an annual loss of £2.5bn in 2014 and is facing a major crisis of confidence and governance; John Lewis on the other hand announced profits of £376m and is happily celebrating its 150th birthday.

The Co-op has recently experienced serious performance failures. Operating profit in the trading businesses is down 71 per cent in the past three years. Sales and profits are down in the grocery business. The Co-op Bank faced even bigger problems. The bank accounted for £2.1bn of the group's £2.5bn loss in 2013. In 2014 the bank was the subject of a rescue plan to address a capital shortfall of about £1.9 billion. The bank had to call upon support from hedge funds and Co-operative Group became only a minority shareholder (Treanor 2014).

The Co-op has been badly managed. This was recognized even by the CEO of the Co-op who assessed 2013 as 'disastrous' for the Co-op. If there was any expectation that mutuality in itself conferred performance improvement, the recent history of the Co-op explodes this assumption. Mutuals can be as badly managed as any other organization. Andy Street—MD of John Lewis—was quite clear on the differences between the Co-op and John Lewis: the difference he argued was management responsiveness and adaptability, and governance: 'The management of John Lewis has the ability to be decisive, quick and effective. We are accountable to our members, but it is the executives who take the decisions.'

Co-ownership introduces tensions that have to be managed; yet management policies may be insufficient to achieve this. JLP managers recognize that a balance must be struck between the polarities of performance and partnership and their attempts to 'find a balance' must be explored and assessed. The JLP difference, managers insist, generates—or *should* generate—competitive advantage. One interviewee commented as follows:

> If you're a believer in partnership then your starting point has to be . . . that the partnership way of doing business gives you a competitive advantage. It gives you a competitive advantage which is sustainable, difficult to copy, difficult to replicate, defensible and a true point of distinction. (Director, 2012)

But this potential must be realized by management: 'I think at worst sometimes the partnership model is used as an excuse to not do those difficult things which would generate that additional return. . . . it should give us the most fantastic advantage, but we struggle to turn that into economic advantage' (Director, 2014).

The JLP is not a charity. It is not an isolated, insulated island of partners selling things to a niche market of people prepared to pay high prices for products. It is a business in a competitive market and it must compete and successfully generate profits if it wants to sustain the model and the pension fund and pay the bonus and invest in the future.

Senior management insists the difference of the JLP model must not only be maintained by commercial success but must be used to *achieve* commercial success.

> It always comes back to how do you use the model to gain some kind of competitive advantage and where might the model be less good in getting competitive advantage? . . . So the model does give us some things around operational excellence. You could argue that the model makes us risk averse. You could argue that the model as I said earlier makes us complacent. There are downsides to the model. (JL director, 2014)

This means that management can take credit for the performance of the JLP and translating potential into reality, but if management has a key mediating role to play in achieving success, in principle it also means that management can—or could—get it wrong—by pursuing flawed commercial strategies which fail to achieve their commercial objectives, or by pursuing policies which succeed commercially but damage the precious differentiator—partner commitment and engagement—and so the capacity for 'discretionary effort', by the inadvertently negative consequences of attempts to make the JLP 'work' more effectively to support business success.

137

This is not the only complication. There is also a tension between maintaining and defending the 'model' and initiating steps to improve performance which could diminish the model, and thus reduce partner engagement and competitive differentiation. As one manager argued:

> I think M&S is a classic example of that: where they threw the baby out with the bathwater, they kept all the wrong things and threw away all the good things. It's often counter-intuitive stuff. It is knowing which part of your legacy is really important. We didn't spend any money; we didn't invest, and we were very self-satisfied. So, in the modern age the combination of that and the model with some proper commercial thinking which, if you think very simplistic, there's a 50 per cent.... If you take the good 50 per cent, which is let's get rid of the civil service mentality; let's get rid of the senior people that only ever worked in one company; let's have some proper auditing of what we do; let's benchmark ourselves against proper retailers instead of saying we're just different. But then let's keep this mad model; let's keep end salary and pensions, even though no one else has kept them; let's marvel in our quirkiness and the fact that we've got the yachts and all the rest of it, and let's start to market it and market the brand to our customers and build. (JL director, 2014)

The ultimate objectives of the business strategies of the businesses are increased efficiency and growth. Both these aspirations are reasonable. They are achieved *via* a series of policies—product range and quality, pricing, customer care policies, store location decisions, logistics, and accessibility and delivery policies (click and collect, for example). But these specific strategic decisions and policies are in turn aimed at achieving two key business objectives which are seen as key to achieving business success, and ensuring a successful business is essential to the achievement of partners' happiness.

One senior manager argued that should the drive for efficiency begin to affect partner attitude or behaviour and thus impact negatively on the customer experience, this would be revealed: 'that would come through in the checks and balances we have set up, so whether that's part of a survey, whether that is customers' footfalls in branches, . . . ' (Director, 2013).

The key point is not that a tension exists—managers know this—but how well they manage it and how prepared they are to being open to, and actively encourage the creation of, the data needed in order to monitor the balance between driving efficiency, and partner engagement. Relatedly, how robust are the mechanisms which ensure managers are held accountable.

Sales of course attract a great deal of attention not least in the media where JLP revenues are taken almost as a bellwether for the economy, certainly for the retail sector—which it usually outperforms. But JLP managers are as interested in the profit figures and especially in *profitability*—profit as a percentage of revenue—which is a measure of how good the businesses are at making money out of the money they receive. Return on invested capital is a crucial measure which supplies an indication of the wisdom of JLP's investment decisions. Both gross sales and operating profit are assessed by the ratio of sales per square foot of selling space and sales per full time equivalent employee. These measures supply information on the effective use of space and the effective use of partners.

In JLP it is normal to find justification for any management initiative in the words of the founder. His statements are perused avidly to find justification; especially if there is a risk that the proposed policy could be defined by fundamentalists as deviating from the Constitution. Current senior managers in their emphasis on efficiencies like to point to the founder's references in his writings to 'ruthless efficiency'. It is clear that partners notice the emphasis on improved efficiencies. The Partner Surveys show that the items gaining the lowest scores concern staffing levels, pay, and the effectiveness of the branch forum.

Nothing illustrates the importance of management's role than changes to opening hours. Sunday trading was introduced into the Partnership in 1999. This was a huge issue for the Partnership because the senior management wanted one thing but the partners wanted another. The issue went to central Council. Ultimately, the decision in favour was taken piece-meal, with a new JL store in Cheadle (with new partners) pioneering the new hours. The decision was taken in the face of considerable opposition from partners who did not want changes to their hours and with considerable cost implications because of the need for new work contracts, yet was unquestionably the right decision. This important development was taken almost in opposition to the preferences of the Partnership; left to itself the Partnership would have chosen to remain as it was and would have declined in consequence. Determined management was required.

Developing plans for the JLP businesses always starts with a re-statement of the original JLP objective: 'the happiness of partners'. But this objective has been subtly repositioned over the period. Gradually, more emphasis was given to the objective of ensuring a profitable and successful business as an essential foundation for the happiness of partners. But this subtle shift (from ensuring partner happiness *within* a successful business to ensuring a successful business as a *prerequisite* for partner happiness) opens up the possibility that the achievement of a successful business or the way the successful business is achieved could be counter to the happiness of partners.

JLP managers recognized the complexity of managing in the Partnership. One Group level interviewee argued as follows:

I think it boils down to our organization being uncompromising on quality, and making sure that the quality of people at senior level that are brought in to deliver some of these functions are really good. One of the things that is very clear in my mind is the quality of the leadership which is driving it. And so my real passionate sense is that we have to have very capable leaders in this business who are able to manage in what you might describe a very three-dimensional way, rather than in a more traditional business model where actually a two-dimensional way (tell or else) is much easier and more straightforward. You need a sixth sense to ensure that partner influences shape proposals in a way which is going to land them successfully. (Director, 2013)

The JLP partners could be engaged and committed as a result of 'partnerhood' or, conversely, by taking advantage of their circumstances complacency is a risk. The frequent management focus on both the 'rewards' and 'responsibilities' of partners reflects these two possibilities. Management has played an increasingly important role in JLP businesses over the last twenty-five years especially with the expansion of business planning. But inadvertently this may have resulted in an enlargement of the amount and scope and frequency of top-down direction.

One experienced senior manager, recruited into the Partnership at a senior level, described her impressions:

I came here with experience of other retail businesses. The basic organizational design of them was in a sense very similar. When I walked into this business it was like a Miss Haversham moment—untouched for 100 years! And I thought how the hell did this happen? I suspect there's a lot in the set-up of the business, the rent that we pay, the proposition, the fact that we're a private company, which has protected it. I think people are beginning to understand that we need to be as good as our competitors in all regards, the Partnership can deliver the icing on the cake. We are now having much more open and honest conversations about some of the downsides of the culture, the sense of entitlement. (JL director, 2013)

Other respondents argued that there could be an unhelpful link between the Partnership emphasis on respect for colleagues and the ability to address issues of performance effectively.

We're not good with communicating bad news. So this whole thing that we're starting to talk about at the moment, about being a learning culture. But if you look at how people reflect and post mortem, it might be done in an ad hoc way, but we don't live and breathe it. (Director, 2013)

Another manager made a similar point using different language of a psycho-analytic kind:

I think there's this parent, Parent–Child thing which is endemic here. The children don't like bad news. As a result there is a danger we don't learn. That's very dangerous because there is a dynamic market place. The issue is especially acute now we're multi-channelled business with multiple formats. (JL director, 2013)

No one argues that JLP managers want to damage the Partnership model or are trying deliberately to dilute democracy or stifle the critical side. But there are people who argue that these trends are occurring partly through the growth of the JLP, partly through the increased dominance of management, partly through the formalization of many aspects of the JLP model, partly by the greater commercial focus.

> It's the bit about respect for the individual. It's the fact that what I love about this company is that we are all equal because my secretary owns as much of the company as I do. So, I may manage her but she has rights in a way and she has rights to be treated fairly and decently by me. She has rights for me to explain why I want what I want and I think it's all about that personal acknowledgement in a way. It's a hugely highly team dynamic kind of environment as well, I think, because your motive is so much stronger than we are as individuals. I think for people that work for it for a long time, it is life changing in a way as well. It's a fantastic club to be in. I think it inspires a pride in you and what you do. I think it attracts people whose personal values align with the business values and perhaps that's the dilemma for people of my age have because they see those business values changing in a way. (Director, 2014)

Against this background, JLP managers must seek to improve efficiencies through policies that engage and enable rather than cheapen and exploit, employees. So the means available to JLP managers are different. And their concern for partners is also characteristic and impressive. For both hard-headed business and moral reasons and because of their undoubted commitment to the JLP values and principles, JLP senior managers take the happiness of the partners very seriously indeed. And of what other business could this be said?

Nevertheless, it is clear that the drive to ensure the success of the JLP divisions however well they are managed, and however true to the constitution and spirit of the JLP difference (and this difference remains important and real) creates potential tension between profit and partner. This is so regardless of how often senior managers insist that this linkage is a positive and mutually supportive one.

Senior management have had to improve the efficiency of the basic business model, and to face economic crises and the gradual emergence of a new form of competition which completely changed the rules of the game—in ways which made some of the historic assets of the JLP potential into disadvantages: extremely expensive flag-ship high street stores. And they had to invest at great expense in their JL stores to make them attractive destinations for the new consumer pastime of shopping, by borrowing money the costs of which had to be covered by increasing profit, while extracting profit from increasing revenues remained difficult. And as if this wasn't tricky enough, while managing these business and organizational balancing acts they also had to ensure that the reputation of JLP—a hugely valuable asset—was not only maintained but actively maintained and developed. For while JLP faced many changes from the external world of the retail business environment, mainly technology-based and increased competitiveness—and internal changes as the JLP improved its systems, its management, organization, and its supply chain—it realized that its core asset—its well-based reputation for fairness, honesty, decency, trustworthiness— must not change. In fact this must become more developed and better known and valued. So another balance was necessary: between business and organizational change, and adaptation, between continuity and the conservation of the principles and values of the JLP and between the changing nature of the JLP model and the forceful presentation of this model in internal and public statements.

Managing Meaning

The job of corporate leadership, writes Peter Senge (1990), is to define reality. And in JLP, to a much greater degree than in conventional businesses, executives have to define and create reality: they have to create or modify conceptions of how the Partnership works in order to help ensure it works in the ways they want. Within the Partnership, and even outside it, they have to define what the JLP is, how it works, how well it works, and how it differs from conventional retailers. They have to disseminate and ensure the pervasive plausibility and acceptance of their definition of management and of their policies and actions.

They have to do this for two reasons. First, because the JLP is inherently a highly moralized institution: many aspects of JLP, many relationships within JLP are subject to explicit morality, much of it formally enshrined in the Constitution or in the explicitly stated JLP principles, others are part of an historical legacy derived from the Founder. So the structure and dynamics, the past, present, and future, the participants in and the institutions of, the Partnership arrive heavily loaded with moral expectations. Managers have to show that what they are doing—and how they are doing it—is consistent with widespread and historic moral expectations. Part of this activity also includes offering (re)interpretations of what these moral frameworks *really* mean. The subtle transformation of partners' rights into partners' responsibilities, or the insistence that what is good for profitability is inherently also good for partners, are examples of management's work of moral reinterpretation.

Secondly, in a moralized organizational world (a world managers actively and energetically seek to articulate and promulgate) JLP managers must ensure their legitimacy and the legitimacy of their actions and plans. So understandably, they interpret and refine these meanings to make them supportive of their purposes, to achieve legitimacy and gain compliance, consensus, commitment, and engagement, and reduce challenge and critique.

JLP managers ensure that their policies and actions are defined and presented in terms of and as consistent with, pervasive JLP moral principles. Management seeks to present their business strategies, and associated efforts to build organizational capacity and increase efficiencies as consistent with the Constitution, with the primacy of partner happiness as an organizational goal, and with the historic purposes of the Partnership. They do this by creating and using a language whereby management purposes are presented as consistent with and as far as possible in the language of, the Partnership's Constitution and history or the words of the founder, but, at the same time, subtly reinterpreting this language to carry and apply the requirements and values of contemporary business purpose and logic. This language—the 'narrative'—asserts the value and priority of some purposes, logics, and strategic directions, and downgrades or rules out other possibilities. Its most significant consequence is that it limits and defines debate either within the management cadre where disagreement is regarded as evidence of management failure, or between management and non-management partners were disagreement is seen as a failure of communication, confusion, or, as a last resort, putting personal interests above the common good: as selfishness.

Senior JLP management stress the morality of their actions. This includes efficiency which, in JLP must be defined not simply as necessary (as in conventional businesses) but also as morally right: management argue that partners are morally responsible for performance: 'Because the Partnership is owned in trust for members, they share the responsibilities of ownership as well as its rewards—profit, knowledge and power'. JLP has three 'Partner commitments'. And number one is: 'Take responsibility for our business success—we take responsibility for delivering the right experience for all of our customers, generating profits for us all to share' (Annual Report, 2013: 18).

But stressing morality also carries risks. One of these is that the functionality of conflict as a potential source of alternative ways of seeing is downplayed and conflict is defined negatively. Dissent may be de-legitimized and viewed as disloyalty. A moralized management context may make disagreement and challenge more difficult and more emotional—challenge is more likely to be discouraged and to be defined as selfishness or betrayal. So a possible, inadvertent and unanticipated consequence of the attempt to define partners' involvement and responsibilities in moral terms might be to reduce and sideline important potential sources of alternative perspectives.

This moralizing of partners' attitudes and behaviour in the JLP management narrative, carries implications for how critique and challenges, perceived—not only by managers but also by non-management partners. As JLP managers seek to avoid or neutralize challenge through the Council, or from elected members of the board, by insisting on the necessity and legitimacy of their emphasis on efficiency measures, they undermine opposition and challenge through the democratic processes and in effect define the role of the democracy as supplying agreement and acquiesence. Since these measures are for the benefit of all, on what basis except confusion or selfishness, can they be challenged?

In conventional businesses the values that characterize work and employment are the values of the market: exchange transactions, market calculations of price and value, the 'morality' and authority of profit, self-interest. And these values are so widespread and so represented and honoured by commentators, government, and so embedded in the language of organizations and the measurements of performance and in the entire fabric of modern society, as to require no special or extra work by management in conventional firms. Their management of meaning is done for them by external agencies. The market rules, in practice and morally. It is a fact of life.

In JLP this is not the case because there is an alternative language which emphasizes wildly alternative priorities: for example partner happiness. This creates a potential dilemma: and to solve this managers have to ensure that their actions are seen as consistent with prevailing systems of JLP morality. This means not only that managers must represent what they do in terms of historic values, but also interpret or reinterpret these values for modern times. It is the moral foundations of the JLP that give the Partnership its competitive edge—and which adds to the appeal to customers. But this difference also supplies the framework within which managers have to act and represent their actions.

Management also want to present the JLP as a modern, efficient, business capable of competing on equal terms with rival retailers. JLP must not be seen as akin to Miss Haversham's drawing room, but as a modern business. The clever solution to this dilemma, a solution which achieves a number of purposes at once, is the 'partner–customer–profit' cycle. This is based on the service–profit chain popularized by Harvard professor James Heskett and his colleagues (1997). They illustrated their model using the case of Sears in the USA but in many ways, although JLP sent out a director to study on the Harvard course, JLP had already developed and honed the model in their own home-grown way.

This cycle, widely and authoritatively emphasized within the Partnership, manages to combine the JLP difference with business efficiency by claiming that the JLP difference is a source of profitability; that being morally better (the 'JLP difference') is better for performance (the principles of twenty-first century retail). But the cycle is important not only because it defines—as it claims—the source of JLP's competitive advantage (and as we know this is more complex and uncertain than the cycle admits) but because by supporting management and its narrative of the JLP, in effect it resolves another dilemma: it defines away potential conflicts between competing logics within the JLP. What is good for profit is good for partners and what is good for customers (efficiency) is good for partners and profit.

Management insists on the importance and legitimacy of the vigorous pursuit of profit. But the JLP business plans always start with a restatement of the JLP's core goal: partner happiness. This too creates a potential dilemma. The solution is to insist that profit is the same as and necessary for, partner happiness, thus eliminating the possibility of conflict between profit and the search for profit and partner happiness, at a stroke.

Profit thus becomes beyond dispute:

> When Charlie became chairman he expressed the Partnership's strategy in these terms, Partners, Customer Service and Profit. I think what Charlie's now trying to say is, he doesn't want people to think about them as separate. They are completely interlinked. So if you're thinking about how to advance profit strategy in the right way, you will be doing the right thing for Partners. And if you're thinking about how to do the right thing for a Partner it will be commercially successful and if you're doing it in the right way, they are just all interlinked. (Group manager, 2013)

But the partner–customer–profit model is not only descriptive; it is aspirational, ideological, and *prescriptive*. It simplifies reality and it asserts a simple mutually supportive, instrumental relationship. It presents a theory, a model of causation: 'partners', who embody the distinctive qualities of the Partnership—the morality and values of the institution—create benefits (for customers) and thus profit—which returns ultimately to partners. So the morality of the Partnership is now a double benefit—good in itself but also good instrumentally in creating benefit (profit). Thus an absolute good (morality in/at work) is translated into something which is instrumentally good: and an end becomes a means. This subtly converts business success and any decision to achieve business success from an important and necessary *precondition* of partner happiness, to the *source* of partner happiness and thus the goal of the business, since the objective of the business is the happiness of partners.

This argument not only posits a process of causation, but by doing so also creates a moral responsibility among those who initiate the process, but it also defuses (rules out) any conflict between the various participants in the process.

One major theme of the JLP dominant narrative is that JLP is a better way of doing business—and that *morally* better means *commercially* better. At best, as managers know only too well, this is only partly true. But the consequence of this assertion is to legitimate and support management's insistence that to receive the benefits of the JLP model, to experience the better experience of being a partner (which are real), is to accept a moral responsibility to produce the extra business benefits or to accept the legitimacy of management actions aimed at improving the efficiencies of the business—efficiencies which are in a sense the rightful dues of the businesses. So it creates a form of contract between partner and Partnership and legitimates management's right to try to enforce this contract. Morality thus becomes contractual: a subtle and interesting transition from the language of morals to the language of the market.

Another application of the contractualization of the JLP legacy is the widespread management message that the extra cost of the JLP model, and the impact of the model on partners (the 'better' way to do business) must ultimately be recoverable through the extra profit achieved by virtue of the value partners generate through their reactions to being treated 'better'. This reinforces the message that management is entitled to extra performance from partners by virtue of the partners' exposure to the JLP model, and that partners have a 'responsibility' to produce this. And so again the language of exchange and contract is laid on top of the language of morality—through the pivotal and ambiguous word: 'better'. The recent emphasis on the responsibilities of partners, aimed to balance the earlier emphasis on rights, is a clear reflection of this new conception of the relationship between the partner and the Partnership.

The JLP difference is also stressed as a privilege for which partners should be grateful and, being grateful, should accept management decisions. And since the Partnership has partners' well-being as the ultimate objective, dissent could only indicate either confusion or a failure to emphasize the common good at the expense of individual cost.

There is a related issue. Currently JLP managers, as noted, prefer to try to manage through consensus and through a narrative which argues that the JLP model has eliminated systemic conflict, that all JLP partners share the same objectives, that management strategies are for the general good, and that any disagreement or critique is a consequence of communications difficulties.

And it is true that the JLP ownership structure and the lack of external investors and the bonus system, the JLP Constitution and values and the numerous benefits available, do significantly reduce the exploitation and tough treatment of partners compared to staff in other businesses. But it is not the case that these features eliminate conflict or the sources of conflict. All organizations are characterized simultaneously to varying degrees by conflict and cooperation. In JLP the balance may be predominantly towards cooperation, but there remain real potential sources of conflict over the relative impact of management decisions or the distribution of rewards. For example, even the JLP pension—much lauded and these days remarkable—could be seen as a mechanism whereby the profits of the business are disproportionately used to reward the few middle and senior management partners at the expense of the many non-management partners and therefore as a source of conflict and disquiet.

But JLP managers' reliance on the narrative of consensus and harmony, may make the expression of challenge or the argument that consensus has limits and that real differences also exist alongside cooperation and consensus, harder to express by partners and harder to hear or accept for JLP managers. The stress on consensus may become so dominant that JLP managers themselves believe it: so any statement that deviates from prevailing orthodoxy (the dominant regime of truth: consensus) is seen as indicative of management failure (to communicate, to persuade) or partner disengagement or lack of commitment. So the actual issue being raised or the alternatives being proposed are seen as symptoms, not as genuine proposals: as indications of dysfunction and management failure.

JLP managers attempt to manage meanings outside the Partnership as well as within. One major common theme is trust. Customers can trust partners and the Partnership because there is a link between the way partners are treated and the way they (and the Partnership) treats customers. The source of the difference are the values at the heart of the Partnership; and the outcome of these values is trustworthiness.

Nowadays, the value of JLP's distinctiveness has been recognized, costed, and thoroughly exploited: the JLP difference is now grounds for competitive differentiation. Marketing experts and management spend time and effort polishing and embellishing the narrative and seeking partner and public (customers') belief in it. Part of the appeal of the partner–customer–profit formula is that it speaks not to the realities of the Partnership but to the narrative. Managers are aware of the crucial importance of building and maintaining the unique JLP brand: unique because it does not lay claim simply to conventional and increasingly dubious commercial qualities of quality or price but to a quality which is increasingly rare: trust.

The famous TV advertisements present carefully and skillfully crafted stories and images defining the relationship between JL and customers—generationally caring, honest, relational, loving, familial. In 2012 the Marketing Director (a post which did not exist at the start of our period) described his tasks in ambitious terms:

> Part of what I've tried to do is build some of the emotion back into the business in terms of how our customers see us. . . . So we always talk about our customers have this trust and love us. Trust we were always good at, love we were very prosaic. . . . We now build on the love which is real because never knowingly undersold is very real. (Marketing Director)

The use and repetition of the word 'love' here is revealing. JL and Waitrose have come top of customer satisfaction surveys of the biggest seventy retailers for many years. Building the brand, maintaining the unique JLP narrative, ensuring that JLP has a place in our hearts because it is decent and fair—to suppliers, partners, and customers—is crucial to the JLP experience and to its success.

One director assessed the brand worth as follows:

What I think we're seeing now is actually what brand is really worth, including the partnership element of that brand. When we valued our brand, at around £1.4 billion, just the brand, the value of the brand if you were to license it round the world. Now, the company who do this for the City said, actually key to this is the partnership element, if you didn't have the partnership element; if you were selling the brand without the partnership element, or someone bought it, and took away the partner element, . . . we'd downgrade the value of the brand to about £700 million. (Director, 2013)

He went on to make a link with the nature of luxury brands:

Looking at the value of our business more like, say, a luxury brand owner would look like, because for them it's the quirk of luxury and it's the quirk of being exclusive. For us it's the quirk of our model which means that we have this amazing trust of the consumer and it's real. This is a different emotion to maybe the emotions in the 1990s when realness was perhaps not as valued as it is now. This difference has been heightened because of what's happened around us . . . the financial disarray, with bankers and the like. (Director, 2013)

Thus, partners and the idea of partnership are revealed as JLP's main strategic asset and the Partnership itself and its unique ownership and employment model are defined as a source of competitive advantage through their impact on partners, and these are assets because of their impact on *customers*— through the trust and affection the model generates.

JLP managers have been successful in creating and disseminating a narrative about the JLP, its nature, and consequences. This narrative insists on the legitimacy and consistency of management actions and partner 'responsibilities' in terms of the Partnership's historic moral framework and expectations. Management have also been successful in reinterpreting core components in this moral context in more modern, reciprocal, contractual terms. The narrative is not nonsense: it is based on reality and real difference—it reflects the history and distinctiveness of the JLP. But it also defines and creates reality— smoothing corners, simplifying, stressing some possibilities while skating over others.

Conclusions

In this chapter we focused attention on the way the task of management is undertaken in JLP; we also commented on the characteristics of the managers themselves. We noted that a prominent feature of the task of managing in this organization was the need to continually balance logics which (potentially) compete. The two most prominent and evident priorities by whose 'laws' managers had to steer were, first, the Constitution and the related set of values and expectations which accompanied the model; second, the increasingly apparent need to compete in the commercial world of retail where the market is in constant flux. In this environment of fluidity, standing still risks going into decline as competitors create new offers and stimulate new forms of demand and expectations. This implies a need to respond with changing service offers, and this, in turn, means carrying partners with you.

Thus, in contrast to conventional shareholder-oriented businesses which rule through hierarchy and command, managers in JLP are expected to meet or indeed exceed commercial rivals while also winning the consent and indeed commitment of the workforce.

Many of the people we interviewed maintained that these dual priorities were not in conflict. Indeed, conversely they argued that the two were mutually reinforcing: the effort expended in bringing partners along with an idea was repaid through effective contribution which in turn resulted in commercial success. This was often described as exploiting the Partnership difference.

Some other interviewees were more cautious, qualified in their interpretations and less certain. They suggested that managing in the Partnership was a more difficult job than managing in other settings. They argued, for example, that the increasing insistence on meeting rigorous financial targets (such as return on invested capital) and indeed outperforming competitors on these same measures was a distortion of the mission. They contended that the targets could take on such prominence, that the Partnership rather than adopting a stance of a genuine 'alternative' to this conventional corporation, was playing along with a set of rules and assumptions which were foreign to the supposed alternative model.

So, in broad and brief terms these were the two cognitive 'camps'. At senior levels the former camp was undoubtedly in the ascendancy. There was a broad consensus that the Partnership approach was indeed a 'better way of doing business'. Better, in that it was morally 'good' (fair, encouraging staff voice to be heard, sharing rewards, trying to be decent). Better commercially as the decent approach also resulted in superior outcomes as staff were more committed and so sought to serve customers well and sought to use their talents to offer creative solutions to commercial problems. This was the dominant view. In the second camp, there were non-believers and doubters. They tended to express their views cautiously.

Institutional theory would suggest that where such competing logics prevail, a number of alternative strategies can be adopted (Mullins 2006; Besharov and Smith 2014). An organization may allow competing sets of priorities to co-exist. This may even find institutional expression in the form of separate units or departments which can concentrate and focus on their prime objective. An alternative approach is to seek to thrash out the competing priorities until a position is reached where one position is reached as the dominant logic (Thornton et al. 2012).

JLP managers have characteristically allowed all of these to operate. The segmented institutional forms are evident: there is substantial investment in the democratic structures; registrars, and the Partners' Counsellor and her office, ensure a level of commitment to JLP principles. Yet, at the same time, a dominant narrative has emerged which insists that JLP managers are able to be winners in the marketplace not only while acting in congruence with Partnership principles but *because* of these very principles. Yet these same managers also know that, in some respects, some hallowed elements of the model are obstructive.

7

Governance, Democracy, and Accountability

Employee-owned businesses tend to raise important questions about governance, democracy, and accountability. These interconnected phenomena are the foci of this chapter with regard to how they play out in the John Lewis Partnership.

The Founder described the Partnership as 'An Experiment in Industrial Democracy' (Spedan Lewis 1948). But is it accurate to describe JLP as a democracy? To what extent, in practice, does it act using democratic principles and methods? How does the democratic character actually work? Have the series of attempts to refresh and reform the democratic side over the past decade served to strengthen or weaken its democratic character?

Whatever the extent of democracy there is the important question of how and to what extent managers are held to account in this organization. Hence, in the later parts of the chapter we widen the focus to include the whole gamut of ways in which accountability may or may not be exercised in JLP. Thus we move from structures to processes and from formal procedures to informal aspects of holding to account.

To put the analysis into perspective, very few businesses in contemporary circumstances would even make claim to being 'democratic'. Democracy at work is, in the contemporary world, rarely an expectation—although at certain junctures in the past the idea of an 'industrial democracy' has been very much in play. There are two main reasons to reassess the democratic credentials of JLP. First, because of the Founder's own claims and objectives. Second, because even today, the managers and partners talk about the business as having democratic 'sides' and democratic structures and even refer to 'the democracy'. They maintain and invest heavily in institutions designed to safeguard and operationalize the Partnership's 'democratic character'. So while many other enterprises—including many of the new social enterprises and mutuals which have spun out of the public sector with publicity around their 'John Lewis-like' nature—are very clear in declaring they are not even trying to operate as democracies, JLP itself does, at times, seek to make this claim albeit often in guarded and provisional ways.

Previous Assessments of JLP Democracy and Accountability

One of the most thorough assessments of democracy in JLP was made by Flanders et al. (1968). They argued that the JLP Constitution requires 'account-ability of management to the managed as a central feature of its democracy, and its excellent committee network is designed to foster the free exchange of information and views between those responsible for decisions and all the other workers in the organisation' (Flanders et al. 1968: 76). To this extent at least, these authors regarded the system as positive. They also point out that the various committees, the registrars and the rest, 'undoubtedly provide an effective means of prompting management not to neglect the human side of its problems and enabling the rank and file to raise their complaints'. Yet, according to Flanders and his colleagues, the system 'is not and was never intended to be, a democratic control *over management*' (Flanders et al. 1968: 187, emphasis added). Conversely, they see accountability as a 'real and all-pervading power'. But, when judged against their own working model of industrial democracy, these authors did not judge it to meet that standard.

Sir Bernard Miller, the then Chairman of the Partnership, in the Foreword to the Flanders et al. (1968) book makes clear how the senior managers of that time interpreted this particular experiment in industrial democracy. It was not the same as that advanced by Flanders and his colleagues. Miller argues that the Partnership does not claim to be 'a definition of industrial democracy; it claims to be one experiment in industrial democracy' (1968: 16). He says it is in fact diametrically opposite to the view of those who 'regard union oppos-ition to management as the prerequisite of any kind of democracy in industry' (1968: 16). The Partnership's answer he says is to keep 'the general body of the Partnership fully and properly informed on what is being done and why, by consultation and by sharing in decisions to the greatest extent that seems practicable' (1968: 16). He further argues that the 'Partnership's democracy is based on the rule of law, the law here consisting of a written Constitution, legally binding through two Deeds of Settlement, Rules and Regulations developed in the light of experience, and the accumulation of precedents in the working of the system' (1968:17).

The Constitution 'does not provide machinery whereby the managed can control the management but the aim and function of the system is to enable the general opinion of the Partnership to express their actual preferences and to influence thereby the decisions of management' (1968: 17–18). So, management, he argues, needs to win the backing and support of partners even though those partners do not select the managers nor direct them.

Allan Flanders and his colleagues used a different benchmark and conception of industrial democracy. They do, however, acknowledge that there are 'different interpretations of democracy' (1968: 28). Key elements, they suggest, include that management do not act in an arbitrary way and that the managed have some control over the conditions of their working lives. But, unlike Sir Bernard and his colleagues, thcy harbour a conception of a 'two systems' approach—that is, not only a top-down but also with scope for a bottom-up approach so that some control can flow in both directions. A problem they have with the JLP system is that it was 'conceived by management and thus introduced from above' (1968: 29).

What Flanders et al. seem to have in mind is the wider industrial relations system in place at the time of writing which was the 'two systems' approach of formal industrial relations based on collective bargaining with trade unions, and an informal system based on work groups and shop stewards. This was the classic, so-called Oxford School analysis (of which Flanders was a part along with Alan Fox) that underpinned the work of the Royal Commission on Industrial Relations chaired by Lord Donovan which was published in the same year as the Flanders book (Donovan 1968). This commission was established to investigate a perceived problem of industrial strife. Its analysis was that the informal shop steward system needed to be counterbalanced by a stronger formal system. When measured against this kind of analysis it is perhaps not surprising that Flanders found the JLP system prone to a risk of 'paternalism'. Iindeed, Flanders characterized this as 'the crux of the dilemma'—that is that employees may want a more independent system. Yet the empirical work of Flanders et al., based on interviews with employees (non-management), tended to find little demand for an alternative independent system though, as elsewhere, there were complaints about pay. And it is true, of course, that when measured against the then prevailing industrial relations system of free collective bargaining over pay and other terms and conditions, JLP employees appeared to have less independent influence. That said, the wider collective bargaining system has since gone into rapid decline.

Without direct influence or control this leaves the 'alternative of accountability' (suggest Flanders et al.) and on this they cite the words of the Chairman in 1966:

> The requirements of the democratic ideal may be equally well and more efficiently met by ensuring that bosses are completely accountable to the workers. This is the principle which is observed within the Partnership. Its management can be and frequently is called upon to account to the Partners for its actions. This adds to the managerial burden. But it does not lead to inefficiency. The manager who knows he may have to account, by chapter and verse, for all he does thinks very hard

before he acts—and he thinks even harder before he fails to act. (Sir Bernard Miller's letter to *The Times* 20 July 1966)

Flanders et al. argue that both employees and managers themselves operate within an all-pervading ideology and this ideology 'acts as cement' (1968: 185) and 'functions as a humane control over management' (1968: 188). It prioritizes the overall interest of the Partnership rather than any particular group. The system of accountability is, they say, 'real and all-pervading' (1968: 187) but it is 'not a control based on sharing power' (1968: 187). Accountability to partners is in terms of business efficiency and the tenets of the ideology, hence, they conclude: 'accountability is in effect control by ideology' (1968: 188). No one can afford to ignore it—'not even the Chairman' (1968: 188).

The Flanders et al. research and analysis took place half a century ago and is a product of its time. We now move on describing and assessing the contemporary system.

The Three Governing Authorities

From the outset, governance and control of the Partnership was built around three governing authorities. These were, and still are: the Chairman, a Partnership Council, and a Partnership Board. Together, these are the governing powers. They are designed to work as a system of checks and balances. The Partnership invests many millions of pounds in operating the elections to the multiple councils, in reimbursing travel and accommodation expenses, in hiring prestigious venues, and in general support of the democratic apparatus. Here, we briefly describe the roles of the Chairman and the Partnership Board before looking in more detail at the work of the Partnership Council which is the pinnacle body in the democracy.

The Chairman combines the role of chief executive and board chairman (Figure 7.1). He is a very powerful figure and carries unusual powers such as being able to appoint his own successor. He is 'accountable' to the Partnership Council. Each of the managing directors of the operating divisions is accountable to the Chairman. The Chairman works with the Group Executive to develop the Partnership strategy. He appoints and can dismiss the managing directors of the constituent businesses and other executive directors.

The Partnership Board is responsible for the management of the Partnership's commercial activity. Members of the board include the Chairman, five directors appointed by the Chairman, five directors elected by the Partnership Council who provide a direct link with the Partnership's democratic structure, and three non-executive directors. The non-elected directors have only been on the board since 2008, hence throughout most of its history the Partnership

Figure 7.1. JLP Chairman, Charlie Mayfield

operated with internal board members only. And it was not until 2014 that the non-executive directors were granted voting rights.

As might possibly be expected, given the demanding and complex nature of a place on the board, even the elected members tend to be managers—and experienced managers at that. The five elected partner (employee) members in 2015 included only one selling assistant, and four managers. In 2016, the five elected members comprised three branch managers and two communication managers. There were no shopfloor ('non-management partners').

The five *appointed members* with voting rights are: the Managing Directors of the main business divisions (Andy Street, MD of John Lewis, Mark Price, MD of Waitrose, and Patrick Lewis, MD of the Shared Services Division), Helen Weir, the Finance Director; and Tracey Killen, the Personnel Director. A sixth appointed director to the board, is a new development. The Chairman has chosen to appoint the Partners' Counsellor, Jane Burgess, onto the board although this position carries no voting rights.

The Partnership Council holds the Chairman to account for ensuring that the distinctive character and the democratic vitality of the Partnership is retained and promoted; and for the commercial performance of the business as a whole. The Council has the ultimate sanction of being able to dismiss the Chairman if it judges that he is failing in these two regards. Notably, under current arrangements, the Partnership Council is not responsible for holding the other directors to account; that is the role of the Chairman.

The Partnership Council has the power to discuss, to ask questions, and to make recommendations on any subject. It elects five directors to the Partnership Board. The Council has a role in influencing Partnership policy and how profits are spent, particularly on things that affect partners directly, like pay, pensions, and discount policies. The Chairman appears before the Council twice a year to report and answer questions on his running of the Partnership.

As has been noted, Spedan's conception of democracy was related to the right to representation. This in turn could either mean simply a right to voice discontent, or more fully, to involve a right to vote and otherwise influence the executive (Bradley and Taylor 1992). Bradley and Taylor suggest that in Speden's own writings he had in mind the former rather than the latter (1992: 48). Yet, in recent times voting has been a feature so in practice it seems the Partnership has been treading an uncertain path between these two conceptions. Equally, it is true that there has been a general trend away from formal voting. The majority of members of the Partnership Council are elected by the entire Partnership and this has been described as 'an exercise of an apparently genuine democratic nature' (Bradley and Taylor 1992: 49). Nonetheless, these authors conclude that 'the power of the council lies in simply confronting management on important issues' (1992: 49).

One of the Partnership Council's duties is to elect three Trustees of the Constitution. They are responsible for deciding the constituencies for Council elections and for ensuring the elections are fair and that the ballot is secret. The Trustees also act as directors of John Lewis Partnership Trust Ltd, the legal entity that holds the company shares in trust for the partners and officially appoints the Chairman and distributes the Partnership bonus. The Chairman and members of the Chairman's Management Committee cannot be Trustees of the Constitution.

The Partnership makes clear that the 'democratic structure' is not intended to act as a democracy per se. The elected partners will—according to current conceptions of purpose—hold the Chairman to account, influence policy and make key governance decisions (about electoral issues and representation). 'Holding the Chairman to account' means having the right to question and challenge the Chairman about Partnership policy and decisions. But while the Council may *influence* decisions it does not *take* decisions and this is very clearly stated and understood. Senior management argues that partners do not attach a premium to decision making. Instead they are anxious to secure the chance to input at the formulation of proposals stage and have a say in the 'how' rather than the 'what'.

The Chairman may appoint holders of particular Partnership posts to the Council. Currently they are the Director of Communications, Director of Legal Services, Company Secretary, and Group Insight Director. Members of the board are automatically members of the Council. One of the senior executives we interviewed had been recently recruited from outside the Partnership and he expressed a clear assessment of the democratic character of the Partnership and how they currently work:

> We are held accountable by the press and the media and non-execs and the Partnership Board. So I think ten years ago, when the business wasn't investing, the Board was probably quite self-satisfied and happy to make no profit on the year. I think those days have gone. These forces keep us honest. But I think now it's more about engaging than actual accountability anymore. Quite often the questions asked become a bit petty. Issues tend to come up about 'my canteen in Cheadle' or about keeping the benefits for the longest serving. And as I say, it's often the wrong way round. It feels like the radicalism is coming from the senior team and not from the representatives. (Waitrose director, 2014)

An important factor which affects the Council's capacity to hold management (through the Chairman) to account is that the councillors are not organized, they are and act as, individuals. There is no collective authority, and so no strength through the power of collective authority. It is true that recently the councillors have been allocated to subunits with specialist areas of interest which could increase their knowledge of these areas and so encourage their ability to question searchingly. But these specialist sub-divisions have been created by and are supported by management; they do not represent increased councillor authority. In fact by dividing the councillors in this way, the Council could potentially be weakened as the possibility of the Council acting as a unified entity is reduced.

Other Democratic Bodies

The Partnership Council sits at the top tier of a multi-level democratic structure. Beneath it are three divisional councils (one for Waitrose, one for the John Lewis stores, and one for Partnership Services). Elections to these bodies occur every three years within constituencies which are determined by the Trustees of the Constitution. Beneath these are Divisional Forums which channel views and opinions from the branch level.

At the branch level there are arrangements in place to promote and facilitate what is now known as 'Partner Voice'. There used to be democratic committees at this level with nominations and elections but these arrangements have undergone a series of reforms. A driving rationale was to make this first level less formal and to reduce the 'them and us' nature of such bodies. One interim arrangement was to call them 'Branch Forums' and these gave way to the current nomenclature of Partner Voice. Branch managers wanted more inclusive bodies which would encourage two-way communication.

Partner Voice is the most local level of engagement (or possibly democracy). The idea is to share knowledge and power between managers and partners in relation to local issues. Each branch (or business unit such as a distribution centre) must have a body representing partners in that branch. The term of office is two years. The Partner Voice body includes the branch manager. Constituencies are decided with the help of the Divisional Registrar. Each partner in a constituency has one vote to 'select a Partner they wish to represent them'. The word 'select' is used at this level and is sometimes explained as different from 'elect' in that all members in a branch are deemed to be candidates and they do not have to 'stand' for election. This is deemed to encourage more representative engagement. Partner nominations (a term used at this level interchangeably with select and elect) are anonymous. While 'ordinary' everyday partners can all be selected/elected, persons actively seeking to be selected are allowed to make this known and are permitted to canvass. Likewise, persons with most votes who do not actually want to serve are not obliged to do so.

Under previous arrangements, the local registrar was often the chair. Now, the meeting itself can decide who will be chair and it can be anyone of their choosing from the business unit—thus it could be a manager or any partner, even if not elected. Each Partner Voice body must also include a responsible manager and this is to be the most senior manager in that business unit such as a branch manager.

There are to be a minimum of four meetings a year. Representatives are given a time allowance 'sufficient to carry out their duties'. The responsible manager is responsible for ensuring that this time is made available. Representatives are supported by a 'Democracy Coach' (note the declared intent to build and maintain a democracy) from the Partnership Councillor's office. In addition, the Democracy Coach attends at least two meetings a year and the Partnership Assurance Lead who has the authority to be present at any Partner Voice, attends at least once a year. If the Partner Voice (here the term is used as a collective noun) judges that the responsible manager is not acting in the best interests of the business unit or is disregarding the views of Partner Voice, they can require the Partnership Assurance Lead or the Democracy Coach to make their concerns known to the manager and to the Divisional Registrar. Ongoing concerns can be escalated up to the Chairman.

The main purpose is to enable partners to influence local decision making. Partners are to be consulted and involved in branch matters. They can question managers on any local issues that affect partners and the branch. They are to share knowledge and power and to use these to create a successful business and a worthwhile and satisfying place to work. The systems are in place to inspire partners' confidence in the effectiveness of the democracy. Agendas for discussion are expected to include whatever partners and their representatives consider as relevant; gathering opinion and feedback from other parts of the democracy; matters delegated by divisional councils or regional forums; and the responsible manager can use the meetings to gather partner opinion on business unit matters. A record of the meeting has to be kept and a copy sent to the Partnership Councillor's directorate. Decisions about who should chair the meeting, who should take the minutes, at what time the meeting is held and the provision for visitors to observe, are all matters delegated to the Partner Voice body itself.

Partners are elected to the second level Forum by direct election from all members of the constituency. The constituencies are designed to ensure that all levels of management are represented. Each business division such as Waitrose and the John Lewis department stores has its own Council so that matters pertinent to that business can be discussed. Representatives of these bodies are elected by indirect election—that is, from and by the second level Forums.

The History of Reform

In general terms, a comparison of present day democratic structures and supporting institutions and those designed by the founder Spedan Lewis nearly one hundred years ago reveals much that is recognizable as similar. The three governing authorities designed by him—the Partnership Council, The Partnership Board, and the Chairman are still in place. The Constitution is still in many ways similar. The registrars and the principles of ultimate purpose are all apparent.

Amendments up to 2004

There were surprisingly few changes to the democracy until the millennium. In 2003, the Chairman and President outlined the nature of the new 'Partnership Council'. There were to be four meetings a year and six regular committees. There were to be sixty-nine elected seats to represent constituencies across the Partnership as a whole. The replacement of the Central Council by the new Partnership Council was said to be 'a move designed to make the democracy more relevant to the business it was set up to support'. The Chairman and the President suggested that 'the new Council's brief differs slightly to that of its predecessor, as its aim is to leave issues that affect the daily running of the two divisions to their respective Councils' and that instead it 'will focus on the strategic direction and character of the Partnership as a whole embodying the spirit of co-ownership' (*Gazette* 2003, number 1177).

This tidying up process took the details of the business of the divisions away from the Partnership Council and was arguably a far more significant shift than the claimed 'slight difference'. The divisional councils do not technically hold the divisional MDs or their management boards to account. The divisional councils are not recognized in the Constitution. Hence, while the move appeared sensible and appeared to facilitate closer scrutiny, it could be said to have taken a major activity away from the Partnership Council.

The 2004 Democracy Project

Prior to the 2004 reforms, each John Lewis Branch had a branch council with elected members, a committee for communication, a retirement committee, and a social committee.

The Democracy Project was in part a response to results from the 2003 Partner Opinion Survey which revealed a surprisingly disappointing evaluation by partners of the democratic arrangements. Partners were asked, among other questions, to express their agreement or disagreement with a statement in the survey that 'Our democratic bodies are effective'. This produced a very low level of agreement—the fourth lowest out of fifty statements. In 2004, the then Chairman, Sir Stuart Hampson, asked the then Deputy Registrar, Ken Temple, to lead a review of democracy. The focus of the project was democracy and engagement at branch level.

The project group formed the view that the existing branch councils were no longer fit for purpose. They saw them as old fashioned and too formal. Branch managers tended to regard branch councils as fostering an adversarial 'us and them' attitude and they were not comfortable with this. While dissent was far from the norm, Christmas and New Year trading hours often triggered some conflicting perspectives. Some branch managers thought that their branch councils would occasionally reject managerial proposals simply to show that they could. They wanted to replace this 'institutionalized opposition' with more of a 'joint problem-solving approach' that was more consensual and unitarist rather than pluralist in nature. The project group worked with three pilot branches in order to devise an alternative design.

The term 'Branch Council' was dropped in favour of the term 'Branch Forum'. This relabelling was suggestive of the shift in nature. A crucial change was to replace the former system which involved nominations and representatives 'standing' for election with a secret ballot which encouraged partners to select any person they judged suitable from their Department to serve as their representative on the Branch Forum. This resulted in many more non-managerial partners being elected.

Under the previous council arrangement, the people who stood for election were usually section managers who served for a two-year term and they were often perceived as using the position as a means of career progression. The old system also seemed to result in long-serving councillors and little new blood. The elected councillors then elected a Branch President. There was a set agenda, minutes of debate and decisions were kept, and the whole system was said to seem stiff and formal. In addition to elected members, there were ex officio members including the Branch Managing Director, the General Manager, the Finance Manager, and the Branch Registrar. These councils met between six to eight times a year on average. Each branch had a visitors gallery and so the total number of persons in attendance was often rather large. Depending on the size of the branch, a typical branch council could have seventy plus people in attendance.

Partners' dissatisfaction with the branch councils may have had many sources—the dominance of the council by managerial representatives is likely to have been an important one and their debates were often seen as being at some distance from ordinary partners' everyday concerns. The Democracy Project team searched for a more collaborative arrangement which would allow partners to express their views. The system pioneered by the pilot branches led to the disbandment of the traditional councils and the launch of Branch Forums. These were adopted throughout the Partnership in 2006–07. As noted above, these forums were in turn eventually displaced in 2012 by Partner Voice. The direction of travel from formality and voting to consultation and information sharing was clear.

The Chairman, commenting on the changes in 2007, said:

> It is a way of summing up the change in the business to say that we want to hear Partner's voices setting the agenda rather than Partners reacting to what management proposes. (*Gazette*, 30 March 2007)

A survey of opinion in the three pilot branches seemed to demonstrate that partners wanted to influence and be consulted rather than to 'take decisions' or to vote on proposals brought by management.

At the Partnership Council in March 2007, one of the delegates maintained that the trial had 'engaged, enthused and empowered' his partners. He went on to use a phrase that has been much used since: 'There's no longer the business and the democracy: now there's one democratic business'. This summation was reinforced by the Chairman, Charlie Mayfield, who said: 'For too long there's been too much separation between the democracy and the business; bringing the democracy to the core of our business must be right' (*Gazette* 28–29 March 2007). This is a notable and crucial shift in meaning. The idea of a separation is henceforth to be discouraged in favour of a unified endeavour—business and democracy as one.

Nonetheless, even in 2015 following the 'Democracy workstream' the role of Partner Voice at branch level continued to be described as to 'hold local management to account for the way they run their branch'. Notably, this is wedded to another role: 'To bring solutions and ideas to make the branch better for customers and Partners alike'.

The complaints about the branch councils seemed to run in two different directions. One criticism was that they were dominated by departmental and section managers who were not fully reflective of non-partner opinion. Yet, a different complaint was sometimes laid—namely that the voting and the procedures tended to stoke an 'us and them' perception with managers having to win consent. This oppositional nature was highlighted in the following remark from one of those involved in the Democracy Project:

> In the branches periodically, the branch managing director would make a proposal such as the proposed trading hours for Christmas. The branch council would usually agree them but just occasionally they would not. It was like stamping a foot and saying, 'Ha ha, we don't have to agree to go back on Boxing Day or whatever'. And it just gave this impression that it was the one against the other. That was something we wanted to change. (Manager, Group, 2013)

Thus, rather different arguments were put forward in order to justify the reform of the branch councils.

The 2008 Commission on Democratic Character

In 2008, the new Chairman, Charlie Mayfield, announced the establishment of a Commission on Democratic Character. In fact the focus was upon the nature and role of the Partnership Council rather than of the democracy as a whole. Mayfield said:

> I have asked the Commission to consider the background to the Partnership's democracy and what it should mean for today's and tomorrow's Partners and to develop proposals to enhance the role of the Partnership Council as the Governing Authority representing the interests of individual Partners. (Mayfield, 2008, Foreword to The Commission on Democratic Character)

The Commission set out certain principles, a particularly notable one being that 'Public opinion is sovereign'. The Partnership Council was said to have three roles: (i) holding management to account (through the Chairman); (ii) influencing; and (iii) decision making. Holding to account is largely done first by holding the Chairman to account for ensuring that the distinctive character and the democratic vitality of the Partnership is retained and promoted, and second, by holding him to account for the commercial success of the business. The Council retains the ultimate sanction: if the Chairman is deemed to be failing in these regards the Council may dismiss him.

The Commission recommended that a change be made in that the Council should only make decisions on governance matters. On commercial and operational matters, it should make *recommendations* to management and then *hold management to account* for the decisions it makes. It also recommended restrictions on the size of the Council so as to allow effective debate. Thus it proposed a total of sixty-seven members. This would be made up of thirty-one John Lewis branch constituencies, thirty-four representatives from Waitrose constituencies, and two from corporate.

The John Lewis Democracy in the Wider Context

Judgements about democratic character depend, to a large extent, on the comparative benchmark being used. A historical perspective reveals wide fluctuations in expectations about employee involvement in decision making at work. At certain phases of the cycle it is taken for granted that owners and managers have the power and will to exercise control and make the decisions. This is the idea of 'managerial prerogative' (Storey 1980). At other times, wider political and economic circumstances impel serious attention to the alternative idea of worker control or at least of extensive worker involvement in industrial decision making.

Following the Second World War, an era of economic growth and prosperity tended towards a new 'settlement' between capital and labour. The trade unions at that time much preferred a stance which allowed them to use collective bargaining as their main *raison d'être* and, in such a mode, they were uninterested in state regulation of terms and conditions, and uninterested also in complicating the bargaining relationship with worker participation or worker cooperatives.

There was, however, another resurgence of interest in industrial democracy in the 1970s as economic conditions worsened and the government set up a Commission under Lord Bullock to make recommendations on Industrial Democracy (Bullock 1977). The Bullock Report proposed legislation that would broadly reflect the German pattern of co-determination with elected trade union representatives on the board of companies. After the ensuing controversy and debate, the proposals lapsed. Since that time the idea of industrial democracy has largely gone into retreat. Later decades saw much more attention being paid to more 'managerialist' approaches such as worker participation through task-based teams and through consultation, and in more recent years in 'employee engagement'.

So, in the light of these historic cycles it can be readily seen that the origins of the John Lewis Partnership experiment lay in a particular period which was very different from the years that followed. In one sense, therefore, some might conclude that the attempt to perpetuate the structures and procedures designed in a period different from contemporary circumstance is an anachronistic and unnecessary project.

But the economic crisis starting in 2008 brought John Lewis even more into the spotlight. Many influential commentators—political and economic—began to talk in more fundamental ways about the need to 'reinvent the firm'—a title used by an influential DEMOS publication (Davies 2009). The search for alternatives was truly on and the John Lewis Partnership was hailed across the spectrum as a worthy model. It was portrayed as a successful and employee-owned firm. The basic ideas were thus given new life and were resurrected in a new positive light. It is in this contemporary context that our examination is conducted and our assessments made.

In the present context, 'democracy at work' remains an unusual concept and it is because the John Lewis Partnership seeks to maintain and enact some version of it that the case is of focal interest (especially as this sits alongside its commercial success and as a highly-regarded business and the notion that these variables seem to be interconnected). Hence, the democratic credentials of JLP merit close attention. We can also see that the issue is complex because the meaning of democracy in a work context remains contested and ambiguous. In the case of the John Lewis Partnership there are interconnected elements: co-ownership (albeit in the form of a Trust settlement); elaborate representative structures; and a conscious and openly declared attempt to share knowledge, power, and profit.

In addition, part of the wider character of the John Lewis Partnership is its distinctive culture, its welfare and benefits package, its investment in a 'registrar' function which seeks to safeguard the Partnership ideals and look after partners, and the investment in a 'critical side' which includes journalism and functions which seek to ensure that managers do not over-prioritize commercial success at the expense of partner interests. All of this sits alongside and separate from a fairly conventional personnel/human resource function.

There is a danger in taking this talk and this idea of industrial democracy for granted. It is notable that in many of the mutuals, social enterprises, and co-owned enterprises that we investigated as part of our research—some of whom took direct inspiration form JLP—that their leaders stated, quite openly and unapologetically, that their organizations were 'not democracies' and they went on to contend that it would be folly to attempt to pretend otherwise or to seek otherwise. Similarly, while many private sector organizations—including the leading and more sophisticated of them—have invested in employee consultation and employee engagement, they would not in any degree claim or even want to claim that their organizations were democracies. In the wider context of contemporary Britain, the notion that a work organization might be or aspire to be democratic is highly unusual and even somewhat idiosyncratic.

It is within this context that we should examine the debates and actions related to 'democracy' within the John Lewis Partnership. While democratic-like institutions exist, are invested in, and maintained, there are also managers who seek to explain the 'meaning' of such activities and institutions. For example, note the following statement from our interviews with senior JLP managers:

> We have now clarified that managers make the decisions. We remain open to challenge and we have to justify our decisions but the fact that we make the decision—possibly after considerable consultation—is beyond dispute.

Despite that, the Managing Director of the JL Division emphasized two core principles:

> First, every partner has a position in the democracy and elects someone who ultimately is judging the senior executive. Every partner must have a vote. The second one, that I believe very strongly in, is that every partner must have a share in the bonus: this is the collective reward piece. So, how people are treated is what you see every day, but I think it all comes from this font of collective participation, actually. What really underpins it ultimately is that this person is a co-owner. (JL Managing Director, 2014)

Here, ownership and democratic voice are twinned closely together. Other directors seemed less certain and were rather unsure. As one pondered:

> Is this is a co-owned autocracy with the veneer of democracy or is it true democracy? I'm not sure if this is a democracy or whether it should even be about democracy. (Director, 2014)

He continued:

> At the moment it feels more like good industrial relations. It feels like people are represented. It makes people feel very involved in their business. I'm not sure, personally, that democracy is fundamental to the outcomes because, at the end of the day, I'm not sure how much it changes that wouldn't still happen. It doesn't really create pensions and the rest. They would happen anyway. (Director, 2014)

Another director reflected on the nature of the input from the democratically elected representatives at the top level:

> I would say that very often the management is more radical than the democracy. The democracy and the individuals who are part of it are often quite conservative with a small c, and even a big C in terms of how they see things. The more radical pro-partnership democracy stuff tends to come from the Board. (Director, 2014)

This could reflect to a large extent the composition of the elected representatives most of whom tend to be fairly senior managers from the branches. One line of argument for reform of the central bodies was that they were stuck in a 'time-warp' of formality and had become ossified. Hence, for example, one view from the centre was that:

> The Partnership Council, the divisional councils the branch councils, I think we felt for a long time that they haven't really kept up; they were old-fashioned, formal and off-putting to the majority of Partners who therefore were in danger of seeing them as terribly irrelevant. (Group manager, 2014)

And then there was the familiar appeal to 'how Spedan would view it':

> If Spedan came back he'd be amazed by how different the business was and proud of how we'd grown fantastically but horrified to find that the Council is the same as he left it fifty years ago with the procedures and the proposing and seconding. So there was a real attempt to modernise the Council. Partners could recommend things to the Chairman. Certain things could only be agreed by the Council. Occasionally Council would turn things down or change things. There was an 'us and them-ness' about it. (Group manager, 2014)

But, despite this conviction of the rightness of the principle of reform there was recognition that getting the detailed practical amendments in place was difficult:

> We found that the line between 'modifying' and 'weakening' is very difficult to find. The purpose of the democratic bodies is often thought to be to act as a counterbalance to management. But, many of us are uncomfortable with that. Yet the way we operated until relatively recently gave that impression. (Group manager, 2014)

Reformers at top level tried to move the Partnership away from that. The Commission on the Democratic Character which reported in 2009 sought to remove some of the formal authority that the Council had retained.

> It was in the Constitution that the Central Council decides matters to do with the use of profit and things that the Chairman delegates like pensions, holidays, sick pay, and partner discount benefits. It left one with the impression that the Council decides these things because it represents the co-owners and a view that 'It's our use of profit and that's what we decide'. Management have done strategy and they particularly run it but when it comes to discount, pensions and holiday that's for the Council to decide. And so it could be argued that in one bound we were free by saying 'management decides everything, what the Council does is it holds Charlie to account for everything'. (Director, 2013)

So now, under the reformed state, the Partnership Council's key role is to influence. 'We'll tweak the words of the Constitution to make it really clear the Council isn't *deciding* what things should be done, rather, the Council is *influencing*. Ultimately the key decisions—even those traditionally seen as within the gift of the Council such as decisions about the amount of partner discount, holiday entitlement, pensions, etc. are now accepted as all for management's decision'. As one manager argued:

Management could consult and come and hear your view but it's got to be Charlie and co who make that decision. And we're still in a process of making that change because there'll be a number of longer-serving Partners who will still think of the Council as where decisions on pensions are made. In reality we wouldn't change the pension scheme without there being some Council involvement so it may be a subtle difference. (Manager, 2013)

A further step could be to remove the Council's own budget which enables it to spend on charity, to look after partners in financial need and to spend on leisure at the clubs and societies:

We haven't quite done that because the budget still sits on its own page in the accounts and we still use it as a way of saying 'well that's a Council budget'. And so the retirement budget and the financial assistance budget remain so it's terribly confusing to Partners as it perpetuates this sense that the Council does have a say over things. We're not rushing to abandon it because we want to keep the sense that the Council is a really important force and Partners' opinion is an important ingredient of the Partnership's success. (Manager, 2014)

Then there is the 'holding to account' function. As one senior manager observed:

Still formally twice a year at the Partnership Council we have a Proposal which is holding the Chairman to account for the results. Now we changed the wording. Away from 'accept the Chairman's Report' to a different principle: 'Supports the Chairman in his leadership of the Partnership'. So the results are part of the picture and you being a good Chairman, all those in favour, all those against. So there is still a little formality. It isn't quite an AGM vote of confidence but the idea we've moved a bit in that direction. So, we are seeking to move to clarity about the Council's role in holding to account; the senior governing authority is holding Charlie to account in more than numbers—it's about what is the Partnership about and is he doing the right thing'. (Manager, 2014)

Some people argue that the reforms tended to weaken the democracy. The case for this thesis is that the Partnership Council lost a number of key features. The specialist committees have been disbanded and the spending power of the Council has been removed. Further, much of the formality of a representative body has been reduced, so, for example, proposals no longer come into the Council like they used to. As one critic lamented: 'there used to be proposals from the floor, proposals from the councillors saying "I propose this and second that" and various other formal devices now all gone'. There are no longer debates between the Council and individual managing directors of the divisional businesses. These used to happen when these managing directors presented their annual reports as did other directors, such as the Director of Building and Services, and the Finance Director used to report to the Council once a year. This used to be published in the *Gazette*. Furthermore, the directors no longer report to the Council and the erstwhile five 'critical directors' are now reduced to just one (the Partners' Counsellor). Moreover, the critical voice of the in-house journalism, most notably the *Gazette*, has been curbed.

Similar points about perceived weakening could be made about the divisional councils. It may appear as though the two managing directors are being held to account by their divisional boards but even here there are doubts. The central interpretation is that:

> Mark and Andy [the MDs respectively of Waitrose and John Lewis stores] technically are not being held to account by those divisional councils because these Councils can't get rid of them. Rather, Mark and Andy are held to account by the Chairman. (Senior manager, September 2013)

There was a large turnover of elected councillors following the reforms of 2009. An unprecedented 75 per cent of councillors were new to the Partnership Council. (This reflected a similar wholesale replacement of representatives when the branch councils were reformed.) There were fears that this had resulted from a 'perceived weakening of the Council'—in other words that experienced representatives had declined to stand under the revised conditions.

Likewise, the reform of the higher tiers of the representative bodies—most notably the changes to the Partnership Council—could also be interpreted as weakening the potential for challenge and a further removal of decision-making power in favour of consultation. Even the senior custodians admit that:

> The Partnership Council now has no decision making responsibility at all. That has been quite hard to land. Now what the Council can do and has the absolute right to do is to recommend a course of action for the chairman, but the chairman makes the decision. (Senior Partner at corporate level)

The narrowing of the engagement towards a consultative stance could be said to reduce the distinctive character of the JLP and reduce the difference with other business. For example, another large UK retailer, B&Q, also has a representative consultative structure. In 2003 it established a multi-tiered consultation framework operating at store, regional, divisional (in geographic terms), and national level. These bodies include formal elections (IPA 2003). Spedan Lewis was aware of potential challenge and of coercive comparisons. He wrote:

> In the John Lewis Partnership, democracy, the sharing of power, has been carried out as far as is practicable. If other people can see how to do it better, let them start another partnership and show how far they are right. (Spedan Lewis, 1954: 10)

Whether, that claim of 'as far as possible' has withstood the recent attempts to reform and refresh is open to question. Increasingly, senior managers have been more assertive about their role and their responsibilities. This is evident in the following quotation from one of the managing directors:

Success is viewed in terms of long-term sustainability. This has to be a business that has a legacy, one that lasts. Senior managers are the custodians playing the long-game. They are not in the short-term, maximising shareholder value, game. What is problematic of course is consistently delivering that and, taking the tough, long-term, focused decisions to enable that to happen. And I'm very clear on that: that's down to our leaders. We cannot leave it to some hope that all partners will suddenly make this happen. (Managing Director)

It seems that the Partnership still wants to keep in play the notion of 'democracy' in some sense and it is prepared to continue to invest heavily in the appurtenances. But the meaning of democracy in JLP has been rethought, reimagined, and recast. So, what difference, if any, does this make? The aim is increasingly seen to compete with commercial rivals on their terms and this includes growth, extended hours trading, and many more such attributes. The processes of decision making seem increasingly and unambiguously in the hands of management. Partner engagement and democracy are tools to enhance the quality of those decisions and the buy-in and commitment to them.

In this context the last word can appropriately be left to a senior manager with a rather cautious and unconvinced view:

For me, the risk, moving forward, is that as we go beyond 90,000 plus partners to 100,000 and beyond, if we don't pay sufficient regard to recognising that, for a partner, the world has moved on, and we invest in the partners to contribute to the business, then we run a risk, I think, that the business ends up being a very different business and the advantage that ownership in the partnership brings to day starts potentially to be diminished. (Senior Manager, 2014)

In sum, there is the optimistic 'one democracy one business' view, and there is this more cautions and concerned view that the new settlement risks exhausting the accumulated capital of the legacy.

A three-year term of office was introduced and the idea was said to be 'to emphasise the special importance and expertise of the role by setting up specialist groups—not the old boring spending committees, spending all the money on pension and retirement but groups similar to select committees' (a view from the Centre). These committees were to have the purpose of building strong relationships with the top team. But that was then. Under new proposals for yet further 'refreshing', these committees have been 'watered down to specialist groups because they're not really like select committees because they cannot hold the directors to account'. Instead they have been redesigned as 'specialist groups with lead directors'.

The above set of recent reforms as with so many others could be seen as simply following the exact logic that stems from precise interpretations of roles. Hence, if a body is holding a director to account then it should not itself be making the decisions. Likewise, if a body does not have the authority to hold a director to account then it cannot be like a select committee and so it becomes a body whose role is to offer ideas. This tendency towards increased precision in the use of language and then following through on the precise logic is wrapped up in related narratives of 'being honest' and having 'adult conversations'.

The specialist groups introduced in 2009 were judged four years later in 2013/14 as 'not having been as successful as hoped'. So the 'stakes were raised' for the Partnership Council. The composition of the Council had always had a management bias but, as the size of the Council has been reduced, the old method of seeking some balance by having one manager and a non-manager for each John Lewis branch, became unworkable when there was only space for one representative per branch. This increased the dominance of managers on the Partnership Council. And given that 'There was always a little bit of nervousness that there aren't many non-management Partners left on the Council', this development is seen as creating a problem.

And yet, the new Council members have to understand the strategy, they have been given more information and the business plans are shared with them. It has become 'slightly more intellectual and so we've frightened off the non-management Partner'. The attempt has been made to steer the contribution away from details of what is happening in a branch to wider issues.

This wider view sits neatly with the new representative structure which sees a typical councillor having a constituency stretching over multiple branches. But arguably it sits less well with an expectation that a core role of councillors is to reflect 'what Partners are feeling in their area . . . it is not meant to be about the detail, we want to hear Partner opinion, that's what the Council should be'. So here is a revised definition of purpose.

One manager argued that 'the most successful meeting of the Council in this current term was last June when we had a session on "What it Feels Like to be a Partner". We just had Partnership Councillors saying what it felt like in their area and Charlie was listening. It wasn't a debate, it wasn't a Q&A session, it was just a download. And that was very powerful' (Partnership Manager, 2013).

But, as with most attempts at reform of the democratic bodies, there could be a downside. One person observed:

> I feel as if we have not had the full buy-in from [the MDs] for all this. Following the succession battle there's just a natural tension that will never go away at the top of the organisation and they're busy running their own divisions. So, the MDs don't

turn up for the Charlie Mayfield show, which we call the Partnership Council and don't say anything because it's all him—he's the one, he's the focus. And so that's bad enough for them and the rest of his team, Tracey, Pat, Marisa, finance, they don't have much of a role to perform other than supporting him. (Manager, Group)

In one sense, the Chairman was said to want the Council to be strong, for example, by giving it more information. The current Chairman attends every Council meeting, whereas the former Chairman, Stuart Hampson, used to attend once a year and sometimes twice a year: but 'Charlie, for the last five years, he's come to every meeting—he is there four times a year'.

It is revealing to hear the assessments made by new directors who had been recruited at senior level from outside the Partnership. For example:

I was expecting, when I first started in the partnership, for it to be much less hierarchal than it was, and actually it was very hierarchal. Some things are coun-terintuitive. So, for example, not so long ago we had dining rooms for senior managers that were separate from the general populous, I was absolutely shocked by that and I . . . hang on a second, you're supposed to be a democracy, what does this mean? (Director, 2014)

Likewise, another argued:

There is a lot of English cultural stuff: parent, child, passive aggressive, all that kind of stuff, wrapped up in this. You're dealing with a lot of people here who have been around for decades who have learned that a partnership model undertakes its leadership accountabilities in a certain way. I've obviously come from a very differ-ent environment and been brought up in a different way. I've seen mercenary cultures in action and I know what they're good at and what they're not so good at. We've got to avoid a culture of complacency and entitlement. (Director, 2014)

One retired very senior JLP manager when discussing the possibility that over recent years the democratic component of JLP has been diluted, argued that: 'this organization was always an autocracy with a profit sharing scheme. There was never much democracy to dilute.' He also claimed: 'Democracy is a con but it's a method where those whose shoes pinch can complain and get something done. However, even that function is now being reduced.'

And while this may sound harsh there is something in this assessment. While the quality and vigour of debate within the Council may have changed (old hands argue that the degree of challenge and critique has reduced) the basic structure and rationale of the Council never intended that the elected representative should make policy: only that they influenced it and chal-lenged (occasionally) those who did. This is not democracy in the purist sense and was never intended to be. And while there is a sense in which the Council can hold the Chairman to account, this power too is greatly vitiated by a number of factors.

Accountability

There are questions to be asked about the contribution of processes beyond the formal democratic structures including, for example, the ways in which the nature and location of authority at a senior level may facilitate challenge and review of senior management.

In this section we consider the extent to which decisions are taken by the wider network of the management team, because in principle, the members of this group can contribute to accountability through their duty to challenge and confront emerging decisions. We have seen a number of examples recently among, for example, the banks where this internal process of challenge failed totally. Catastrophic decisions were seemingly supported by executive and non-executive directors who saw their role in terms of loyalty to the CEO rather than loyalty to those whose funds they were negligently wasting. Hence, accountability is not simply a matter of formal mechanisms, it is also essentially a process of top team dynamics.

Accountability is centrally important because, only if it is robust and effective can the balance that JLP managers stress as crucial to their stewardship of the JLP be properly positioned and maintained. The main components of this balance are: ensuring the success of the businesses, and ensuring the survival of the model. These are the two prime criteria by which the performance of JLP management will be judged, and for which they need to be held accountable.

Accountability is important not simply because it includes active monitoring but because the process (when robust) has authority and sanctions, so it supplies challenge and critique and a potential corrective or alternative to management decisions.

Does the Partnership Council hold management accountable? To hold someone accountable it is necessary that their actions are fully revealed and apparent, that the consequences of their actions apparent, and that the people holding the actors accountable are able to assess these actions thoroughly and radically and have the authority and willingness to be able to require changes in policies and/or apply consequences. This requires that the principal or their representatives have an agreed right and the ability and authority to oversee managers' stewardship of the business and the Partnership—and sufficient authority to impose sanctions and to require alternative or remedial actions. Regardless of the frequent references to democracy and accountability in JLP statements, arguably the Council does not, in this sense, hold the Chairman or management accountable.

Holding the Chairman to account is supported by the ultimate sanction: to remove the Chairman. But it is hard to imagine ways in which this totally unlikely threat could be employed to any practical benefit in discussions of, or challenges to, JLP policy or performance. Although such a threat sounds significant, its implications are so catastrophic that it becomes virtually unusable and meaningless.

As our research revealed, much of the business handled by the Council concerns relatively local and restricted issues. The only actual decision-making authority that remains relates to issue of governance. Tellingly, policies relating to partner discounts on goods get more attention than investment policies.

The Council does not hold senior management accountable because, despite the claims of the JLP website, few of the key players believe that this is what it is really meant to do. Some councillors may raise awkward questions and there have been times when managers have admitted to getting things wrong and when councillors' reactions to a proposal have forced a modification or even rethink. But getting a rare wigging from councillors is not the same as being held to account by shareholders at an annual general meeting, or by non-executives at a board meeting (when non-executives remember and implement their proper responsibilities). When shareholders challenge board strategy or complain about performance, it matters greatly. As owners, their views count. Although *in a sense* partners are owners, their views count for less—precisely because they are only owners (or owners' representatives)—'in a sense' and not fully. So it is not surprising that the Council does not hold management (the Chairman) to account because this is not its role; it is a sounding board, an opportunity for partners to express their views.

Yet conversely, JLP management is exposed to an internal process of scrutiny and challenge which managers in conventional businesses would find remarkable. The Council allows and encourages the partners' representatives to give voice to partners' concerns. However if JLP senior management is exposed through the Council to internal challenge in ways managers elsewhere are not, they are also *not* exposed to the processes of systematic accountability that is expected in conventional businesses where shareholders and their representatives (non-executive directors) have the right, the capacity, and the authority to challenge, critique, and when appropriate to demand action. So, the JLP is at the same time both unusually participatory and unusually non-accountable.

One of the main reasons why the Council finds it difficult to hold management accountable is because management has successfully disseminated a dominant conception of what the JLP is and how it works and the priorities it must pursue, which plays a major role in constructing the context within which the Council works. This 'narrative' describes the world of the organization, and represents a pervasive, powerful body of ideas which is largely taken-for-granted within the Partnership as part of a natural order and which tacitly or explicitly offers 'the power of truth, the potency of rationality and the promises of effectivity' (Miller and Rose 1990: 10).

This significantly diminishes the space in which partners or their representatives can develop and articulate a critique of or an alternative to, the prevailing management argument. Management argue that there is no alternative to their strategy and their focus on growth and improved performance; that the success of the Partnership benefits all partners; that decisions about the allocation of JLP's profits are made by neutral, committed, and trustworthy managers with the continued success of the Partnership as their priority, that profit and partners' happiness are mutually supportive and not opposed. And they argue that it is councillors' duty to overcome their personal interests and to show commitment to the Partnership and the Council by accepting and supporting managers' decisions. So a hegemonic silence is created since dissent and challenge are either neutralized by the dominant perspective or ruled out as indicating a failure of trust in or commitment to, the JLP's values and principles.

The narrative insists that the nature of the Partnership requires the commitment of partners and their representatives to the common good. Management has created an overwhelming conception of the Partnership not only as special and unusual, and with which partners are fortunate to be associated, but as an organizational entity in which, since it is committed to the achievement of partner happiness, and since a proportion of profits are redistributed to partners, conflict between management and partners is ruled out as something which by definition cannot occur.

This prioritizes the collective at the expense of the individual. But conflict—or at least disagreement—is possible, around the *distribution* of the profits of the business. The focus on harmony has the consequence of undermining dissent. Since the system is co-owned and run for mutual benefit, disagreement and opposition can only occur through misunderstandings and poor communication, or through people, or sub-units, giving priority to their own parochial interests at the expense of the benefits for the whole: selfishness. Although occasionally individuals may suffer, this is for the benefit of the group as a whole and so individuals should demonstrate their commitment to the greater good by compliance with the policies in question. Since management policies are designed to achieve common shared benefit, councillors find themselves without grounds on which they can criticize these policies unless they argue that somehow the policies are flawed or defective. They may be able to question the means (although this will often require technical, expertise, information, specialist support, and confident judgement and knowledge which they will probably lack) but they cannot question the ends. The narrative also defines the democracy, a particular form of democracy, one in which the democracy supports the business itself.

While the JLP narrative is based in reality, it also *creates* reality. It essentially represents a managerialist, idealized conception of the JLP (trusted expert management, an harmonious organization with shared purpose) and a managerialist conception of the Partnership itself, in that the essential JLP difference—co-ownership and shared rewards—is rationalized not in terms of morality or decency but instrumentally: treating people decently is good (or must be made good) for business results. And achieving results is defined as at the heart of the goal of the Partnership—partner happiness. So the 'difference' of the Partnership has been translated into the language and values of the conventional corporation: it has becomes a different means to the same end. A classic analysis of the nature of power by two celebrated American political scientists, Peter Bachrach and Morton Baratz, captures much of the nature of this dynamic. In their analysis of the nature of power, they ask whether it can be understood only when embodied in, and expressed in concrete decisions; they contend that it is not, and they explain their reasoning thus:

> Of course power is exercised when A participates in the making of decisions that affect B. But power is also exercised when A devotes his energies to creating or reinforcing social and political values and institutional practices that limit the scope of the political process to public consideration of only those issues which are comparatively innocuous to A. To the extent that A succeeds in doing this, B is prevented, for all practical purposes, from bringing to the fore any issues that might in their resolution be seriously detrimental to A's set of preferences. (Bachrach and Baratz 1962: 948)

There are grounds for suggesting that this analysis captures much of the essence of the normal business with regard to the operation of the Partnership Council in relation to its role of holding managers to account.

However, as we have noted, there is another mechanism through which the balance sought by managers and partners might be achieved: the Partnership Board. In principle, the members of the board are expected, and required, to think independently, to critique and challenge and to subject any proposed strategy to stringent risk analysis on behalf of the business as a whole and its shareholders—the partners. But, we need to be mindful of the many recent cases of malfunctioning boards outside the Partnership which nodded-through strategies and decisions which, recklessly risky, destroyed share-holders' assets and often the business.

Such pathologies result not from aberrant individuals or exceptional circumstances but are a *normal* consequence of features of the business organization. Confident leadership can discourage critique and challenge; emphasis on teamwork and loyalty can close down debate and restrict open analysis; hierarchy can limit the flow of 'negative' feedback up the organization; careerism can encourage excessive support for flawed leadership policies; respect for the leadership can result in a search for data to support the leader's policy preferences. These are potential tendencies in any board that the board and its leadership must work to negate and avoid.

How confident can we be that the Partnership Board is able to avoid these various pathologies, will be open to challenge to the strongly embedded dominant narrative, and be able effectively to ensure that strategic decision making achieves an acceptable balance between the preservation of the Partnership model and its constitutive elements, and business priorities? To answer this we need to assess the possible contribution of the Partnership Board.

It is difficult for the elected members to argue against the intellectual and managerial authority, analyses, and arguments of the appointed members. For these appointed members not only speak with the authority of their leadership positions and their personal authority, experience, and expertise based on many years of success at senior levels within the Partnership, but also their proposals have been carefully and thoroughly prepared by dedicated expert advisers,discussed at the boards of the respective businesses (and so carry considerable weight), and considered by the Chairman's Committee which comprises the Chairman and the appointed directors.

This group meets frequently to develop strategy, business plans, and budgets and to review major operational and management issues, financial results and forecasts and proposals for capital expenditure. So the elected members are, when faced with draft business plans, being invited to react to carefully constructed proposals. Furthermore, although nominally of equal status as members of the Partnership Board, the elected members are in reality inevitably formally subordinate to the appointed directors—a factor which must impact on their confidence.

There can, however, be occasional instances of success for elected partners. In his history of the Partnership, Peter Cox notes the difficulty the elected representatives had in settling into their board roles. 'They all found it difficult to acquire confidence at first among the intellectual big-hitters around them on the board, but gradually gained it. Some felt under intense—if usually unstated—pressure to agree to a board proposal. Once, when they baulked at the imminent closure of a specialist unit, they were *read the riot act*—but they got their way and the unit is still open some years later' (Cox 2010: 287, emphasis added).

There are also three non-executive members of the Partnership Board. They add weight to the emphasis on the commercial, business objectives of the JLP since all three come from outside the Partnership and despite whatever levels of personal sympathy for or admiration of the JLP model, their experience, expertise, and values are very clearly in favour of conventional business arrangements and objectives. In as much as they behave as proper non-executive members of the board, their prime concern should be the protection of shareholders' interests—that is, in this case, partners' interests. But since in the prevailing narrative, partners' interests are probably defined in terms of the business success, partners' (shareholders') interests are normally translated into a concern for management performance and management objectives.

The most important influence on the behaviour and functioning of the board is the Chairman. When we asked the previous Chairman how he saw his main responsibilities, he replied that it was to safeguard the Partnership. And the current Chairman would also see the role in this way. We heard from a number of respondents that the Chairman does actively seek to protect the JLP model and its component elements in the face of strategic proposals from divisional MDs which he saw as going too far (and many of our respondents saw some recent proposals as breaching their conception of the inviolate components or principles of the JLP model).

To argue that the Chairman is meant to play a key role in achieving the desirable balance, and that incumbents of the role recognize and accept this responsibility is not the same as *achieving* this balance. They may be swayed excessively one way or the other, for example, by persuasive divisional managing directors, so the most likely direction is in favour of commercial priorities.

The other, executive members of the Partnership Board are long-term JLP people, thoroughly marinated in the JLP values and committed to its principles. But they are also committed to the continuing improvement of the performance of the businesses. And they are fully committed to, indeed responsible for and champions of, the dominant JLP narrative. So they share the prevailing view that the definition and achievement of the balance can be left safely to management.

Currently, the formal position (echoed by our respondents) is that there are two lines of defence of the Partnership. First, that the Partnership Council, Partnership Board (especially the elected members), and the Chairman will argue in favour of the interests of partners and of the Partnership (these are not of course the entirely same thing). The second line of defence is that the integrity and commitment and values of senior management, especially the long-term JLP people, will ensure the protection of the JLP. (Newcomers from outside are regarded understandably, as less reliably committed.)

There is a certain amount of myth-making in—and about—the JLP. Part of the myth is that the JLP is uniquely accountable, consultative, transparent, and democratic; in fact in some respects (the *Gazette* letters, the Council's ability to question the Chairman, the elected members of the board) the JLP *is* unique. But these features do not constitute an unusual degree of accountability; indeed in some respects the JLP lags behind conventional practices, governance structures, and standards in conventional firms.

To the extent that the survival of the JLP depends on the integrity and values of incumbents of key positions, it is vulnerable. Respondents often told us that JLP had been lucky with its leaders. While we agree, it worries us: the persistence of the JLP needs to be assured by more than the vicissitudes and capriciousness of personnel selection processes: it requires firm, institutional support.

If this question of balance is not resolved, it is likely to be revealed in three types of issue. First, if there is insufficient power, confidence, and authority in the Partnership representative side, the businesses will be more liable (subject to the restraint of senior decision makers—an uncertain long-term guarantee) to adopt strategies which stretch or breach the principles. Second, in the face of continuing and increasing pressure for efficiencies and cost reductions, the remaining elements of the JLP will continue to be eroded. The 'rights' of Partnership will continue to be translated into 'responsibilities' and the democratic constituent will continue to lose power and traction albeit remaining as a potential irritant. Recent and current tendencies towards the use of contract labour will appear increasingly attractive in the face of pressure on costs. Third, with increasing competition and a squeeze on profitability, issues will arise which act as lightning rods for disagreements and conflict.

The pension is sometimes regarded as an indication of JLP's benevolence, as a striking demonstration of the JLP difference. And there's no doubt that it is increasingly unusual. There are times when senior managers seem to see the pension as a benevolent allowance rather than as the right due to owners. A potential conflict opens up between investment which grows the business and pension and bonus payments which reward current and past partners. In the annual negotiations around the division of the profit, pensions have tended to receive less than their due.

As we noted in Chapter 5, until very recently, the chairman of the pension scheme's trustee board was the JLP Finance Director, thus allowing a potential conflict of interest between the investment needs of the Partnership and the benefits of partners. While historically the JLP Finance Director was required to protect JLP assets and to be part of the 'critical side', recently the role has been redefined in favour of a greater focus on commercial efficiency. And recent finance directors have been appointed from outside the Partnership presumably to bring into the JLP some skills, experience, or attitudes which JLP required but was seen to lack, and which were more available or better developed outside the Partnership. This is possibly one indication of a shift in the historic emphases of the JLP.

It is hard to escape the conclusion that while in theory the profits of JLP belong to the partners, senior management takes the firm view that it is their prerogative to decide what to do with them. They decide on the distribution of the Partnership's profits between the three sources of demand, and the relative importance of these. It also seems, from the statements of JLP managers, that distribution of profits to partners, through bonus or pension payments, are both a reward for effort and an indication of JLP benevolence. However, it could be argued that they are more than this: that they are a right.

This may be little more than quibbling but the issue becomes more significant when it comes to the extent to which the principal is able to constrain or influence the agent's powers in this and other areas. In other words, it raises questions about accountability. Management, as we have seen, is firmly committed to growth. This means partners' funds are being invested in the future and management argues that this is necessary for survival and success. Managers exercise a free hand in strategic decision making, especially in comparison with shareholder-owned companies where shareholders can come together and form pressure groups and organize.

What ability do the partners of JLP have to question or constrain senior management strategic decision making which involves spending partners' funds on future expansion and future profits? The constraints on management are relatively modest outside of extreme and highly unlikely circumstances of total management loss of legitimacy, and the power of the Chairman is remarkable in terms of modern standards of governance. The extent to which the principal is able to control its agents is not simply or solely a matter of constitutional propriety or compliance: it is also practical. The extent to which senior managers' strategic decision making is open to challenge and assessment from partners will affect the *quality* of strategic thinking. This is why governance issues are so crucial.

The fact that the rights of the principals may be increasingly dominated by the rights of the agents—the right to manage—could be seen as a manifestation of what the founder presciently regarded as a common and universal feature of management—that management power will grow unless checked— 'human nature being what it is, management is more or less warped by selfishness' (Preface to the Rules). But if there is such an universal tendency (the numerous governance failures in conventional firms would lend support to such a thesis) in the case of the JLP a further contributing factor might be that over the past twenty-five years management in JLP has played an increasingly significant and critical role in designing and expediting the success of the JLP businesses. While publicly JLP management seeks to argue that the success of the Partnership is a result of the nature of the organization and its principles, in fact management also presents itself—at least implicitly—as playing a major role in expediting this success.

The principal/agent distinction may seem arcane and legalistic. But it is very real and represents yet another tension for JLP managers to manage. Management references to the objectives of the Partnership as 'where commercial success is a driving force but where the needs of customers, partners, and long-term financial ambitions *are balanced*' the recent introduction of the expression 'partners' reasonable expectations', the decision to invest large amounts of the available funds in growth projects, all indicate management decisions on the allocation of profits and their attempts to justify these.

179

Although the Partnership presents itself as an accountability-based democracy, and indeed has an elaborate and active democratic structure, it is in reality a benign autocracy in terms of its day-to-day management. The Chairman has significant power to make policy and implement it.

Conclusions

We began the chapter with questions about whether JLP does or could claim to be a democracy and the extent to which it acts using democratic principles and methods. We asked how the democratic character actually works in practice and finally we asked whether the various attempts to reform and refresh the democracy over the past decade have served to strengthen or weaken the vibrancy of the democratic side.

We set about answering them by commencing with a description of the current arrangements for participation and decision making. We then reviewed the story of the various attempts to 'reform', 'refresh', and 'update' the original democratic arrangements in order to arrive at this current state. These reforms and their underlying rationales help reveal different interpretations of purpose and of nature. In the third section we made an evaluation of the changes and here we drew upon data from our interviews with managers and elected councillors.

Is JLP a democracy? If the benchmark is the Bullock Industrial Democracy proposals which emphasized the importance of workers on the board then there is a case to be made. The Partnership does have elected worker representatives on its main Board sitting alongside the executive managers and the non-executive directors. Indeed, until very recently, the non-executive directors did not have the right to vote whereas the staff representatives did. In addition, there is the Partnership Council which is primarily elected and which has ultimate power to hold the Chairman to account and to dismiss him from office.

Further, the democratic structures extend throughout the whole Partnership and down to every level. As described earlier, there is a four-step structure with elected representative bodies from the branches (Level 1), through regional level (Level 2), the divisions (Level 3), and the Partnership-wide level (Level 4).

In addition, unlike many mutual organizations, let alone PLCs, the Partnership does talk about itself as a democratic enterprise, managers and staff (partners) appeal to the democratic ideal and this kind of appeal is never or very rarely denied or challenged outright—no one states in public 'We are not a democracy' in the same stark way that we heard stated in other mutuals and social enterprises.

On the other hand, the case against the claim to it actually being a democracy in practice has a number of elements. Managers make most of the key decisions. This fact has increasingly been clarified rather than clouded or obfuscated. Most elected representatives on the senior bodies are managers and there are very few non-management partners on the Partnership Council. Also, regardless of the existence of formal democratic structures, this chapter has identified not only some questions about the validity of some of these— for example the claim that the Council holds the Chairman to account through its right to remove him/her—but also about the strength of democratic and accountability processes in the face of the dominant management narrative.

Then there is the crucial question about the direction of travel. Have the many attempts over the past decade or so to 'reform' and refresh the democracy served to strengthen or weaken it?

The results of the first Partner Opinion Survey in 2003 indicated that they did not feel engaged in the democratic structures. Senior managers' response to this was to redesign the methods of engagement at branch level. The numerous committees were rationalized and the main branch council was redesigned as a 'Forum'. Nominations and standing for election were disbanded and in their place partners were asked to select any member of their department to serves as their representative. The Forum to which these representatives were elected became less formal and was reshaped more as consultative bodies sharing ideas jointly with managers about how to improve the business and the partner experience together. This redesign was described as 'more honest'. Surveys suggested partners were more content with the new arrangements, but whether the redesign resulted in a downgrade of the potential for robust challenge—which is arguably implicit in the idea of democracy—is open to question. The subsequent further reforms in 2012 which resulted in the removal of the Forums in favour of Partner Voice, is expressive of the same trend, but pushed further.

8

Conclusions

In this final chapter, we pull together the main strands of the book. The chapter is organized under the four main themes outlined in Chapter 1:

1) What are the crucial elements of the JLP model, how is leadership exercised and how, within such a model, are managers held to account?

2) What are the implications of the model for business performance?

3) How do managers view the nature and importance of partner engagement and democracy?

4) What are the lessons to be drawn from this case example of stakeholder-oriented organization for policy makers and practitioners and can the positive attributes of the model be replicated elsewhere?

All four themes are crucial elements of the idea of an 'alternative' model to the modern corporation as discussed in Chapter 1. If there was to be a shift to the kinds of alternative forms as advocated by Mayer, Hutton, and others then these are the kinds of issues that would need to be explored and resolved. Thus, the JLP case carries importance beyond its own manifestation.

The Crucial Elements of the Model, Leadership, and How Managers Are Held to Account

Unlike conventional businesses, the Partnership spends a great deal of time, trouble and expense sustaining an elaborate and impressive structure of democratic forums. Furthermore, as Chapter 7 demonstrated, senior management have recently spent time and trouble trying to simplify and refresh these democratic bodies. The democratic structures within the Partnership undoubtedly play a major role, not least in supplying a vehicle for partner 'voice' and in providing, at the very least, a reassuring symbolic underpinning for the culture of the organization.

However, of the JLP's many contradictions, one that is especially notable is that while the organization is highly participatory (through the democracy and the elected members of the board) it is not very accountable. Management can be questioned and challenged, but this is not the same as being rigorously held to account.

Critics claim that senior management has reduced accountability (for example, by reducing the number of 'critical side' roles) and that they have sought to define the role of the democratic element in terms of support for management strategies. But management continues to regard the Partnership Council as a potential source of challenge and so works hard to persuade the Council (and partners as a whole) of the sense and inevitability of the adopted strategies. And management's success in conveying a dominant narrative in effect vitiates the degree to which it is challenged and held accountable. But, ultimately, this success weakens management by restricting the possibility of confronting potential alternatives to the dominant view to any serious degree.

Accountability is crucially important in the Partnership. This is partly for the usual reasons—that management be accountable to owners for the use of, and distribution of the profits from, their funds. And given that the Partnership's commitments to the various demands on profits are considerable (not least because of investment plans) and that difficulties in raising profitability have proved intractable, the distribution of JLP profits is likely to become increasingly contentious within the Partnership. To date, such discussion has been muted, and management's insistence that it can be trusted to pursue the common good through its expertise and experience, largely accepted. But management know only too well that this confidence is based on continued success. And success means satisfying all the demands on profits. When, or if, that changes, debate could increase and at this stage the issue of accountability will become critical.

But the other reason—unique to the Partnership—why accountability is crucial is because JLP management must be accountable for the *preservation* of the Partnership, and for the proper and acceptable positioning and achievement of the balance between commercial priorities and the happiness of partners, between the survival of the businesses and the survival of the core 'difference' which gives the businesses their competitive edge, between the principles and values of the Partnership and the principles of the market which, despite the protestations of management can at times be remain distinct, different, and even opposed.

There are those who argue that recent years have seen some erosion of the central JLP difference. As we saw from the oral histories in Chapter 2 this is contentious. Such changes as have occurred were closely associated with a re-invigoration of the JLP businesses. But, ultimately, the only bulwark against any future inroads into the JLP difference, or an abandoning of the balance between partnership and commerciality (which is in itself the source of the Partnership's competitive appeal) can only come not from the integrity and commitment of individual senior managers, but from real and robust institutional structures and processes of accountability. These institutional arrangements must be capable of challenging, and if needs be checking, the policies of management. The survival of this well-intentioned and worthy institution depends on the existence and vitality of its structures and processes of accountability. So, on this measure we conclude that there is more to be done.

But what about the record on performance outcomes? Have the shortcomings on accountability been compensated for by exceptional performance?

The Performance of the JLP Businesses

Is the JLP really a better way to do business? In some ways, absolutely. When, in the wider economy operating under conventional rules, trends such as zero hours contract jobs show a relentless increase (700,000 and rising), then a firm that is genuinely committed to treating staff as partners with a suite of component benefits including bonus payments, sabbaticals after twenty-five years, and a pension, is unquestionably better in the *moral* sense. But what about the other sense—better in *performance* terms? Is JLP a superior performer? And does being *morally* better result in better *performance*?

One of the major themes of this book, echoing the insistent claims of JLP managers, is that the JLP model, for a number of reasons, bestows competitive advantage but that this point is partly true and partly aspirational. And it is because of this mixed blessing that managers regard it as a key component of their JLP destiny to ensure the conversion of this potential benefit into performance advantage. But, as we have seen, this conversion, especially if it is defined in terms of the achievement of an advantage that equals the extra cost of the JLP employment model, is a daunting challenge. And paradoxically, some of the obstructions come from the very same model that confers the potential benefits. This is one of the major complexities faced by JLP managers.

It is an indication of management success, especially in the face not only of dramatically increased competition, but also of radically transformed competition, that when measured alongside the performance outcomes of its competitors, the Partnership has fared very well. In a tough market where many retailers have folded and other have lost sales, JLP has been noted as bucking the trend.

But what about profitability? As JLP managers are acutely aware (see Chapter 6) while sales are crucial—for this generates revenue and acts as an immediate barometer of the success of the buying, merchandising, and sales activities—they are not sufficient: it is margins that count as well. Profit matters of course because it supplies the funds that support investment, bonuses, pensions, and other costs. But profit *margins* matter, too, as an indicator of JLP management success in controlling costs and also as a sign of the wisdom of their investment decisions. Growth and investments plans and decisions must ultimately be assessed in terms not of the sales they generate but the profitability of those sales.

As we saw in Chapter 5, while revenue increased at an impressive rate, retained profits remained relatively flat. It will be recalled, for example, that retained profits in the financial year 2007/08 were £130m and yet, despite a very significant increase in sales from £6,763m to £10,172m in 2013/14, retained profits declined to only £102m. On conventional assumptions, the low-ish level of profits could be seen as a serious problem that needs to be fixed. But, we question whether it is in fact a problem for this type of organization or could it be viewed as a sign of appropriate management behaviour and priorities?

In one sense, even for this kind of business, low-ish profits could be viewed as a 'problem' because they mean the Partnership cannot afford to fulfil its ambitions plans at the speed it would like. It is another kind of problem if managers respond to the figures by actions which then threaten the reputation or the model.

For the past twenty-five years, JLP management has been struggling to reduce costs and improve efficiencies. They have made considerable progress but by reference to their goal of 'recovering' the cost of the Partnership in improved profit, they have, to a degree by their own targets, failed. But in our view, this target was always an illusion and, worse, was misguided. There is no reason why the extra cost of the Partnership should be precisely balanced and neutralized by the conversion of the JLP 'difference' into extra efficiencies or profit to equal the additional cost, despite it having in general terms, a real positive impact on attitudes, commitment, and behaviour.

Given that the JLP is officially committed to partner happiness, the bonus is certainly a factor in their happiness but so are the other benefits as are, in varying degrees, the other components of the JLP model (all of which add to costs). The decent way in which partners are treated and managed (in contrast to staff in many other retailers both online and in high-street stores) means that some ways of reducing staff costs are out of the question. So, the JLP model, which in various ways contributes to partners' happiness, reduces profitability (and increases sales), and the avoidance of a range of management practices used by other retailers to increase efficiencies limits a number of profit-enhancing strategies.

Thus, while low profitability may be a source of difficulty in terms of finding funds for JLP's commitments, it could be seen not as a sign of poor management or of management failure, but of management success—at ensuring, in broad terms, the achievement of the over-arching goal: partner happiness. Partner happiness is not simply a question of the size of the bonus. Partners 'own' the JLP so in theory it is perfectly reasonable for them, through their agents, JLP management, to agree to a level of profit which may be less than is achieved by others but which balances the need for a sufficient level of profit with partners' enjoyment of all the components of the JLP model.

Hence, the low-ish level of profits can also be seen as a sign of strength and conviction: that managers are not prepared to go the 'Tesco route', that there are steps (conventional responses to improve efficiencies) that they are *not* prepared to make; that they accept that the JLP integrity must be preserved (for if that goes, so does the JLP competitive difference and advantage) and that the model (partners' happiness) is real and still important to them, and that partner happiness is partly defined in terms of how the JLP works, and how people are treated.

It is neat and very convenient to insist that the JLP model is good for business but it is more (and in one sense less) than that: it is also good in its own terms. From the point of view of the survival of the JLP *qua* JLP, the important point about these figures is not simply what they reveal about the mixed impact of the JLP model, but also about how managers react to them. While JLP managers may use the financial metrics of conventional businesses to monitor performance and inform their reactions, this is not the same as accepting that these metrics are the *only* language in which the business performance of the Partnership can be discussed and assessed.

The JLP, uniquely, says its prime objective is the happiness of partners. Although senior managers insist, understandably, that this requires and depends on a successful business, they must remember that profitability is a simulacrum of the real success objective, and not the objective itself. There may be a risk that JLP managers for whatever reason measure success and themselves in the language and values of conventional businesses while the whole point about the JLP is that it addresses fundamentally different priorities. The JLP with its mantra of 'a better way to do business' introduces a moral dimension to business process and assessment, not simply an instrumental one—a moral focus which other firms lack. 'Better' in the moral sense means much more than simply a potential source of competitive advantage and this should not be masked by reference only to the commercial implications of the JLP but lauded proudly as a virtue in itself. And these figures show that JLP managers still respect and value this moral sense of 'better'. So, overall, on this measure we conclude that the Partnership has been a success.

Managers' Views of the Nature and Importance of Partner Engagement and Democracy

JLP managers are convinced that partners are more fully engaged and committed than employees in other businesses and that this engagement has positive consequences for the performance of the business. This is not an empirically-based conviction: it is an article of faith. It is not derived from research, and anyway, such research as is available (covering partners/employees but not the other stakeholders) is limited and equivocal. Even the Partner Survey (to the extent that this instrument measures the correct variables and takes account of the significant effects of managed and differential expectations) supplies variable and uncertain support. But this does not matter because the whole edifice of the JLP knowledge and understanding of itself is predicated on the assumption—the certainty—that the elements of JLP success—growth, sales, customer satisfaction levels—are based on the consequences of the JLP model. This book has offered numerous examples of managers' conviction of this belief.

The possible positive indicators associated with employee ownership will vary somewhat with the work situation. In a customer-facing situation the positive outcomes may be enhanced customer service. In a warehouse, the out-turn may include productivity and higher levels of accuracy in order fulfilment. In all contexts they would include reduced rates of absenteeism, turnover, sickness, and possibly, more positive results in employee attitude surveys.

One of the rationales for employee-owned enterprises is that workers in such enterprises will be more engaged and therefore more productive in a variety of ways. The suggestion is that workers in such enterprises will think and behave differently: that they can be expected to act more like 'owners'. So they will be more customer (and market) focused as they see the customer rather than the boss as the source of their economic futures; they would be willing to make sacrifices in hard times in order to sustain the enterprise. They are willing to expend what JLP managers tend to describe as 'discretionary effort'. They might be expected to be more willing than an employee in a conventional firm, to 'go the extra mile'.

Of course JLP managers know very well (and some made this point) that they could easily improve the performance of the businesses not by treating partners, suppliers, and customers well, but by treating them badly. The JLP model adds considerably to business cost. And the JLP's values and principles restrict or limit managers' ability to take actions (or anyway to the same extent) as their colleagues in competitor companies which would reduce costs or increase margins. But they also know that these business benefits would be short-term and would destroy the critical differential on which the distinctive market positioning, reputation, customer appeal, 'brand' and business performance are based. To make this point is not to argue that JLP managers' commitment to the JLP model is necessarily based on this instrumental calculation: many are genuinely committed to the JLP model in its own right. They know it has costs and they are convinced it has benefits.

The most important source of evidence for the plausibility of this conviction relies less on any data about partners' behaviour or attitudes and more on data concerning the performance of the businesses, especially the performance of Waitrose and John Lewis measured against their competitors in terms of revenues and growth over the past twenty years, as presented earlier in this book. The latest results at the time of writing (2015) were overall sales at £10.9bn which represents an increase of 5.7 per cent on the previous year. Overall, revenue is up by 5.6 per cent at £9.7bn, and this despite a highly competitive business environment for food retailing which includes the highest level of food price deflation in the UK since the 1970s. The rise of discount grocery retailers has added to demands for value and increased price competition across the industry. Waitrose profits dropped to 3.9 per cent, John Lewis profits rose to 7.1 per cent.

There has also been consistent year on year growth in partner numbers: from 76,800 in 2010 to 93,800 in 2015. The year 2015 saw the addition of thirty-three Waitrose shops (including twelve Little Waitrose and five Welcome Break shops) and three John Lewis stores including the massive full range department store in central Birmingham (a 'regional flagship'). There are eight more JL stores in the pipeline. Large, modern distribution and dot. com fulfilment centres were opened and investment in technology and what is termed 'omnichannel' retailing is increasing at pace—at around 37 per cent of total capital expenditure.

JLP managers are also interested in the profit figures and especially profit as a percentage of revenue. Both gross sales and operating profit are assessed by the square foot of selling space and by full-time equivalent employees. These measures supply information on the effective use of space and the effective use of partners. Both sets of figures for 2013 show an improvement on the previous year. The trends are upward: both John Lewis and Waitrose report that from 2009 to 2013 efficiencies in use of space and use of partners increased.

But there is something curious. If there is a positive link, as claimed, between the JLP model and partner behaviour, it seems this link (engagement, discretionary effort) attaches more to one component of management's priorities (customer service, quality) than others (profitability, efficiency). The JLP model's contribution to organizational performance stems from enhanced individual partner 'engagement' rather than, enhanced efficiency. Indeed, as noted earlier, some managers even argued that partners' commitment and system efficiency could be negatively related, because individual effort covers-up process and system inefficiencies.

Not surprisingly, in the face of the constant emphasis on, and reference to, the distinctive nature of the Partnership as an employer ('It's your Partnership', JLP Annual Report, 2015), partners' expectations for their jobs and employment are high. Staff newly inducted into the Partnership when new branches are opened or acquired, consistently award higher scores on all question items including crucial questions such as 'I would recommend the Partnership as a great place to work'. This advocacy question achieved a 92.9 per cent average positive answer in the new branches compared with 88.6 per cent in existing branches (still an impressively high score). If engagement can be indicated by attitude survey response rates, then the JLP scores are very high—averaging around 96 per cent.

One area where direct comparisons can be made between partners and non-partner employees is in the warehousing/regional distribution centres (RDCs). Waitrose is serviced by four regional distribution centres, some of which are operated by JLP partners and some of which are outsourced to a provider company (Kuehne and Nagel). Productivity is measured by cases picked per hour. The results show that the contractor company is just as productive as the partner-operated sites. Managers tend to argue that the real 'Partnership difference' is felt not so much in these support roles but in the customer-facing settings of the selling floor. That said, it is interesting to note that on the partner attitude surveys, the two telephone contact centres tend to have the highest scores even in comparison with the selling stores on virtually all thirty-five questions. Again, this may be a consequence of differential expectations. Call centres are not normally the most congenial of work environments and the effort put into managing these by JLP seems to be well regarded by staff.

Data were assembled which identified the highest scoring branches in the Partnership attitude surveys. Analysis was made of the verbatim, free text, responses in order to try to understand what partners in these branches thought about their local management. Key themes reported were: personal qualities such as showing trust and respect for partners, and being open and honest. When interacting with partners these branch managers were seen to take an interest in the partners, deal with questions in an open manner, and listen to partners. They also gave feedback and were seen to manage performance. The pattern of results seems to indicate a positive association between positive employee attitudes, good management, and above average sales growth.

Across the Partnership, sickness absence is lower than average compared with the retail sector as a whole. The retail sector average in 2012 was 6.8 per cent and average rates across the economy in 2012–13 were 7 per cent (CIPD 2015).

In Waitrose, the sickness absence rate hovered around 3 per cent between 2010 and 2013, the John Lewis Department store rate is broadly the same. Corporate staff and those in Partnership services have lower rates around 1 per cent. The average sickness absence rate in Waitrose in 2013 was 3.32 per cent, this was a slight increase over the 3.08 per cent of 2012. In 2014, the Partnership spent 56 per cent more than similar organizations on the creation and delivery of partner development. In a sector notable for its high turnover, the Partnership has achieved an above average length of service for partners of over nine years (for partners over the age of 22, thus not counting student temporary employment).

The results of partner satisfaction surveys conducted in the JLP in 2011, 2012, 2013, and 2014 show positive overall results compared to an external benchmarking sample of 337 organizations. The survey shows for each of the thirty-five questions a comparison with median and upper quartile responses of similar questions by employees of the benchmarking sample. For eighteen of the questions the satisfaction of JLP partners is higher than the upper quartile of the sample and for six other question areas the answers are over the median of the sample. Surveys in JLP are increasingly focusing on engagement, since management considers that engagement, rather than satisfaction, is correlated with business success. Enhanced performance, customer service, retention, and absence are all factors linked strongly with employee engagement in JLP. Some of the items to measure engagement, such as the question 'I would recommend the Partnership as a great place to work' place JLP in the top 10 per cent of the benchmarking sample. And an important indicator is that 75 per cent of partners agree that 'We create real influence over our working lives' (2014 survey). Nevertheless, for ten of the survey questions, the satisfaction of JLP partners is lower than the median of the sample. The survey shows relatively low marks on some items where one might expect an employee-owned advantage: teamwork, communication, acknowledgement, participation, ideas welcomed. JLP managers explain those lower satisfaction levels as stemming from higher expectations among JLP partners. There could be a related reason. Managers appear to be increasingly making the important decisions, and these attitudinal scores may be reflecting recognition of that reality.

It seems that although JLP managers are able to engage partners in day to day work, it is more difficult to engage them in participation on democratic bodies. Between half and two-thirds of partners are not active participants in the councils.

JLP has been pragmatic on the question of pay differentials. The highest salary in JLP is limited to 75 times the average pay of a selling partner (a huge contrast with the 7.8 to 1 differential in the businesses of the Spanish Mondragon cooperatives). These higher pay differentials in JLP have enabled it to attract high-performing managers from competing firms. Hence, JLP is not reliant on internal promotion. Access to leading-edge knowledge is made available and the competition among managers means that there is far less scope for complacency.

We have argued that although some supporters and commentators (and occasionally JLP managers themselves) have argued that the success of the JLP is a simple consequence of the JLP model, in fact the model creates a potential which must be carefully directed and managed. This argument may well also apply to the link between model and partner engagement: this is not a necessary or automatic response but must be crafted and supported by management at central and local levels. For example, without such management there is a tendency for co-owned businesses to become too complacent. This suggests that the resolution of the dilemma posed earlier—is the success of the JLP a result of the impact of the JLP model, or of partners' 'experience' of the model as mediated by managers?—is that it is both. Partner engagement, despite managers' insistence, is a response to managers' actions and sense making. If this is true, it also carries the worry that if positive engagement is a response to managers' management of meaning, in theory heavy-handed or clumsy management action could damage this precious quality.

In other words, the experience of share ownership on its own is not enough: for positive employee attitudinal and behavioural outcomes to be realized, employee ownership must be complemented by increased employee participation in decision making and innovative human resource policies (Klein 1987; Kruse et al. 2004).

In John Lewis, managers took active steps to manage the co-ownership model. They introduced changes to and simplified the partner democracy structures and procedures. They invested heavily in communication of the meaning of the Partnership: the 'narrative'. And they constantly and actively sought to manage the way partners knew and understood their roles and contribution and to interpret and continually reinterpret the 'meaning' of the Partnership for partners.

The way JLP partners respond to their experience of the Partnership is broadly in line with research on employee-owned firms which has indicated that for employee ownership to have an effect on worker behaviour there needs to be additional supportive HRM and management practices (Kruse et al. 2004; Kaarsemaker and Poutsma 2006)—an active, highly professional management which can construct a shared reality, reframe understandings and expectations so that these mechanisms appear to help deliver employee voice and support a consensual view of the Partnership and its strategic business direction.

In emphasizing the importance of management we do not argue that single-minded commercial management is the determining factor. The lesson from

JLP is that a particular, highly context-aware, mode of managing is crucial. A significant number of managers with extensive experience earned in other companies have been brought in to JLP at senior levels because of their proven technical skills. Not all of these entrants have flourished or even survived. They tend to be rejected by the system if their approach is too out of line with the accepted ways of working and modes of behaving. Innovation and fresh ideas are expected but they have to be introduced in harmony with JLP norms and values even if in some respects newcomers bring ideas and practices from outside, for example, recently, ideas and practices associated with external systems of business measurement and monitoring.

Thus, each of the prongs of employee ownership is required (intrinsic/emotional attachment to the idea of being an owner, the accrual of financial reward from ownership and associated effort, and the participation which ownership rights confer) but on their own these may still not be enough. We have added not so much a fourth prong but rather a governing inner-contextual factor—the influence of skilled management in harnessing the employee ownership idea, breathing life and meaning into it, investing in the necessary support systems to make it real, and, most of all, communicating a sense of direction and legitimacy to a version of industrial democracy which is viable and sustainable in the wider contemporary changing context.

Overall, through a combination of an application of the model and its enhancement by managers, partner behaviour does seem to be impacted in a positive manner.

The Replicability of the JLP Model and the Wider Lessons

So we come to perhaps the most important question of all: can the model and the approach be copied by others? Should it be imitated? Is this the type of alternative to the conventional corporate form that so many have sought to find? What are the wider lessons even in the absence of complete replication?

The power of the JLP model lies not simply in the effect it generates (with clever management) on partners, and ultimately customers, but that this benefit is hard to copy because it derives not only from history, not only from a number of interlocking principles and structures, but also from the bedrock of shared ownership. So the question of replicability is fundamental.

One senior manager expressed the underlying idea neatly: 'if you're a believer in partnership then your starting point has to be that the partnership way of doing business gives you a competitive advantage. It gives you a competitive advantage which is sustainable, difficult to copy, difficult to replicate, defensible and a true point of distinction'.

The replicability of the JLP model is a crucially important issue because it is the possibility of achieving the perceived benefits of the JLP in other businesses that creates much of the interest in knowing about and understanding the JLP.

However, the issue of replicability depends on the resolution of a prior issue: is it desirable to replicate the model? If it is not seen as desirable to replicate the model there is little point in considering whether it is possible. And there are two aspects to the desirability or attractiveness of the model: the moral case (treating people better) which for many is very attractive (and as we have argued, an attraction for many JLP customers); and the practical utility case (achieving superior business performance through the model). These are of course the two senses of 'better' that are conflated in the maxim: 'a better way to do business'.

Although it is necessary to distinguish and separate these two senses of 'better', they must be reintegrated. For the thesis on which JLP is based insists that treating people better creates business benefit. And there is good sense in the insistence on the importance of this argument for if the JLP model was only attractive and justified because it was *morally* better (i.e. treated its staff better) and did not have any implications for better commercial performance, it would attract relatively few followers.

Sales performance relative to conventional competitors adds to the allure of the model. But the record on profitability might diminish the attraction for those parties seeking maximization of return. The reduced impact on profitability might reduce the attraction of the model, and this book has described JLP managers' ceaseless efforts to translate the consequences of the JLP model for partner engagement into JLP profitability. But the model adds to JLP costs, constrains the range of options available to management, excluding or at least severely limiting the ability of JLP managers to degrade employment terms, outsourcing, to increase the intensification of labour and so increase profitability by reducing labour costs. Morally 'better' may add to business benefit but in a sense it clearly also *constrains* management behaviour—and rightly so: that's the point.

However, as argued in the section on the impact of the JLP model on business performance, while it is true that JLP businesses tend to lag behind their competitors in profitability when calculated on an annual basis, the results (and the assessment of the relative merits for business performance of the JLP model and that of 'conventional' businesses in the UK/US context at least) might be different when averaged over a longer period. For, as we have recently (2015) seen, at least one of the highest performing competitors— Tesco, the paradigmatic representative of the principles of the conventional business model—incurred the biggest loss ever recorded on the UK high street (£6.4bn) as a result of huge reductions in the value of its property portfolio and stock. And the relevance of this loss is not only that it affects the relative assessment of JLP's profitability but more significantly it raises the possibility that the Tesco failure was not accidental but a consequence of the Tesco business model with its total preoccupation with achieving quarterly profit figures to satisfy shareholders and earn managers their bonuses.

Any assessment of the desirability of the JLP model is therefore inherently complex and must take account of the time period. One central component of this complexity is that different stakeholders may well have radically different assessments of the desirability of the JLP model. So it is important not only to consider the attractiveness of the JLP model, but to consider: attractive to whom? It is necessary to identify the different attitudes of different audiences or groups of stakeholders. Indeed it is precisely this issue: which groups benefit from the conventional business in the UK/US model and from the JLP which becomes central. For, while the conventional firm in effect, if not in its publicity, identifies and emphasizes the shareholders as the category of stakeholder who must benefit from the operations of the business, the JLP places emphasis on a *range of stakeholders* and seeks to balance the distribution of benefits and advantage to them all. The conventional firm defines its responsibilities as massively if not exclusively to shareholders (with senior managers benefiting from satisfying shareholders' expectations); JLP defines its responsibilities and commitments to partners, suppliers, customers, and the wider community.

In the UK, politicians and many commentators have advocated the model as one which public sector organizations could emulate (although it is not certain that such recommendations are based on full knowledge of the JLP model, or represent an enthusiasm to recreate all components of the model). And certainly lots of managers in conventional businesses would love to be able to re-create the partner engagement and customer confidence/trust enjoyed by the JLP businesses. But it is unlikely that they would be prepared to pay the price associated with the model: the restrictions on management rewards and authority, and especially the ownership arrangements.

During the writing of this book we discussed the premise of such an 'alternative' with a range of people. A memorable encounter was with a group of investment bankers in the City of London. We wanted to understand their likely responses to these options and their view of the possibility and desirability of a serious alternative to the shareholder value priority. For most of them, the responses were fairly predictable: unless the alternative delivered higher or at least equivalent out-turns for shareholders and themselves as agents they maintained that there would be very little interest. A few were intrigued and were attracted to the moral case but even these few were sceptical of such an alternative gaining traction among their colleagues and business acquaintances. The implication is clear. Those who continue to benefit disproportionately from the status quo would not be easily persuaded to change; indeed they would actively resist it. Thus, in a parliamentary democracy it may be necessary to consider legislation and regulation to lay-down a revised set of rules and expectations.

One reason for the paradox that while the JLP model and its businesses are widely admired, and the links between the model and the performance of the business generally recognized and valued (especially by customers), managers and decision-makers in conventional firms may be less enthusiastic about the model even if they accept the thesis (possibly especially *if* they accept the thesis) that the model creates business benefit. For what is obvious about the JLP model is that it affords fewer possibilities for managers to enrich themselves partly because of the principles and constraints of the JLP model but also because managers' enrichment in conventional businesses is through bonus systems and share option arrangements tied to the achievement of business results and increases in shareholder value, which are denied JLP managers because of its ownership structure.

The answer to the question whether the JLP model is replicable is clear. Yes, ensure you understand all the components of the model and then install them. Simple. But the fact that the question is raised indicates that there is a significant sub-text—the real question is: is it possible to replicate the JLP and to achieve and enjoy the benefits of the JLP model without going the whole way, without giving the business away? This is the key question.

Within the Partnership, managers differed on this. Some argued that it was possible to cherry-pick components of the model and to achieve a high proportion of the benefits in terms of employee and customer attitudes without the JLP ownership model, or with a more acceptable version of the ownership arrangements: for example profit-sharing. These were the senior managers who defined the model as a set of techniques that they could, having worked with them, take with them and apply elsewhere. But even these informants accepted that applying the model elsewhere would place serious and, difficult demands on managers.

> Well, the three components (profit sharing; knowledge; and power) make for a partnership model, so you can, in principle do that anywhere. I could make other businesses feel similar to the partnership if I went to another job. So I could go to Sainsbury's now and I could say, right, we're going to have a staff profit-share scheme and it's going to be more widespread than the current one where just the management, senior management will have something. And, to give them their dues, Tesco and Asda do have some kind of profit sharing. So you could replicate that. Knowledge, is there any reason why you can't share knowledge? Not really. Being publicly quoted is a bit of a problem, but within constraints, no reason why you couldn't share knowledge. Power, absolutely no reason at all why you can't say to your management, before we take this decision we want you to engage the staff and make sure they are on board. So could you operate in a similar kind of

way? Yes. Could the management be expected to comply? Probably not. Why? Because it's just so much easier to say, 'Look, you just do what I say, I don't want to hear about it.' (JLP Director, 2014)

But others saw the model as a set of mutually supportive elements, which made it impossible to pick just some elements.

> ... the clever thing about the Partnership is it's not actually one big thing, it's lots of little things that make a big thing. That's not a very technical response but you understand what I mean. I just ... I'm not very comfortable saying it's this or it's that. I think one of the reasons why the model is so hard to replicate in some ways is it's a whole raft of stuff that, if you add it all together, it creates this thing ... (Director, Group)

> So they are all intertwined. I think there is a philosophical level issue which is probably linked to the replication issues. For me, having 25 years in retail and other organisations, this legacy type paternalism and how it works feels just like and entirely different kind of place. A unique feature I think is the journey, you also need to have lived inside retail and its cut-throat-ness. You always have to understand that, before you can understand the legacy which is why I think it's difficult for some one in 2011 to say, 'we have become a partnership', because the strangeness is complete insanity with John Spedan Lewis relative to other people of his age in terms of giving everything he had away. And that's sort of the unreplicability—if there's such a word—of the model. (Manager, 2011)

> There are paternalistic people and there are altruistic people but there's giving up everything you own to the point where all his descendants have nothing. That part in a sense is not replicable—at least not normally.... Features such as the benefits, the houses, the yachts, the anonymous letters in the *Gazette* so anyone can 'slag off the chairman'—these are all part of the total picture. In theory they are replicable but in the real practical world most unlikely. (Manager, Group, 2014)

In practice, there are occasional examples of business owners setting up JLP-type arrangements but, unlike Spedan Lewis, without ceding total share ownership.

One case in point is AG Parfett & Sons cash and carry business in the north west of England. It describes itself as a John Lewis style mutual since it changed from being a family owned business. In 2008 the family sold 55 per cent of the shares in the business to an Employee Ownership Trust which holds the shares on behalf of the employees. The Trust is committed to buying the remaining 45 per cent of the shares in the future to achieve the aim of Parfetts becoming fully employee owned. The employee-owned shares are held in trust and administered by a trust board. When we visited the company for a set of interviews in 2013 we found general approval but no marked shift in behaviours or attitudes. In part this was because the transfer of ownership is only partly achieved to date and in part because there was appreciation of the way the family firm had been traditionally run. There was appreciation that the new co-ownership arrangement had prevented buy-out by a hedge fund.

Another example is a wire-fencing and wire connector company based in Sheffield. This company, Gripple, is employee-owned by means of monthly debits from wages and salaries so that all employees buy a £1,000 stake in the company. Extra shares can also be bought and sold.

In a number of these cases there has been an at least partial attempt to learn directly from JLP. Indeed, sometimes past employees of JLP were involved in applying the lessons. But in none of these cases has the JLP model been replicated in full.

Our view is that the JLP ownership arrangements are fundamental to the JLP model and to its impact on partners and on customers, and while it is possible that the application of selected elements of the model may have short-term beneficial consequences, the full benefits for staff behaviour and customer confidence can only be achieved in situations where common ownership ensures not only that managers can make long-term investment decisions, but also employees can be confident that regardless of the good intentions and principles of managers, they are protected from the risk of outside interests taking over the business and imposing a new employment and management regime.

Management's good intentions are worth nothing if the business can be taken over by people with a radically different management philosophy. The senior management of Cadbury were committed to the Quaker management principles of the business. But they were also legally required to protect the best interest of the shareholders when faced in 2009 with an increased bid from Kraft. As the Cadbury Chairman commented, 'fiduciary duty had to overcome emotional instinct'. Despite promises made to protect the workforce and facilities, these promises were rescinded within a few weeks of the take-over and one of the plants was closed and its work offshored to a cheaper location.

Unlike some other retailers, JLP partners are not working to support enormous debt liabilities incurred by private equity owners, are not working to generate a surplus for the owners who may be more interested in the money that can be extracted from the business than its long-term health and survival. As one director observed:

> You would need an endowment in a trust to defend the model. At the end of the day this is a capitalist world and financial forces will take over, because no one's going to protect it. It has to be underwritten, and if this business hadn't been underwritten it would've gone the way of the building societies. The partners would've found a way of taking £15,000 each and not worrying about anything else. That really would have happened, I think. It's a bit like capital punishment; people will vote for it unless you put in checks. I think you have to underwrite. (Waitrose director, 2014)

The shared ownership basis of the JLP is not the only factor generating the trustworthiness of the business and its managers: the culture, Constitution and principles, and institutions are also very important. These elements identify and lay an emphasis on the values that characterize relations within the JLP and between JLP and the customers and suppliers. The knowledge that the business is protected from the risk of take-over by managers oriented towards shareholder value, is a crucial underpinning of partner and customer confidence.

This psychological and moral implication of JLP's ownership is crucial. It is hugely important as a source of the 'discretionary effort' of which managers are so conscious and so proud. And it is a foundation on which to build the ubiquitous JLP narrative of difference, trust, and decency. One manager argued that one limit to the take-up of the model elsewhere is that top managers, in general, would not be satisfied with the deal. Furthermore, he made the important point that the replicability of JLP was limited by the complexities of managing within the JLP:

> When I have been involved in recruiting from outside I have been amazed at these really ridiculous personal incentives which candidates have. Many of them find the cost of a move here too much to contemplate. So recruitment in at senior levels will continue to be a challenge for us. If it was that easy to be like us, all retail businesses would be partnerships, and they're not, we're the only one. Partnership elsewhere seems to work more easily in small enterprises. But you don't see it in larger businesses, I think it comes back to this downside: entitlement, complacency, ingrained behaviour, how do you basically performance manage and/or create a culture which manages the downside risk of that in a big business? Because in a small business, your DNA will be such that everybody feels as if, and actually you'll be exposed if you're not performing. In a big business, there's a lot of people that can hide, and fold their arms and move the other way, and you have to develop a process that means everybody feels a tap on their shoulder if they're not performing. So I think there's a lot that is challenging in big businesses, around managing the downside of performance in a values based partnership business. (JLP director, 2014)

Conventional management thinking—especially from 'market fundamentalists' would argue that shared ownership, and protection from the threat of take-overs, releases the JLP business from the discipline of the market. The positive side of this could be the ability of JLP managers to make long-term investment decisions which invest resources that would elsewhere be diverted to shareholders. And it is possible to point—as JLP managers do—to investment decisions which reflect this freedom. However, as noted above, does this freedom from external shareholders also carry a degree of freedom from the sort of scrutiny and challenge which contributes to the processes and quality of senior management debate within the Partnership? Does it mean JLP managers are therefore less disciplined than other managers? Colin Mayer argues that the research suggests that this disciplinary function of take-overs has been exaggerated: '. . . hostile takeovers are not so much about correcting poor performance or disciplining bad management as changing the strategy of middle-of-the-road performers so they become top performers' (Mayer 2014: 103).

In any assessment of the possibility of replication of the JLP model it is necessary to distinguish between the image and the reality of the JLP: how it works and how management operates to make it work. This reality is far more complex, subtle, and complicated and to a degree contradictory than the comments and assessments of many advocates might suggest. Management action, carefully crafted to comply with JLP values and principles is required to accentuate the positives and neutralize the negatives. In these endeavours recent and current management have been very successful. Management must balance commercial priorities and requirements and partners' interests, and achieving this balance is a constant challenge. So, replicating the JLP—if it is possible—is going to be a more complex business and require a great deal more management skill and understanding than some advocates recognize.

One way in which the model underpins success is through the internal and external perception—carefully and vigorously supported and mobilized by management—of the JLP as a moral entity where the normal, exploitative relations between employer and employee, between business and suppliers, between business and customers, is replaced by a clear and alternative relationship of fairness, decency, and trust. This conception of the JLP is vigorously and cleverly packaged and disseminated through extremely expensive advertising and is also promoted internally. It has a real basis: partners and suppliers are treated very differently than their equivalents outside and it is in marked contrast to the same relationships in conventional retailers which are overtly exploitative and in some cases explicitly advocated and regarded as virtuous by those who insist that the only moral responsibility of a business is to its shareholders.

Many competitors envy JLP the reputation it has achieved, its appeal to customers, the commitment of the partners. They would like to emulate these. But they would probably prefer to do this without emulating the JLP's shared ownership. So if they are interested in emulating the JLP, it is to find techniques which can assist them to achieve this priority. This will be as ineffective as it is ironic: for the whole point of the JLP and the source of its success is that it is not simply and solely committed to one set of stakeholders. The JLP is not a consultancy package, or a collection of management, communication, reward, and participation techniques focusing on sharing profit, knowledge, and power. It is much more than this: it is fundamentally a set of serious commitments and responsibilities towards its key stakeholders, responsibilities and commitments which are ensured by the underpinning ownership structure.

199

Mindful of this, one director was pessimistic about replicating the model elsewhere:

> Replicable elsewhere? Dream on. The way of working here is based on the efforts of an eccentric genius of the early to mid-last century and is grounded in that. It would be very hard to reinvent it in the current world. It doesn't mean you couldn't but absolutely you just need to, as you guys do, understand the beast you're dealing with and cultures and what those are about. It's hard to convince politicians of that. (JL director, 2014)

Despite the attractions of elements of the JLP model after over 100 years, the JLP is still a unique organization. True, as noted, there are organizations that have made some attempts to replicate some elements of the model, but the JLP still stands alone: admired, yes, but from a distance.

But the importance of the JLP may not lie in the extent to which other firms copy it. It could be more than this—that it represents a bold attempt to manage and negate some of the dysfunctionality and pathology of the model of business and business ownership that dominates in the USA, the UK and, to an extent in many other countries, where the interests of any stake-holders other than shareholders are not simply neglected but actively and purposefully over-ridden; where businesses can be bought and sold simply as financial assets, where value extraction dominates over value creation and where the morality of the casino and the skills and cleverness of financial engineering dominate over the skills required to build organizations capable of supplying goods and services to their customers.

The true significance of the John Lewis Partnership is that managers are expected to meet a set of stakeholder needs which go beyond short-term gain. These managers are not beholden to quarterly performance targets set by external investors. JLP managers are expected to balance a range of interests. Their adherence to these wider interests is not solely underwritten by formal structures. Indeed, we have argued that formal accountability is in many respects limited. But, despite this, the management cadre collectively, mainly do attend to the wider array of interests—partner bonus payments, pensions, investment in new and refurbished stores, investment in new channels and technology—in a balanced way. This set of behaviours reflects an organizational culture which differs in a positive way from the many examples of avaricious and unprincipled corporate behaviour. Collectively the management cadre act in an unconscious as well as a conscious way to sustain the 'better way of doing business'. From where does this culture derive? It is not the result of a culture change programme. It is not the result of consultancy packages. It is not a set of glib exhortations or smiley face badges. It stems from a long-term process of *sedimented behaviours* which have matured over many years of experimentation and learning from successes and failures. The behaviours have been tested under fire—not least, for example, in the responses to the economic crisis of 2008. The expected behaviours are both conservative and radical. Trading in particular requires a fine nose for risk and innovation; the balancing force from the Partnership guardians. When times have been tough this balance has been tested and the Partnership has learned. Indeed, the immediate economic and trading environment looks especially tough and so new tests lie ahead. And, as the present generation of managers which has learned to embody and live these values retires, there is a risk that the informal self-policing at the top could be compromised. To offset that risk, it is vital that the process of transmission of values and behaviours to new recruits and to the new rising talent is handled with care.

Final Considerations and Lessons

In this final chapter we have reviewed four crucial themes: how managers are held to account; the impact of the model on employee attitudes and behaviours; the implications of the model for business performance; and whether and how this alternative model could and should be replicated across the economy. As we noted, all four themes are crucial elements of the idea of an 'alternative' model to the modern corporation.

A few additional comments which stand above these separate segments are appropriate. While we have been critical of some of the workings of JLP we have also tried to make clear that everything is relative. Our criticisms have normally arisen when we have compared everyday practice with the ideals of the Partnership. But, even with regard to these 'lapses' (the forays into outsourcing for example), another basis for comparison, as we noted earlier, would be with its competitors. Such comparisons usually result in a more favourable view of the Partnership. For example, Sports Direct, which has over 400 stores in the UK, has the vast majority of its employees on zero hour contracts. The boss, Mike Ashley, is a billionaire and even after floating the company on the stock exchange has retained around 62 per cent of the shares personally (Titcomb 2013). Even a major company such as Next, which is broadly comparable to JL in terms of turnover and number of employees, product categories, and with a mix of stores and online, indicates the nature of the counterfactual. Next, is single-minded in its pursuit of shareholder value. It restlessly opens and closes stores, acquires and disposes of businesses at will.

These companies make no bones about where their priorities lie. Maximizing return to shareholders is the name of the game; all else is a means to an end. Such companies exert some market pressure on alternatives such as JLP. Their pricing of labour has implications for cost comparisons and cost pressures. Other competitors, some operating on a massive scale such as

Amazon.com, pay miniscule taxes in the UK or indeed elsewhere and thus exert yet further pressure on JLP attempts to offer fair rewards. A force-field analysis might show downward pressure on JLP arising from the kinds of competition noted, but conversely, upward pressure is felt by even these competitors due to legal requirements and by labour market forces. There has been associated near-collapse of labour resistance (Fraser 2015). During periods when labour legislation is relatively weak in its effects, and when labour markets are slack, when access to the labour pool has become international, the exercise of comparative advantage through a 'high-road' strategy of human resources is somewhat stymied. On a wider front, the malfeasant behaviour of Volkswagen with regard to noxious emissions, and the behaviour of numerous banks with regard to rate fixing and exploitative relationships with their clients are all too clear indicators of the dangers of a narrow profit-seeking stance.

There are many lessons to be learned from the John Lewis case; here we pick out six key ones.

The first is that the success of the model is not an automatic and direct consequence of the model. Making the model 'work', converting the JLP potential into reality takes considerable, and constant, management effort and ingenuity. And the achievement of JLP management is precarious and unstable and requires the constant balancing of opposed forces. So the JLP is if anything, more complex to manage then conventional businesses. The pervasive neo-liberal narrative insists on the necessity for, and benefits from, the unrestricted exposure of businesses to the take-over market. This narrative postulates the moral and practical (to shareholders if not other stakeholders) benefits of businesses being unrestrictedly available to potential purchasers. This prevalent and pervasive view, defines firms solely in terms of the primacy of shareholders' interests and their protection by the firm's executive arguing that this is both virtuous and necessary for corporate efficiency and corporate performance. Colin Mayer authoritatively disputes this argument showing that corporate take-overs are rarely a response to poor performance and rarely lead to improved performance.

The second lesson the John Lewis Partnership teaches is that finding ways to restrict the full-blooded play of neoliberal dynamics does not curtail success but creates the grounds for solid growth and performance: restricting the free-for-all in selling and buying businesses, protecting the interests of stakeholders other than shareholders, and creating patient shareholders with a long-term interest in growing the business rather than extracting value, assists business performance, underpins employee protection and confidence, and builds customer trust.

The third lesson is that JLP creates trust among stakeholders: customers, suppliers, and staff because of its genuine and reliable commitment to them. Many businesses claim their commitment to customers and staff; many insist on their trustworthiness. But, as Chris Argyris has noted, with respect to corporate values, we must be careful to distinguish between espoused values and the values that actually underpin decisions: the values-in-use (Argyris and Schon 1981). All too often, when firms are committed to maximizing shareholder value and when that priority conflicts with other commitments, there is no doubt which will dominate: commitments to customer service, the well-being of staff, or customers' interests rapidly decline.

Some players may be genuine in their commitment, but this counts for very little when corporate predators buy the business (possibly making all sorts of—worthless—reassurances) and replace previous commitments with policies of value-extraction.

A fourth and possibly most important lesson (which even some of its advocates and admirers don't want us to learn by trying to define it as an eccentric if charming niche phenomena) is that the JLP can represent a counter to and an alternative for, the dominant model and theory—not only of the firm, but also of the ways in which and the ease with which businesses can be bought and sold solely for the benefit of speculators and shareholders and at the expense of other stakeholders.

A fifth lesson is that managing in this 'counter way' is more complex than managing in a conventional PLC driven solely, or mainly, by maximizing shareholder value. As we saw, when describing the internal debates about controversial choices in earlier chapters, senior managers in such a stakeholder firm are required to account for their strategic and their tactical decisions across a broad front. Thus, disputes and debates are not just about what constitutes sound judgement about commercial advantage (e.g. whether and how much to invest in online retailing, or whether and how much to invest in a big store refurbishment programme or a chain of small stores in new locations) rather, the senior players are additionally open to public challenge on a much wider canvass. Thus, they face (emotionally-charged) challenges on staffing matters: outsourcing and offshoring are contested; seizing trading opportunities which involve the employment of non-partners is likewise contested. Most especially, decisions about how much revenue to allocate to pensions, how much to partner bonus, and how much to investment, have to be defended. The first of these may reward or penalize past partners, the second may privilege or disadvantage current partners and the last of these may work in favour of future partners.

The final lesson is that treating workers decently is not simply a matter of additional cost. When, in 1914, Henry Ford announced that he would pay his workers the remarkable sum of $5 a day, his fellow business leaders were initially horrified: surely low wages were necessary for high profits? But Ford was arguing an alternative logic: that high wages were smart for business because high wages turn workers into consumers. And for many years after the Second World War this logic—a virtuous circle of growth—that business success and worker well-being were mutually supportive, not opposed, was dominant. This was a period of rapidly increasing worker productivity during which the objectives of the firm were described by senior executives in terms of 'stakeholder capitalism', and the need to balance the interests of *all* stakeholders, to maintain 'an equitable balance' among the various groups involved in a business.

But, from the 1970s, something changed in the USA—and the UK—although productivity continued to increase during the period 1973–2011 (by 80 per cent), average wages rose on average only 4 per cent, while corporate profits spiked to the highest proportion of national income for sixty years. A new era had dawned and a new philosophy dominated management thinking. In such a context, the importance of the John Lewis model and example in practice takes on an increased status. The general absence of any imagined alternative makes this one all the more significant. The general retreat from the aim to create more decent employment standards again makes this case all the more important.

It is something to be celebrated that the JLP is not only committed to serving and protecting the interests of partners, suppliers, and customers—and even better that they have managed to make these commitments underpin a lively and successful business. This has not been an easy task; and as we have noted, there remain real tensions which must be balanced (not *solved* at the expense of one of the polarities as seems to be happening at the Co-op where new senior management apparently lack an awareness and understanding of the importance of *balancing* oppositions). But, the most important lesson from the JLP is a simple one. It is a lesson that applies to the business model that is so prevalent currently in the UK and the USA, and yet one that was noted by Franklin D Roosevelt in reference to the global economic crash of the 1930s: '*We have always known that heedless self-interest was bad morals, we now know that it is bad economics.*'

References

ACAS (2011). *Annual Report 2000–1*. London: Advisory, Conciliation and Arbitration Service.

Ackers, P. and J. Payne (1998). 'British trade unions and social partnership: rhetoric, reality and strategy', *The International Journal of Human Resource Management* 9(3): 529–50.

Adams, F., G. Tabak, and G. Hansen (1993). *Putting Democracy to Work: A Practical Guide for Starting and Managing Worker-Owned Businesses*. New York: Berrett-Koehler Publishers.

All Party Parliamentary Group on Employee Ownership (2011). *Sharing Ownership: The role of employee ownership in public service delivery*. London: All Party Parliamentary Group on Employee Ownership.

Altuna, L. (2008). *La experiencia cooperativa de Mondragon. Una síntesis general*. Eskoriatza: Mondragon unibertsitatea.

Alvesson, M. and H. Willmott (2002). 'Identity regulation as organizational control: producing the appropriate individual', *Journal of Management Studies* 39(5): 619–44.

Appelbaum, E. and R. Batt (2014). *Private Equity at Work: When Wall Street Manages Main Street*. New York, Russell Sage Foundation.

Argyris, C. and D. Schon (1981). *Organizational Learning*. Reading, MA: Addison-Wesley.

Bachrach, P. and M. S. Baratz (1962). 'Two faces of power', *The American Political Science Review* 56(4): 947–52.

Bacon, N. and Samuel, P. (2009). 'Partnership agreement adoption and survival in the British public and private sectors.' *Work, Employment & Society* 23(2): 231–48.

Barrick, M., G. Thurgood, and T. Smith (2015). 'Collective organizational engagement: linking motivational antecedents, strategic implementation, and firm performance', *Academy of Management Journal* 58(1): 111–35.

Bataille-Chedotel, F. and F. Huntzinger (2004). 'Faces of governance of production cooperatives: An exploratory study of ten French cooperatives', *Annals of Public and Cooperative Economics* 75(1): 89–111.

Batstone, E. (1983). 'Organization and orientation: a life cycle model of French cooperatives', *Economic and Industrial Democracy* 4(2): 139–61.

Batt, R. and E. Appelbaum (2013). *The Impact of Financialization on Management and Employment Outcomes*. Kalamazoo, MI: Upjohn Institute.

Battilana, J. and S. Dorado (2010). 'Building sustainable hybrid organizations: The case of commercial microfinance organizations', *Academy of Management Journal* 53(6): 1419–40.

References

Ben-Ner, A. (1984). On the stability of the cooperative type of organization. *Journal of Comparative Economics* 8(3): 247–60.

Berle, A. A. and G. C. Means (1967). *The Modern Corporation and Private Property* (2nd edn) New York: Harcourt Brace.

Besharov, M. L. and W. K. Smith (2014). 'Multiple institutional logics in organizations: explaining their varied nature and implications', *Academy of Management Review* 39(3): 364–81.

Blackhurst, C. (2011). 'Will being biggest really mean best for John Lewis?' London *Evening Standard* 10 March.

Bradley, K. and A. Gelb (1983). *Cooperation at Work: The Mondragon Experience*. London: Ashgate.

Bradley, K. and S. Taylor (1992). *Business Performance in the Retail Sector: The Experience of the John Lewis Partnership*. Oxford: Oxford University Press.

Brignall, M. (2015). 'Has John Lewis lost the digital plot?' *The Guardian* 31 January.

Bullock, L. (1977). Report of the Committee of Inquiry on Industrial Democracy. C. 6706. London HMSO.

Cabinet Office (2011a). *Open Public Services*. London: The Cabinet Office.

Cabinet Office (2011b). *Our Mutual Friends: The Case for Mutuals*. London: The Cabinet Office.

Cathcart, A. (2009). 'Directing Democracy: The Case of the John Lewis Partnership'. PhD thesis, School of Management, University of Leicester.

Cathcart, A. (2013a). 'Directing democracy: competing interests and contested terrain in the John Lewis Partnership'. *Journal of Industrial Relations* 55(4): 601–20.

Cathcart, A. (2013b). 'Paradoxes of participation: non-union workplace partnership in John Lewis', *International Journal of Human Resource Management* 25(6): 762–80.

Chang, H.-J. (2011). *23 Things They Don't tell You about Capitalism*. New York: Bloomsbury Press.

Chang, H.-J. (2012). 'It's time to start talking to the City', *The Guardian* 20 February.

CIMA (2014). *Building World Class Businesses for the Long-Term*. London: Chartered Institute of Management Accountants.

CIPD (2015). *Absence Management*, London: CIPD.

City Company Law Committee (1977). *A Reply to Bullock*. London: City Company Lawyers.

Coates, K. (1976). 'The background to the new movement: some questions and some arguments', in K. Coates (ed.), *The New Worker Co-operatives*. Nottingham: Spokesman: 11–33.

Coats, D. (2013). *Just Deserts? Poverty and Income Inequality: Can Workplace Democracy Make a Difference?* London: Smith Institute.

Cornforth, C. (1995). 'Patterns of co-operative management: Beyond the degeneration thesis', *Economic and Industrial Democracy* 16(4): 487–523.

Cox, P. (2010). *Spedan's Partnership: The Story of John Lewis and Waitrose*. Cambridge: Labatie Books.

Crouch, C. (2011). *The Strange Non-death of Neo-liberalism*. London: Polity Press.

Davies, W. (2009). *Reinventing the Firm*. London: DEMOS.

Donovan, L. (1968). *Report of the Royal Commission on Trade Unions and Employers Associations*. London: HMSO.

Dore, R. (2000). *Stock Market Capitalism: Welfare Capitalism: Japan and Germany versus the Anglo-Saxons*. Oxford: Oxford University Press.

Dore, R. (2008). 'Financialization of the globabl economy', *Industrial and Corporate Change* 17(6): 1097–112.

Economist Intelligence Unit (2010). 'Re-engaging with Engagement: Views from the Boardroom on Employee Engagement', *The Economist* London.

Eisenhardt, K. (1989). 'Agency theory: an assessment and review', *Academy of Management Review* 14(1): 57–74.

Estrin, S. and D. C. Jones (1992). 'The viability of employee-owned firms: Evidence from France', *Industrial and Labor Relations Review* 45(2): 323–38.

Flanders, A., R. Pomeranz, and J. Woodward (1968). *Experiment in Industrial Democracy: Study of the John Lewis Partnership*. London: Faber & Faber.

Fraser, S. (2015). *The Age of Acquiesence: The Life and Death of American Resistance to Organised Wealth and Power*. New York: Little, Brown.

Gamble, A. (2014). *Crisis Without End? The Unravelling of Western Prosperity*. London: Palgrave Macmillan.

Gray, J. (2010). 'Book review of Chang "23 Things"', *The Guardian* 29 August (http://www.theguardian.com/books/2010/aug/29/ha-joon-chang-23-things).

Guardian (2012). 'Millions of working families one push from penury, Guardian research finds', *The Guardian* 18 June.

Hales, C. (1986). 'What do managers do?' *Journal of Management Studies* 23: 1.

Hall, P. A. and D. Soskice, eds (2001). *Varieties of Capitalism. The Institutional Foundations of Comparative Advantage*. Oxford: Oxford University Press.

Hernandez, S. (2006). 'Striving for control: democracy and oligarchy at a Mexican cooperative', *Economic and Industrial Democracy* 27(1): 105–35.

Heskett, J. L., E. Sasser, and L. A. Schlesinger (1997). *The Service Profit Chain*. New York: Free Press.

High Pay Centre (2014). 'FTSE 100 bosses now paid an average 130 times as much as their employees', http://highpaycentre.org/blog/ftse-100-bosses-now-paid-an-aver age-143-times-as-much-as-their-employees.

High Pay Commission (2010). 'What are we paying for?' High Pay Commission and Incomes Data Services.

Hird, C. (1981). 'The crippled giants', *New Internationalist Magazine* 106 (December).

Hood, C. (1991). 'A public management for all seasons', *Public Administration* 69: 3–19.

Hutton, W. (2015a). *How Good We Can Be: Ending the Mercenary Society and Building a Great Country*. London: Little Brown.

Hutton, W. (2015b). 'Once, firms cherished their workers, now they are seen as disposable', *The Observer* 21 August.

Incomes Data Services (2014). 'Executive remuneration in the FTSE 350—a focus on performance-related pay', London: A Report for the High Pay Centre, October.

IPA (1992). *Towards Industrial Partnership: A New Approach to Relationships at Work*. London: Involvement and Participation Association.

IPA (2003). *Informing & Consulting your Workforce: B&Q—Listening to the Grass Roots: Case Study*. London: Involement & Participation Association.

References

Jenkins, J. (2007). 'Gambling partners? The risky outcomes of workplace partnerships', *Work, Employment & Society* 21(4): 635–52.

Kaarsemaker, E. C. and E. Poutsma (2006). 'The fit of employee ownership with other human resource management practices: Theoretical and empirical suggestions regarding the existence of an ownership high-performance work system', *Economic and Industrial Democracy* 27(4): 669–85.

Kalleberg, A. L. (2015). 'Financialization, private equity, and employment relations in the United States', *Work and Occupations* 42(2): 216–24.

Kasmir, S. (1996). *The Myth of Mondragon: Cooperatives, Politics and Working Class Life in a Basque Town*. New York: State University of New York Press.

Kay, J. (2012). *The Kay Review of UK Equity Markets and Long-Term Decision Making: Final Report*. London: Department of Business Innovation & Skills.

Kemeny, T., D. Rigby, and A. Cooke (2013). 'Cheap Imports and the Loss of U.S. Manufacturing Jobs.' London: LSE, Spatial Economics Research Centre.

Klein, K. J. (1987). 'Employee stock ownership and employee attitudes: A test of three models', *Journal of Applied Psychology* 72(2): 319.

Knights, D. and H. Willmott (1999). *Management Lives*. London: Sage.

Kochan, T. and P. Osterman (1994). *The Mutual Gains Enterprise*. Boston, MA: Harvard Business School Press.

Kraatz, M. S. and E. S. Block (2008). 'Organizational implications of institutional pluralism', in R. Greenwood, C. Oliver, and R. Suddaby (eds), *The Sage Handbook of Organizational Institutionalism*. London: Sage.

Krugman, P. and R. Wells (2010). 'A resurgence of financial folly,' *New York Review of Books*, 13.

Kruse, D., R. Freeman, J. Blasi, R. Buchele, A. Scharf, L. Rodgers, and C. Mackin (2004). 'Motivating employee-owners in ESOP firms: Human resource policies and company performance', *Advances in the Economic Analysis of Participatory and Labor-Managed Firms* 8: 101–27.

Lawrence, F. (2014). 'Why Supermarkets are on the way out', *The Guardian* 7 October.

Lazonick, W. (2014). 'Profits without prosperity: stock buybacks manipulate the market and leave most Americans worse off', *Harvard Business Review* September: 47–55.

Lewis, M. (2014). *Flash Boys: Cracking the Money Code*. London: Allen Lane/Penguin.

McCarthy, J. E., P. B. Voos, A. Eaton, D. L. Kruse, and J. R. Blasi (2011). 'Solidarity and sharing: Unions and shared capitalism', in E. Carberry (ed.), *Employee Ownership and Shared Capitalism: New Directions in Research*, Labor and Employment Relations Association, Urbana-Champaign, IL: University of Illinois.

Martinez Lucio, M. and M. Stuart (2005). '"Partnership" and new industrial relations in a risk society: an age of shotgun weddings and marriages of convenience?' *Work, Employment & Society* 19(4): 797–817.

Mayer, C. (2012). 'Why "short-termism" in markets is a very British problem', *Financial Times* 20 July.

Mayer, C. (2014). *Firm Commitment: Why the Corporation is Failing Us and How to Restore Trust in It*. Oxford: Oxford University Press.

Mazzucato, M. (2012). 'If the eurozone is serious about growth, it can have it', *The Guardian* 17 May.

Meek, C. B. and W. P. Woodworth (1990). 'Technical training and enterprise: Mondragon's educational system and its implications for other cooperatives'. *Economic and Industrial Democracy* **11**: 508–28.

Meister, A. (1974). *La participation dans les associations*. Paris: Editions Ouvrières.

Meister, A. (1984). *Participation, Associations, Development, and Change* New Brunswick, NJ: Transaction Publishers.

Miller, P. and N. Rose (1990). 'Governing economic life', *Economy and Society* **19**(1): 1–31.

Mintzberg, H. (1973). *The Nature of Managerial Work*. New York: Harper & Row.

Mitchie, J. (2012). *Mutual Advantage? The Future Implications of Mutualism for Employment Relations*. London: ACAS.

Miyazaki, H. (1984). 'On success and dissolution of the labor-managed firm in the capitalist economy', *The Journal of Political Economy* **92**(5): 909–31.

Morales, A. C. (2004). 'La dirección en la empresa de trabajo asociado: una revisión de estudios empíricos', *CIRIEC-España* **48**: 99–122.

Mullins, D. (2006). 'Competing institutional logics', *Public Policy and Administration* **21**(3): 6–24.

Münkner, H. H. (2000). 'Corporate governance in German cooperatives: What happened to Co-op Dortmund?', *Review of International Co-operation* **92–3**(4): 78–89.

New York Times (2010). 'How superstars' pay stifles everyone else's', *New York Times* 25 December.

Nuttall, G. (2012). *Nuttall Review of Employee Ownership*. London: Department of Business Innovation & Skills.

Pache, A. and F. Santos (2013). ' Inside the hybrid organization: selective coupling as a response to competing institutional logics', *Academy of Management Journal* **56**(4): 972–1001.

Paranque, B. and H. Willmott (2013). Cooperatives: Saviours or Gravediggers of Capitalism? Cardiff, Draft Paper.

Paranque, B. and H. Willmott (2014). 'Cooperatives—saviours or gravediggers of capitalism? Critical performativity and the John Lewis Partnership', *Organization* **21**(5): 604–25.

Park, R., D. Kruse, and J. Sesil (2004). 'Does employee ownership enhance firm survival?' *Advances in Economic Analysis of Participatory and Labor-Managed Firms* **8**: 3–33.

Peston, R. (2013). *How Do We Fix this Mess?* London: Holder.

Pettigrew, A. (1985). *The Awakening Giant: Continuity and Change in Imperial Chemical Industries*. Oxford: Blackwell.

Pollitt, C. (2014). 'Managerialism Redux?' Keynote address to the 2014 EIASM Conference, Edinburgh.

Porter, M. E. (1985). *The Competitive Advantage: Creating and Sustaining Superior Performance*. NY: Free Press.

Potter, B. (1891). *The Cooperative Movement in Great Britain*. London: Swann Sonnenschein and Co.

PwC (2015). *Executive Pay: Review of the 2015 AGM Season* London: PwC.

Reay, T. and C. R. Hinings (2009). 'Managing the rivalry of competing institutional logics', *Organization Studies* **30**(6): 629–52.

Rucci, A. J., S. P. Kirn, and R. T. Quinn (1998). 'The employee–customer–profit chain at Sears', *Harvard Business Review* January–February: 82–97.

Senge, P. (1990). *The Fifth Discipline: The art and practice of the learning organization*. New York: Doubleday.

Spear, R. (2004). 'Governance in democratic member-based organizations', *Annals of Public and Cooperative Economics* **75**(1): 33–60.

Spedan Lewis, J. (1948). *Partnership for All: A thirty-four year old experiment in industrial democracy*. London: Kerr.

Spedan Lewis, J. (1954). *Fairer Shares: A possible advance in civilisation and perhaps the only alternative to communism*. London: Staples Press.

Stewart, R. (1976). *Contrasts in Management*. Maidenhead: McGraw-Hill.

Stiglitz, J. (2003). *Globalization and its Discontents*. New York: Penguin.

Storey, J. (1980). *Managerial Preprogative and the Question of Control*. London: Routledge.

Storey, J. (1992). *Developments in the Management of Human Resources: An Analytical Review*, Oxford, Blackwell.

Streeck, W. (2014). *Buying Time: The Delayed Crisis of Democratic Capitalism*. London: Verso Books.

Thornton, P. H., W. Ocasio, and M. Lounsbury (2012). *The Institutional Logics Perspective: A New Approach to Culture, Structure and Process*. Oxford: Oxford University Press.

Titcomb, J. (2013). 'Ashley sells £106m in Sports Direct shares', *The Telegraph* 24 October.

Treanor, J. (2014). 'Co-operative Group's terrible year leads to growth slowing in wider movement', *The Guardian* 22 June.

Van der Krogt, D., J. Nilsson, and V. Host (2007). 'The impact of cooperatve risk aversion and equity capital constraints on theor inter-firm consolidation and collaboration strategies', *Agribusiness* **23**(4): 453–72.

Wall Street Journal (2012). 'The $100 million giveback', *Wall Street Journal* 7 February.

Webb, S. and B. Webb (1920). *A Constitution for the Socialist Commonwealth of Great Britain*. London: Longman.

Whyte, W. F. and K. K. Whyte (1991). *Making Mondragon: The Growth and Dynamics of the Worker Cooperative Complex*. New York: Cornell University Press.

Wilkinson, R. G. and K. Pickett (2010). *The Spirit Level: Why Equality is Better for Everyone*. London: Penguin.

Wolf, M. (2014). *The Shifts and the Shocks: What we've learned—and have still to learn—from the financial crisis*. London: Allen Lane.

Name Index

Subject Index

　and performance 184
　strategic objectives of JLP 132, 133, 135
performance
　Co-operative Society 136
　employee-owned firms 67
　and executive compensation 12
　failures, and US/UK model of the firm 6
　JLP 184–7
　　1990–1999 29, 72, 73
　　2000–2005 33, 73, 74–5, 76–7, 78, 79
　　2003–2004 81, 82, 83, 87
　　2005–2009 88, 89
　　2006/07 (2007)–2014/15 (2015) 106
　　2007–2015 performance summary 102
　　2010–2014 96, 100, 101–7
　　2014/15 performance relative to
　　　competitors 104
　accountability 174, 177
　capacity building 137
　comparisons 35
　Gazette 47
　and growth 108, 117, 119–20, 122
　high performance culture 44, 45
　impact of JLP model on performance
　　16, 20
　management and 131
　of managers 172
　meaning, managing 146
　measurement 20
　partner engagement 187, 188, 189, 190
　pension scheme 110, 112
　registrars 44, 45
　replicability of JLP model 193, 195, 198
　strategic objectives 133–4, 135
　and takeovers 199, 202
　see also profits; sales
Peter Jones 24, 27, 29, 31, 83, 136
petrol retailers 37, 77
Philippines 22
planning *see* business planning
Post Office 52, 55
poverty 3
power
　and accountability 154, 175, 178
　Chairman 154, 179, 180
　employee-owned firms 66, 67
　management 179
　nature of 175
　partner proposition 40, 76
　Partnership Council 171, 180
　registrars 48–9
　replicability of JLP model 195
　sharing 158, 164, 168
'Powered by our Principles' slogan 37
Price, Mark 36, 155, 168
pricing 36, 88, 90

principal–agent dynamic 34, 66, 70, 111, 179
private equity 3
profits
　and accountability 174, 178, 179, 183
　and bonuses 18
　capacity building 136, 137, 138–9, 141
　Constitution 25
　Co-operative Group 136
　dangers of profit-seeking stance 202
　and democracy 164
　distribution 27
　and growth 110, 124
　and investment 30, 34, 35
　Marks and Spencer 103
　maximization 57, 61, 135
　meaning, managing 142, 144–5, 146
　Morrison's 124
　as motivator 10
　mutuals 60
　partner–customer–profit cycle 19, 36,
　　144–5, 147
　　business plans 88, 96
　　employee-owned firms 50
　　growth 116, 120
　　Sears 58, 144
　partner engagement 188
　partner proposition 38
　Partnership Council 156
　pension scheme 110, 111, 112
　performance 185–6
　purpose of JLP 20, 132–3, 134–5, 136
　replicability of JLP model 193
　retained profits 34
　shareholder value 7, 8
　sharing 195
　Tesco 124, 194
　timeline
　　1952 72
　　1990–1999 29, 72
　　1997/8 29
　　2000–2005 33, 74, 76, 77, 80
　　2003–2004 81, 82, 83–4, 85, 86, 87
　　2005–2009 88
　　2008–2012 89, 90
　　2010–2015 94–5, 97, 100–1, 103, 105,
　　　107, 124
　　2015 23
　UK, historical perspective 4
　wages vs 204
Public and Commercial Services (PCS) union 64
Public Relations officer 73
public sector 9, 53, 54–5, 64, 194
purpose
　of employee-owned firms 57, 70
　　mutuals 60
　　social enterprises 60
　　worker cooperatives 68